Ethnic Associations and the Welfare State

Social Work and Social Issues
Columbia University School of Social Work

Ethnic Associations and the Welfare State

Services to Immigrants in Five Countries

Shirley Jenkins, Editor

Columbia University Press   New York   1988

Columbia University Press
New York   Guildford, Surrey
Copyright © 1988 Columbia University Press

Printed in the United States of America

Library of Congress Cataloging-in-Publication Data

Ethnic associations and the welfare state: services to immigrants
in five countries / Shirley Jenkins, editor.
p.   cm.—(Social work and social issues)
Bibliography: p.
Includes index.
ISBN 0-231-05690-7
1. Social work with immigrants—Cross-cultural studies.
2. Emigration and immigration—Societies, etc.—Cross-cultural
studies. 3. Immigrants—Cross-cultural studies. 4. Welfare
state—Cross-cultural studies. I. Jenkins, Shirley. II. Series.
HV4005.E86   1988   87-20995
362.8—dc19   CIP

Hardback editions of Columbia University Press are Smyth-sewn
and printed on permanent and durable acid-free paper

To my grandchildren
  Christopher
  Kate
  David

Contents

Preface

This book extends the line of investigation followed in my earlier work, *The Ethnic Dilemma in Social Services* (1981). That study asked how, when, and where ethnicity can and should be a factor in social service programs. In this volume, the question raised is whether the organization and delivery of services to new immigrants, and by implication to other ethnic groups, would not be facilitated if their own ethnic associations were part of that process.

The work of implementing this study was greatly facilitated by a generous grant from the Charles H. Revson Foundation, in response to a proposal prepared jointly by me and Mignon Sauber, research director of the Community Council of Greater New York, where the field study was undertaken. For this head start I want to express gratitude to Eli N. Evans, president of the foundation, Bernard M. Shiffman, executive director of the Community Council, where I worked during my sabbatical year, and to my long-time friend and collaborator, Mignon Sauber, who codirected the New York field study with me. Specific acknowledgements for work are made in notes to the individual papers.

Studying immigrants of seventeen different ethnic groups puts one in an international frame of mind, and it seemed natural to ask whether the phenomenon of ethnic associations participating in service delivery was not also present in other countries with significant new immigrations. Collaborators from four countries were recruited for replication studies and analyses of the role of ethnic associations in their own homelands. I am grateful to the coauthors for their scholarship, care, and cooperation. Acknowledgement is made to Drs. Bard Bothe, deputy director general of welfare, Ministry of Welfare, Public Health and Culture of the Netherlands, who facilitated the paper on that country. I also appreciate the support of former Dean George A. Brager of the Columbia University School of Social Work, who made funds available from the Lois and Samuel Silberman Fund, which supports the school's publication series, "Social Work and Social Issues," and the continuing interest of Ronald A. Feldman, the present dean.

If international population movements continue, and all indications are that they will, then ethnic associations are likely to be a growing sector of future service delivery. This book is dedicated to my grandchildren, Christopher, Kate and David, for reasons of affection and because they are also part of the future—of a time when, it is hoped, both commonalities and differences among peoples will flourish in welfare states.

Ethnic Associations and the Welfare State

Services to Immigrants in Five Countries

1.

Introduction: Immigration, Ethnic Associations, and Social Services

Shirley Jenkins

The movement of people across national borders is not a new phenomenon, nor is the tendency of newcomers to come together in ethnic associations based on race, religion, language, common cultural heritage, and consciousness of kind. What is new is that both immigration and ethnic associations are taking place in countries with large institutionalized social welfare programs and professional social work bureaucracies. This raises several questions. First, are the benefits of the welfare state available to immigrants, refugees, and temporary workers? Second, even if they are eligible for help, how can newcomers negotiate the system to obtain needed services? Finally, can the ethnic associations, in their role as mutual support groups, become a conduit for the delivery of social services to immigrants and refugees? As a corollary, what linkages exist, or can be forged, between ethnic associations and the formal voluntary and public social service system?

The new immigration to the United States in the last two

Shirley Jenkins is professor of social research at the Columbia University School of Social Work.

decades has generated thousands of ethnic associations, with a range of purposes and programs. My general hypothesis is that the ethnic associations can be an important link between the old life and the new, broader than the family group but narrower than the formal organization. In the case of new immigrants and refugees, this is particularly important because of the dislocations they have experienced and the need for rapid acculturation. The present study will show that ethnic associations are indeed fulfilling a number of social service functions. If this continues and they prove to be effective, then it may be that the traditional categorization of service providers in the United States as being either secular or sectarian, public or voluntary, may have to be modified to include an "ethnic" component as a further classification.

This book examines the potential of ethnic associations as deliverers of social services to new immigrants. It does that by reporting field studies of new immigrant associations in five countries that have substantial provisions for social welfare; hence the title, *Ethnic Associations and the Welfare State*. The main focus is on the United States, where a study of thirty associations, including seventeen different ethnic groups, was undertaken in New York City (Jenkins, Sauber, and Friedlander 1985). This study was then replicated in England, Israel, and the Netherlands, and supplementary information obtained on associations in Australia.

The inclusion of international material flows from the social context of the subject itself. Immigration is international by definition, and ethnic groups differ from each other, but the significance of the ethnic tie, and the propensity to associate with others of like background, appear in all countries studied. Social welfare provision is widespread, but entitlements vary from country to country. Material from five countries makes it possible to compare ethnic associations as they operate in their various settings.

One conclusion from the comparative analysis is that although the roles and potentials of the associations vary in different countries, depending on the national structure of welfare systems, in all settings the ethnic associations have made important contributions. The primary considerations are that they provide access to new immigrants and help point the way to an ethnic-sensitive practice.

How the associations function in service delivery depends on several factors. Five of these, which in research terms could be conceived of as the "independent variables," are as follows:

1. The nature of the new immigration.
2. The ethnic characteristics of the groups.
3. The nature of the ethnic associations.
4. The social welfare entitlements.
5. The social welfare system.

All of these help shape the role of the ethnic association in service delivery. These factors will be discussed separately in this introduction, mainly in terms of the American experience, but with some cross-country references.

Immigration to the United States

The impetus for this study is the new wave of immigration to the United States in the last two decades, and the dramatic shift in the ethnic composition of new arrivals. Asians and Hispanics are now the majority of all newcomers. In 1986, a year dedicated to the restoration and renewal of the Statue of Liberty in the New York Harbor, it might have been more appropriate to clone the "Lady" with suitable replicas in Miami, Loredo, and Los Angeles. The welcoming words might have to be altered, however, to fit the new arrivals and the new trends in immigration legislation. In fact, different messages might be needed for the various categories of newcomers: resident aliens, refugees, temporary workers, and the undocumented.

The Newcomers

Economic improvement has been a powerful force behind much of the world movement of people, and this latest wave is no exception. Internationally, the North-South gap between the "have" and "have-not" countries is very wide, and poverty-stricken people of Central America, other areas in the Caribbean,

Mexico, and parts of Asia are pushed from their homelands by lack of opportunity, and pulled to developed, industrialized countries to improve their economic status. One event that opened the immigration process to the new ethnic groups was the passing of the United States Immigration and Nationality Act of 1965, which significantly changed restriction on entry. Quotas that had previously tied numbers of visas to a percentage of nationals who were in the country almost half a century ago were abolished, and an even-handed number of 20,000 immigrants from each country was legislated. This law and later revisions were a response to our greater international involvements following World War II and to the worldwide shifts in power attendant to its aftermath. The twain of East and West were meeting, and could not be disentangled.

In addition to economic pressure, the continuing political upheavals, wars, and civil unrest abroad resulted in large numbers of refugees who sought residence in this country. Refugee policy has been an arm of foreign policy, as well as a humanitarian response to need. There was national recognition in the United States of the fact that refugee needs for entry are in fact different from those of ordinary immigrants, and vary depending on political circumstances. As a result the Refugee Act of 1980 agreed to admit refugees outside of planned quotas. This act was essentially designed for the entry of persons coming, under international agreements, from the place of first asylum, such as the refugee camps. It was not deemed applicable to the large numbers who arrived directly (e.g., Cubans and Haitians), and a special time-limited category of "entrant" was devised for those groups.

Another factor affecting the movement of people is the demand for seasonal and other short-term labor to perform specific jobs, usually agricultural. In the United States the extent of contract labor is a controversial issue. Proposals to raise the numbers admitted under labor contracts are supported by agricultural interests and opposed by sectors of organized labor.

The last group, undocumented aliens, includes both people who enter legally and overstay their visas and those who enter without visas, mainly the "feet" people who cross the borders. Some come, and leave when their jobs run out, but many others set up households, work, raise families, and live for many years in a precarious status as "illegals" with unresolved futures.

NUMBERS

Exact figures on total immigration to the United States are difficult to come by, in part because of unsystematic record keeping, and in part because of categories that are not mutually exclusive. A report of the National Research Council is aptly titled *Immigration Statistics, A Story of Neglect* (Levine, Hill, and Warren 1985). Final figures in 1983 report that there were 559,763 immigrant aliens admitted to the United States. Of these, 336,799 were new arrivals, and the rest, 222,964, were aliens who were adjusted to permanent resident status in the United States, presumably including former refugees. Exempt from numerical restriction (primarily close relatives of U.S. citizens) were about 34 percent of new arrivals and 78 percent of adjusted-status cases. In addition, there were about 57,000 refugees and 2,900 asylees, here for political reasons (U.S. Department of Justice 1983).

Estimates of undocumented aliens in the United States range from under one million to over twelve million. The differences can be explained in part by political motivations to under- or overstate the figures, by differences in who is counted as illegal, by a lack of real data, and by ignoring mortality as well as emigration back to the home country.

One data-based estimate uses a residual technique, subtracting legal aliens known to the Immigration and Naturalization Services (INS) from the total number of resident aliens reported in the 1980 census (with modifications to account for deficiencies in the data). The final estimate indicates that approximately 2.06 million undocumented aliens are included in the 1980 census, about 55 percent of whom are Mexicans. Current controversy over the Immigration legislation of 1986 (Simpson-Rodino Act) is particularly concerned with the issues of the undocumented and their impact on the American labor market, as well as on concepts of civic unity.

ETHNICITY

Immigration data are primarily defined by nationality. Ethnic data on immigrants, however, are far more complex and much less precise, but also far more informative for predicting the adaptation, acceptance, and adjustment of newcomers. Ethnicity has been variously defined, and since the term has been frequently used it is worth clarifying its meaning, which is often more apparent to "insiders" than to "outsiders" (Merton 1972). One definition is that of Schermerhorn (1970;12) who defines an ethnic group as a "collectivity within a larger society having real or putative common ancestry, memories of a shared historical past, and a cultural focus on one or more symbolic elements. . . . A necessary accompainment is some consciousness of kind." Among the symbolic elements are physical contiguity, language or dialect, religion, features, kinship patterns, and nationality, or any combination of these. Using this definition, it can be seen that immigrants from a single nation may be of different ethnic groups, or conversely, persons of the same ethnic group may immigrate from different national states. In spite of the difficulty of precision in definition, "ethnic group" is a telling category in relation to service delivery. Race and class are also important, but matters of lifestyle, custom, culture, and beliefs are often better understood by reference to the ethnic designation of the people in question. Such designations are also subject to fine-line separations—the *Harvard Encyclopedia of American Ethnic Groups* (Ternstrom 1980) includes over one hundred categories, discussed in alphabetical order, from Acadians to Zorastrians!

As already noted, in the United States the immigration legislation of 1965 sharply altered the ethnic composition of new arrivals. An analysis that compares data for fifteen years prior to that law and fifteen years after shows a growth in Asian immigration from 6.5 percent to 29.7 percent of the total, and a drop in immigration from Europe from 46.7 percent to 23.3 percent (Tobier 1982). The newcomers from Asia are the fastest-growing minority in the United States. They are from at least a dozen countries, speak different languages, have certain racial characteristics in common, and have varied cultural, political, and class backgrounds. Also of particular ethnic importance are the large numbers of newly arrived Hispanics, who join citizens of Spanish background already here in making up what is projected to be shortly the largest minority group in the country. Although Hispanics are also from different countries, the common language (although with differing accents and vocabulary) and many similar traditions and customs mean there is probably more justification for grouping Hispanics, in ethnic terms, than there is for the more disparate newcomers from Asia, who include Filipinos, Koreans, Vietnamese, Indians, and Chinese, among others.

The History of Immigration Policy

Immigration policy seeks to rationalize national interests and to control national borders. This is not to say that the national interest is unidimensional. The United States has been ambivalent in its immigration policy for a century, and has vacillated between acceptance and exclusion, depending on the strength of the interest groups. A brief review of immigration policy will highlight the ethnic themes in the legislation.

The history of the peopling of the present United States territory is closely linked with the history of immigration policy, supplemented by territorial acquistion. The ethnic base of the original settlements was a limited one. A classification of surnames in the 1790 census shows that virtually all of the white immigrants were from northwestern Europe, mostly from the British Isles (78.9 percent). Thus as far back as colonial times the ethnic die was cast. The earliest colonists set the mold for a national Anglo-Saxon image.

In the colonial years and the early period of the republic, the goals were the same—to people the country and to provide a substantial source of labor, available for both agriculture and skilled occupations. The "open door" policy prevailed and encouragement was given to the free entry of settlers from abroad. From 1820 to 1880 over ten million people immigrated to the United States, an estimated 95 percent of whom were from northern and western Europe. Although the slave trade was abolished by Congress in 1808, it did not actually end until the Civil War, and the peopling of the United States included large numbers of blacks from Africa and their progeny.

In spite of the growing negative attitudes toward newcomers, as expressed in the anti-Irish and anti-German nativist movement, immigration burgeoned; in the three decades from 1881 to 1910 about 17.7 million people entered the United States. There was a change in national origins, however, from the "old" immigration from northwestern Europe to the "new" immigration from southern and eastern Europe. The restrictionist movement developed racist theories of the presumed inferiority of these newcomers. The major feature of this period was the introduction of national quotas in the immigration acts of 1921 and 1924, which set national quotas at 2 percent of the foreign born of the nationality recorded in the 1890 census (later revised to relate to the 1920 census). The Chinese Exclusion Act of 1882 was already in force, and aliens ineligible for citizenship (i.e., nonwhites, particularly Chinese) were not allowed to enter. This system favored northern and western Europeans, who comprised about 82 percent of the total allowable quota.

World War II and its aftermath forced certain changes in immigration policy. The Chinese Exclusion Act was repealed in 1943, and a token quota was given to Chinese immigrants. Global policies were forcing realignments which altered American foreign policy and, as a consequence, American immigration policy. This was reflected in the 1965 immigration legislation, which abolished national quotas and put an end to the special Asian discriminatory restrictions. An overall ceiling of 290,000 visas was determined, 120,000 for the Eastern Hemisphere, the latter to be limited to 20,000 per country. They were to be distributed subject to preferential treatment for designated family members and persons with specific skills. In 1976 the differences between the Western and Eastern Hemispheres were abolished and the same preference system applied to both. With the passage of the Refugee Act in 1980, the overall ceiling was reduced to 270,000, with substantial members of refugees entering outside the immigrant quotas following processing by the international refugee organization.

Following extended national discussion and dispute, the Immigration Reform and Control Act of 1986 (Simpson-Rodino) was signed into law on November 6, 1986. Unlike earlier legislation which primarily dealt with quotas, entry, and exclusion, this new law was concerned with circumscribed areas of punishments and rewards. There are two main provisions: penalities, for employers who hire undocumented aliens after November 6, 1986; and amnesty for undocumented aliens who can prove they have lived continuously in the United States since 1981. The latter group can then receive first temporary, then permanent status, and eventually citizenship. Those who can prove continuous residence since 1971 can receive permanent status upon documentation. There is also a legalization program for a limited number of farm workers (350,000) and one for certain Cubans and Haitians with residence since 1981.

The bitter conflict over the legislation centered on the civil (escalating to criminal) penalties applied to employers. According to some critics, the concern is that they might be led to discriminate in employment against all Hispanic workers, regardless of status. A further criticism has been made of the feasibility of implementing the amnesty program, because of the difficulties that the undocumented, who have lived for so long in hiding, would have in proving continuous residence, and the subsequent danger of deportation should their efforts at legalization fail.

This brief review of immigration legislation shows how it responds to national, social, political, and economic forces. Movements of people, however, may only be contained, but not fully controlled, by immigration legislation. In recent years economic, political, and legislative developments have together resulted in what is probably the most multiethnic population of new arrivals in the history of the United States. Domestically, cultural pluralism has increasingly been accepted as a fact of American sociological life, superceding the discredited and never viable "melting pot" theory. Nonetheless, the new arrivals have presented a range of new problems, including questions related to the delivery of social services.

Ethnic Associations

One way of characterizing ethnicity is to describe it as a concept that combines an interest with an affective tie (Bell 1975). This may be the rationale for the recent proliferation of ethnic associations, a type of organization common to many societies and particularly evident in times of heavy migrations. The ethnic association is a special type of voluntary association because of the affective tie, and a special type of self-help group because of the nature of the common interest. This may be particularly meaningful if a society is involved in affirmative action, where membership in one or another ethnic group may offer certain advantages in relation to specific needs.

A distinction can be drawn between what an ethnic association is and what it does. In terms of what it is, an ethnic association can be defined as an organization formed by individuals who consciously define themselves as members of an ethnic group within a larger context. Thus it is distinguished from an organization that operates without ethnic identity. It fulfills needs common to persons of its defined group, and typically sees itself as part of an ethnic community. In terms of what it does, an ethnic association may exist for a wide variety of reasons: social, recreational, political, cultural, professional, business, service, or a combination of some or all of the above. It usually has a core of members, but nonmembers may also be involved. The key elements are the base in a self-defined ethnic group, the voluntary nature of the association, and the goal of mutual benefit.

The association can be distinguished from an ethnic agency, which is an established social agency with a primary commitment to members of one or more ethnic groups. The ethnic agency operates service programs and usually has professional staff. It may or may not have a membership base. Operations are usually under a board of directors, and both public and voluntary funding may be received. One type of service may be offered, such as foster care, or there may be a range of services in a multifaceted program. One study that sought to operationalize the definition of the ethnic agency described three key variables characteristic of its operations: the incorporation of cultural components of the ethnic group; a consciousness of ethnic identity; and a policy on mixing or matching by ethnic group in all areas of operations (Jenkins 1981).

Although interested in social-service delivery, the present study looks further than the ethnic agency, and examines some voluntary ethnic associations which may or may not be committed to solving the social problems of members. The attempt is to reach some groups that are just beginning to recognize the needs of newcomers, as well as others with active programs. The focus is on associations with a potential for service delivery.

Although ethnic associations are not a new phenomenon in the United States, they have reemerged with the rise in immigration, in particular for new groups with distinct cultural patterns. One study, for example, identified more than five hundred Mutual Assistance Associations (MAAS) created by the Indochinese refugee community in the United States from 1975 to 1980. These associations had various functions, the main ones being social/fraternal, educational/cultural, and political (Bui 1981). Another study of Indian associations reported that they were organized in functional categories, but within each category divided into Indian language groupings, which were almost entirely mutually exclusive (Fisher 1980).

Most of the research on ethnic associations tends to be descriptive and focused on a single group. Sassen-Koob (1979), however, has undertaken comparative work on Colombian and Dominican associations. Her findings are that the relative similarity of the culturally ideological variables, involved in both groups by virtue of the attribution of a common Hispanic identity, tend to be outweighed by the structural variables which differentiate the immigrant groups, such as class and rural or urban origins. Thus the association of the middle-class urban Colombian will be different from that of working-class Dominicans from rural areas, even though both are of Hispanic background.

Where they are actively involved in service delivery, ethnic associations can have important community roles, and can stretch their activities beyond their local situations. An example of this is the convening of the first National Conference of Haitian Community Centers in New York in 1985, an initial step in forming a national network of groups concerned with problems of Haitians. Representatives of about fifty Haitian community centers across the country gathered to discuss issues of mutual interest—including housing, employment, language, and immigration counseling (Haitian Centers Council 1985).

The ethnic associations discussed in this study include both voluntary organizations of immigrants who are financially independent and groups of refugees who have access to special public funds to aid members toward self-support. Both groups, however, face a complex and bewildering set of social service entitlements which they must digest if they seek help for members in need.

Entitlements for Newcomers

A model to illustrate entitlements for newcomers in this study would have to be multidimensional. Countries differ from each other in their social welfare systems, and internally they offer a wide range of benefits. Newcomers differ from each other in legal status, and this differentially affects eligibility for many of the benefits. In the United States some benefits are national, and others depend on state and local governments. Newcomers with special needs are often unaware of their entitlements, and are in need of help to facilitate communication and gain referrals to the proper channels.

In the United States some entitlements are universal, such as social security, and some are means tested, such as public welfare. Newcomers are disadvantaged by contributory programs, such as unemployment insurance, until they can qualify for benefits, and in the absence of a national health program they are uncovered on arrival and at particular financial risk if they experience accidents or illness. Even though resident aliens have most of the social service entitlements of citizens, many fear deportation until citizenship is achieved, and others fear that relatives may not be admitted if they become dependent on welfare. Legal immigrants are usually a minimum burden to the social welfare budget; they are mainly young, with skills and work capacity, and often enter under family preferences, implying resident relatives.

For refugees, the situation is very different. They enter with assumed entitlements and with the commitment of the federal government, under the Refugee Act of 1980, to help them to be self-supporting. In fact, this has meant federal reimbursement to states and localities for support of refugees, where needed, for three years, and for special help for instruction in English, job training, and other programs.

Entitlements for undocumented aliens present a legal and moral dilemma. United States immigration law and social service law are not congruent in philosophy or execution, and may often work at cross-purposes. Federal authorities are responsible for excluding the undocumented, but if they enter the country the social service system has to carry out certain health and welfare functions for all persons in need, regardless of legal status. In particular hospitals and schools have responsibilities for service delivery. The issue is particularly clouded with regard to entitlements of children of the undocumented, who may be citizens by virtue of birth, but whose family caretakers may be illegal residents. For example, the rights of such children to foster care is not challenged—the problem is whether they have the right to care from their own parents, who may need income support.

The impact of the substantial new immigration on social service programs in the United States is difficult to estimate. Many programs are contributory, and there is input as well as output—indeed one of the complaints heard from advocates for the working undocumented is that they pay heavily in all forms of taxation, but are barred from most forms of benefits. One study has examined the situations of three types of newcomers—legal immigrants, refugees, and the undocumented—with regard to three types of programs where data are available: income transfer, health, and education. In general, legal immigrants were found to be about average for the country in contributions and utilization of benefits; refugees were below average in contributions and above average in utilization; and illegal immigrants were below average in both contributions and the utilization of benefits (North 1983; 272). This study is concerned with the impact on new arrivals of the existing benefit structure. It is worth noting, however, that there is a two-way interaction. Just as immigrants must respond to the social-service system, so the system itself may change in response to the needs of these new client groups.

Global Factors

The inclusion in this volume of papers that report on ethnic associations in England, Israel, the Netherlands, and Australia is no afterthought. All four variables discussed in this introduction—

immigration, ethnicity, ethnic associations, and welfare entitlements—are phenomena of international import. Both immigration and migration reflect the movement of people in response to
global events. Single-factor explanations of "pushes and pulls"
are too simplistic, economic determinism too mechanical, and
political and religious freedoms too ideological to be fully explan-
atory of the world movements of people. In addition, sharp distinctions between "permanent" and "temporary" often fail, and
even "legal" and "illegal" are not always mutually exclusive
categories.

Immigration Policy
        The review of American immigration legislation shows the
relationship between national interests and the entry of newcomers. Each of the papers included here refers to legislation relevant
to each country's situation. In Great Britain, for example, severe
labor shortages after World War II prompted the heavy recruitment of West Indians, but when these shortages were relieved
legislation was designed to regulate immigrant inflows. The special
relationships with former colonies, however, as well as commit-
ments to Commonwealth members, have complicated British efforts to control immigration. It has been noted that "the debate
on immigration in the United Kingdom centers as much, if not
more, on political, cultural, and ethnic issues, rather than on
economic ones" (Tapinos 1983:55).
        In Israel, there is the least ambiguity toward new immi-
grants. Populating the newly created state with Jewish entrants
had high priority for the government, and policies to implement
this goal are explicit. The "law of return" gives Jews the world
over the right to emigrate to Israel. This is backed up by economic
incentives all the way from entry of duty-free merchandise for
settlers to subsidized airlifts and a substantial period of support for
language instruction and acculturation.
        In contrast, after World War II, the Netherlands was felt by
many to be overpopulated, and emigration by Dutch inhabitants
was encouraged and did occur. Both political and economic factors
worked to counter this movement. The entry of repatriates in the

aftermath of Indonesian independence, as well as of Moluccans from Java and students and residents from Surinam, composed the political immigration. In addition, the recruitment of migrant "guest workers" from Mediterranean countries in the 1950s and 1960s was designed to relieve labor shortages for unskilled and semiskilled workers (Penninx 1984).

Finally, in Australia, there have been shifts in immigration policy. There was a formal end to the White Australia Policy in 1973, although it had been dismantled in the mid-1960s, and a substantial refugee influx from both Southeast Asia and parts of Europe (Cox 1983). Thus the countries examined in this study have had different immigration experiences. All have been affected by both domestic and international events, often with unintended consequences.

ETHNICITY

One of the unintended consequences of the new immigration has been the changes in the ethnic composition of the receiving countries. A *New York Times* article, "Race Issues in Europe," comments on these changes:

> Western Europe is coming to face a problem of national identity new to the modern age. It has to do with the arrival of huge numbers of migrant workers in the last quarter-century. By now, some of them have settled down and have no intention of leaving. The rising generation of their children hold citizenship in their new homes by right of birth.
>
> This is creating problems of assimilation and community frictions that Americans know well but that challenge basic assumptions of old Europeans who were quite content to run other societies in Africa and Asia but are finding it hard to deal with what they consider exotic aliens in their own countries. (Lewis 1985).

In comparing the situation in Europe with that in the United States, the article continues:

> Racism, which many Europeans thought was a peculiar fault of Americans, has developed in countries that believed they were above it without noticing that they took national identity as one race for granted.

In Great Britain, ethnic differences are a key factor in the reception of and attitudes toward the new immigrants. Primarily

of West Indian, Indian, Pakistani, Chinese, and African backgrounds, much of the immigration in that country has centered
on the accommodation of these ethnic minority groups in the
heretofore homogeneous white British population. There is much
of the same racial ideology in the Australian setting, but the size
of the continent, and the need to populate it, provide a different
context for the discussion of ethnic immigrant groups.

Israel may be the most ethnically diverse country in existence for its size, a result of its active absorption process. With
religion the unifying element, the Jewish population of Israel
(about 83 percent of the total) originated in over eighty different
countries. Although there are wide differences in customs and
language among many of the eighty countries, two general groupings emerge: the Ashkenazi—Jews from Europe, the United
States, Canada and other Western countries; and the Sephardic—
Jews mainly from Asia and Africa. There are historical differences
between the two groups, as well as political, economic, and class
differences in their situations in Israel.

The Netherlands had experienced a major post–World War
II influx of repatriates, primarily from Indonesia (Penninx
1984;345), and their assimilation was considered to be relatively
successful. Groups who arrived later were of different ethnic backgrounds, e.g., Moluccans, Surinamese, and migrant workers from
Mediterranean countries, particularly Turks. These groups have
not fared so well in adaptation to the Dutch society.

Ethnic Associations

The cross-national papers included here all report the same
growth of ethnic associations as has occurred in the United States,
following the rise in postwar immigration. As in this country,
these associations are involved in a range of activities, and probably a minority would say their main concern is social services.
How these associations function in response to the perceived needs
of their members varies, depending in part on the structure of
social services in each country. The associations all have the potential, however, for both access to entitlements and communication with members of their own groups, two critical factors in
reaching persons in need of help.

Comparative Entitlements

There are wide variations in the service systems and welfare entitlements among the five countries in this study. Furthermore, within each service package, new immigrants and refugees may occupy positions of more or less preference than do citizens. It is understandable, therefore, that there has not been substantial empirical work comparing immigrant entitlements.

Another way to approach this question is to follow a deductive method and develop a typology of immigrant needs and a model for meeting them, regardles of national setting. Cox (1985) has taken this approach, in raising the question of whether or not it is possible to develop an international perspective on migrant welfare based on an understanding of the migration phenomenon, which would provide a model for appropriate preventive and remedial services.

In developing this model, Cox sees migration-integration as a process with four basic stages: premovement, transition, resettlement, and integration, or becoming an integral part of the new environment. At each of these stages, there is a series of variables affecting outcome. Cox (p. 76) suggests that the following six independent variables are involved:

1. The background of the group and the nature of its migration.
2. The nature of previous contact with the host society and consequent prearrival attitudes, on both sides.
3. The socioeconomic and political context on arrival.
4. The prevailing host society attitudes.
5. The nature of the ethnic-group development.
6. The economic status of the group.

Dependent variables, or outcomes, are "...first, the nature of the social problems likely to emerge during integration, and second, the nature of welfare developments that will occur both within the immigrant population and in the host society" (Cox 1985:75).

This approach has particular relevance for this study. Cox's concern is with welfare outcomes, and one of the independent variables he uses is the nature of ethnic group development, in particular the ethnic association. Cox states, in discussing this phenomenon, that the nature of the ethnic group developments is to some degree predictable on the basis of an understanding of the nature and likely impact of the previous four variables. It is also highly important as a variable in its own right in that the nature and degree of development of the ethnic group is highly significant in a welfare context (p. 77). Cox then goes on to suggest certain propositions relating to ethnic development. He hypothesizes that ethnic associations will be stronger if the culture of the immigrants is distinctive and cohesive, if the host society has negative attitudes toward the group, and if the political climate appears to be controlled by a dominant group. On the other hand, ethnic associations will be weaker if migration has been involuntary and if there is a difficult economic climate for newcomers on arrival.

This study of ethnic associations presents data relevant to several of the hypotheses suggested by Cox, and also develops a typology of associations based on field interviews. The study of thirty associations in New York interviewed ethnic leaders of seventeen different groups and asked about the perceived needs of group members; the ethnic association's history, structure, and services; aspects of identity and acculturation; and linkages with the formal service system. The replication of this study in England, Israel, and the Netherlands and the review of the situation in Australia provide a base for testing the model. The cross-country comparative paper indicates how national differences affect the role of ethnic associations in relation to social service delivery systems.

References

Bell, D. 1975. "Ethnicity and Social Change." In N. Glazer and D. P. Moynihan, eds., *Ethnicity, Theory, and Experience*, p. 169, Cambridge: Harvard University Press.

Bui, D. June 1981. "The Indochinese Mutual Assistance Associations." In *Bridging Cultures: Southeast Asian Refugees in America*, pp. 167–180, Los Angeles, Calif.: Asian-American Community Mental Health Training Center.

Cox, D. 1983. "Refugee Settlement in Australia: Review of an Era." *International Migration* 21(3): 332–44.

Cox, D. 1985. "Welfare Services for Migrants: Can They Be Better Planned?" *International Migration* (March), 23(1): 73–95.

Fisher, M. P. 1980. *The Indians of New York City: A Study of Immigrants from India.* (Columbia, Mo.): South Asia Books.

Haitian Centers Council. *Newsletter* (Spring 1985), vol. 2, no. 1.

Jenkins, S. 1981. *The Ethnic Dilemma in Social Services.* New York; Free Press, pp. 43–74.

Jenkins, S., M. Sauber, and E. Friedlander, October 1985. *Ethnic Associations and Services to New Immigrants in New York City.* New York; Community Council of Greater New York.

Levine, D. B., K. Hill, and R. Warren, eds., 1985. *Immigration Statistics: A Story of Neglect.* Washington, D.C.: National Academy Press.

Lewis, F. "Race Issues in Europe." *The New York Times,* Nov. 8, 1985, p. A35.

Merton, R. K. 1972. "Insiders and Outsiders: A Chapter in the Sociology of Knowledge." *American Journal of Sociology* (July), 78,(1): 9–47.

North, D. S. 1983. "Impact of Legal, Illegal, and Refugee Migrations on U.S. Social Service Programs." In M. M. Kritz, ed., *U.S. Immigration and Refugee Policy,* p. 272, Lexington, Mass.: Heath.

Penninx, R. "Research and Research Policy with Regard to Ethnic Minorities in the Netherlands: A Historical Outline and the State of Affairs." In *International Migration* (Winter 1984). 22:345–366.

Sassen-Koob, S. 1979. "Formal and Informal Associations: Dominicans and Colombians in New York," *International Migration Review,* vol. 13, no. 2.

Schermerhorn, R. A. *Comparative Ethnic Relations: A Framework for Theory and Research.* New York: Random House, 1970.

Tapinos, G. P. 1983. "European Migration Patterns: Economic Linkages and Policy Experiences. In M. M. Kritz, *U.S. Immigration and Refugee Policy,* p. 55, Lexington, Mass.: Heath.

Ternstrom, S., ed. 1980. *Harvard Encyclopedia of American Ethnic Groups.* Cambridge, Mass.: Harvard University Press.

Tobier, E. 1982. "Foreign Immigration." In C. Brecher and R. D. Horton, eds., *Setting Municipal Priorities, 1983,* p. 163. New York: New York University Press.

U. S. Department of Justice, Immigration and Naturalization Service. 1983. *Statistical Yearbook of the Immigration and Naturalization Services.* Washington, D.C.: GPO.

2.

Ethnic Associations in New York and Services to Immigrants

Shirley Jenkins and Mignon Sauber

The faces of New York are changing. Census data confirm what has been apparent in the streets, the classrooms, and the hospital emergency rooms. There is a new wave of immigration to the United States, and New York City continues to be a major place of settlement. Some newcomers are from developing countries, others from industrialized areas. Some come with professional and technical skills; others do not. Some come from countries in turmoil, others from nations at peace. They come both as individuals and family groups, and they share the common human needs of the population in general. But the newcomers also have special needs related to their language and cultural patterns, their customary life-styles and their perceptions of others. Furthermore, they experience the trauma of separation from their homelands and the problems of coping in a new community.

This paper is based on the study *Ethnic Associations and Services to New Immigrants in New York City,* by Shirley Jenkins, Mignon Sauber, and Eva Friedlander (Community Council of Greater New York, 1985). The study was funded by the Charles H. Revson Foundation, Eli N. Evans, president.

Shirley Jenkins is professor of social research at the Columbia University School of Social Work. Mignon Sauber is associate executive director for research, Community Council of Greater New York.

The question of the "fit" between the needs of these various groups of newcomers and the existing human services systems in New York is the context for this study. The basic question is the role played by ethnic associations, which historically have been concerned with, and responsive to, the needs of their respective groups. Are ethnic associations today helping newcomers, whether refugees or other immigrants, to meet basic human needs? And if they are helping, are they relating to the formal social-service system?

In designing the study, it was recognized that the situations of recent immigrants are both similar to and different from those of past waves of arrivals. There are similarities, in particular, in the "pushes and pulls" that motivate people to improve their way of life and seek both economic, educational, and political opportunities. But there also are differences that relate to potential service needs. One difference is the ethnic composition of the new immigrant groups. The major changes in the United States immigration laws that occurred in 1965, and the evolving policies pertaining to refugees that were legislated in 1980, altered the racial and ethnic composition of newcomers. In New York City approximately four-fifths of immigrants in 1979 came from Central and South America, the Caribbean, Asia, and Africa (Tobier 1982:181). They comprise what Bryce-LaPorte (1977) has called the "visible ethnics," and these groups entered a society with a long history of discrimination against people of color. At the same time, they entered a rapidly changing economy where they must compete with native workers for jobs and services.

On the positive side, newcomers came to a society that has experienced affirmative action and where the ethnopolitics of recent decades has meant that minorities have recognized the advantages of developing their own organizations as sources of services and rewards. Few knowledgeable observers currently view the "melting pot" concept as a viable goal. Cultural pluralism as an ideology is a more widely accepted philosophy. Although there have been some reversals in this trend, there still exists a basis in the United States for the legitimation of differences and the toleration of a variety of cultural expressions.

The general hypothesis in this study is that ethnic associations can be an important link between the old life and the new, and between primary-group family ties and formal bureaucratic structures. Interviews with leaders of ethnic associations explored how these associations:

- came into existence, and their goals, then and now;
- perceive the needs of the newcomers among their constituents;
- work toward acculturation of their members;
- help their members relate to their ethnic identity;
- offer direct help or other assistance to newcomers; and
- interface with the formal service structure.

Altogether leaders of thirty associations in New York City representing seventeen ethnic groups were interviewed. The groups included Cambodians, Chinese, Colombians, Cubans, Dominicans, Greeks, Haitians, Indians, Israelis, Italians, Jamaicans, Koreans, Palestinians, other Arabic-speaking people, Poles, Russian Jews, and Vietnamese. Interviews were conducted in English, Spanish, Korean, and Chinese.

Study Design

The study design undertook work on at least three levels: a descriptive report on ethnic associations, their history, the people served, and the nature of services; a study of linkages with the formal service system; and an analysis of group ethnic identity. The goal was to develop a typology of associations that could be used in planning service delivery to newcomers.

Study resources were only adequate for the field interviewing of thirty associations, and their selection from the hundreds of possible settings was a difficult task. There was no sampling frame from which to draw a representative sample, and in fact representativeness could not be accomplished without more information about the nature of the organizations. The sample, therefore, is purposive, selected according to multiple criteria which took account of the following:

1. Demographic data on the numbers of each group in the immigrant populations in New York.
2. A telephone survey of over one hundred associations, listed in various directories, with preliminary screening questions on their activities and membership.
3. References to government funding agency lists of ethnic associations who are in receipt of public grants.
4. Suggestions from the study's advisory committee, made up of academics, human-services agency directors, and representatives from a range of ethnic associations and agencies who have expert knowledge of their communities.

For each association selected, there was validation by reference to two independent sources of information on the association's authenticity, its relevance to the study, and its acceptance by its own ethnic community. For some groups, because of size, or to insure diversity, two or three associations were included; for others only one. In all cases field interviews were conducted with the director or head of each association; in several cases additional contacts were made with staff. There is no claim to complete coverage of all ethnic groups in the city, but the major categories of newcomers are included.

Interview Instrument

The interview instrument was a thirty-six-page questionnaire, which incorporated both structured and open-ended questions. It was organized in three main parts: the history and characteristics of the associations, identity and acculturation issues, and service roles. In the last section, respondents were asked specifically about perceived needs and services in the areas of housing, jobs, training, health, family supports, the elderly, youth, children and schools, women, mental health, finances, and legal help.

Interviewers included doctoral students in social work and sociology, all with master's degrees. Several were involved in ethnic research themselves, and they were diverse in background.

The group included men and women who were black, Chicano, Chinese, Dominican, and Korean. The study's senior research associate, an anthropologist with extensive interview experience, conductd about one-third of the interviews herself, and supervised the field operation.[1] Three training sessions were held for the interviewers, as well as a debriefing session following four months in the field.

Analysis of Data

After careful editing of the interviews, with return calls if needed, a plan was developed for analysis. There were several options, and it became apparent that there was a need for two sequential approaches in analyzing the various aspects studied. To study the associations, the focus had to be on each case in the sample. For classification purposes, these were grouped by ethnicity, nationality, and region. To study services and linkages, however, the data had to be related to the present service system operating in New York City, and the service data were therefore analyzed under the appropriate service categories such as housing, jobs, health, and so forth. This requires the reader to make a conceptual shift between the discussions of the associations and their differentiating factors and typology, and the later discussion of the associations as they relate to human services; but the analysis is faithful to the multifaceted concerns of the research.

Interviews with the Formal Provider System

As a context for understanding some of the information collected through the interviews with ethnic association leaders, interviews were also held with key specialized agencies of the existing formal human services system who had particular concern with services to new immigrants. Included were the Human Resources Administration; the Board of Education; the Health and Hospitals Corporation; the Department of Mental Health, Mental

1. Interviews were conducted by Eva Friedlander, senior research associate, Young Hee Ahn, Thomas Bryant, III, Amelia Chu, Anneris Goris, R. Tony Sainz.

Retardation and Alcoholism Services; Catholic Charities Diocese of Brooklyn; the Federation of Protestant Welfare Agencies; and the New York Association for New Americans. The purpose of these interviews was to learn the perceptions of the established sector regarding the needs of new immigrants, the resources available to meet their needs, and their expectations of the potential for service linkages between the formal agencies and the ethnic associations.

Organization of the Report

This paper is organized into seven sections: an introductory section on the study design; a section giving demographic content relevant to an understanding of the new arrivals in New York City and trends in programs for refugees and entrants; a section on the ethnic associations themselves, outlining their history, origin, purposes, and structure; a section analyzing differentiating factors, presenting a typology of ethnic associations; a section on issues of identity and acculturation as strategies for coping; a section examining the question of ethnic associations and human services delivery; and a section presenting the study's conclusions and recommendations.

Throughout the study it must be remembered that the core of the information presented comes from extensive interviews with a purposively selected group of thirty associations. These associations can in no way be fully representative of all newcomers in New York City or, indeed, even of all newcomers in the particular nationality group from which they were formed. They were carefully selected, however, according to the criteria noted. Another limitation of the interviews is that the respondents were the leaders of these associations who could only share their own perceptions of their functions but could not actually speak for all their membership or constituents. They are, however, the recognized spokespersons. Given these limitations, what is included in the report is a wealth of descriptive information about a variety of ethnic associations, a proposed typology for study of these associations, and an assessment of their role in facilitating social service delivery.

Demographic Trends

Changes in immigration legislation, as well as changes in the politics and economics of the nations of the world, are reflected in the changing ethnic patterns of New York City. Demographic data not only provide a picture of the situation that newcomers enter, but also help to explain some of the problems they face.

Census data for 1950, 1960, and 1970 show New York City to have 7.8 to 7.9 million people, but in the 1970s New York City began to lose population, which by 1980 was down to 7.1 million, a loss of over 800,000 or 10.4 percent. This trend has been attributed both to a net outmigration from the city and to a decline in the rate of natural increase.

Accompanying this decline in population was an even sharper drop among children under 18 (-21 percent); there were modest increases among those aged 25 to 34, an age group into which many newcomers might fall. The population aged 75 or older also increased over the decade.

The most visible change between 1970 and 1980 in the population was among racial and ethnic groups. Using census categories, the greatest loss was among white non-Hispanics who went from 63 to 52 percent of the city's total population. The black, non-Hispanic group meanwhile grew from 21 to 28 percent of the population, and the Hispanics from 16 to nearly 20 percent.

This is the background against which data on New York City's foreign born must be viewed. In approximately the same numbers as New York City's populations declined, immigration to New York City increased; between 1970 and 1980 there was an influx of 800,000 to 850,000 persons (Tobier 1982:179). By 1980, there were an estimated 1.67 million persons of foreign birth living in New York City. This figure from the 1980 census is considered conservative, given the absence of an unspecified number of undocumented aliens who may not have been included in the census count. One estimate places the total number of undocumented persons in New York City between 400,000 and 500,000 (Tobier 1982:187). Some of these persons are included in the census figures and some are not. A census study estimates that 234,000 undocumented aliens had been included in the 1980 population counts for the state of New York, and suggests that this number accounts for a majority of the undocumented (Passel and Woodrow 1984). A panel of the National Academy of Sciences has recently supported this estimate, and does not believe that there has been a substantial increase since 1980. The question of the specific dimensions of the undercount for New York City remains unanswered for both the undocumented as well as for the overall immigrant population.

Even on the basis of the available 1980 census data, the recent growth in New York City's foreign-born population is dramatic. There were some 233,000 more foreign-born living in New York City in 1980 than in 1970, an increase of 16 percent over the decade. As a result, by 1980 nearly one in every four (23.6 percent) New Yorkers was born outside the United States (see table 2.1).

Large as this increase was, it represented only 5 percent of the growth in the foreign-born population nationwide. Between 1970 and 1980 the total foreign-born population of the United States increased by nearly 4.5 million, or 46 percent. With this growth nationally, the proportion of the country's foreign born living in New York City declined—from nearly 15 percent in 1970

Table 2.1. Total Population and Foreign-born Population, United States and New York City, 1970–1980

			Change, 1970–1980	
Population and Area	1970	1980	Number	Percent
United States				
Total population	203,210,158	226,504,800	+23,294,642	+11.5
Foreign born	9,619,302	14,079,906	+4,460,604	+46.3
Percent total	4.7	6.2		
New York City				
Total population	7,894,798	7,071,639	−823,159	−10.4
Foreign born	1,437,058	1,670,199	+233,141	+16.2
Percent total	18.2	23.6		
New York City as Percent of United States				
Total population	3.9	3.1		
Foreign born	14.9	11.9		

SOURCE: *U.S. Census of Population: 1970.* Final report PC(1)-C1, U.S., table 68; and PC(1)-C34, N.Y., table 81. *U.S. Census of Population: 1980.* Final report PC80-1-C1, U.S., table 79; and PC80-1-C34, N.Y., table 116.

to about 12 percent in 1980. Nevertheless, New York City continues to house a disproportionate share of the country's foreign
born. In 1970, New York City accounted for 3.9 percent of the
total population of the United States, but housed nearly 15 percent
of the country's foreign-born population. In 1980, it housed 12
percent, while its share of the total population had dropped to 3.1
percent.

There were also substantial shifts in the ethnic makeup of
the foreign-born population of New York City between 1970 and
1980, and these roughly reflect the changes in the United States
as a whole. The most notable change is the increase in the share
who are Asian and from the Americas, and the smaller proportion
who are of European birth. U.S. census data for 1970 and 1980
show that the percentage of Asians in New York City's foreign-
born population went from 7 percent in 1970 to 13 percent in
1980, while for the Americas it changed from 24 percent in 1970
to 39 percent in 1980. The percent who were of European birth,
on the other hand, decreased from 56 percent in 1970 to 35
percent in 1980. National trends were in the same direction, but
there were some important differences, with New York City continuing to hold a greater attraction for some immigrant groups
than for others.

Included among the foreign-born population of 1.67 million in New York City in 1980 are some 944,000 who arrived in
the United States in 1965 or subsequently. The four largest nationality groups among them were Dominicans (10 percent), Jamaicans (8 percent), Chinese (7 percent), and Haitians (5 percent).
With 1.67 million foreign-born, and almost 1 million recent immigrants, there is a fertile population for recruitment to the growing number of ethnic associations in New York City.

The Associations

The thirty ethnic associations interviewed in New York included
groups with very different immigration histories and circumstances of arrival, cultural backgrounds, languages, national and racial

origins, and legal statuses and entitlements. Members may be resident aliens, refugees, entrants, visitors, or undocumented aliens. So it was not unexpected to find that the histories and goals of these associations varied greatly, reflecting the special circumstances of each group. The brief description of the associations that follows provides background information for the typology developed and the discussion of social service roles. The initial categorization of the descriptive data will be regional, with national origin noted under each region.

Asian Associations

Ten of the thirty associations interviewed comprised people from Asian countries: three were Chinese, three Korean, two Indian, one Cambodian, and one Vietnamese. The last two are refugee groups.

CHINESE

Chinese immigrants to the United States have come in several waves, and the ethnic associations interviewed reflect both the old and the new. The residential concentration of New York Chinese in the Chinatown neighborhood has meant that several social agencies and community centers have developed ethnic programs as part of their overall activities, but these were felt to be outside the purview of this study, confined as it is to ethnic associations.

Oldest among the Chinese associations interviewed was an organization founded in 1886, four years after the U.S. Chinese exclusion legislation. The original purpose of the group was to provide job referrals and help with translation for early Chinese immigrants, and to mediate conflicts between the Chinese community and the other ethnic groups in New York. This original purpose remains, but their program has been expanded to include educational, social, and recreational activities. The organization includes sixty family associations (characteristic of the Chinese social structure), twenty-four business organizations, and some recommended individual members. The association has a board of nineteen members elected by representatives of the family and business groups, and a four-person leadership. The association does not receive any public money, but is self-sufficient with its investments, endowments, contributions, and school fees. The association relates to the old established organizations in the community, and mediates between local business and government officials. Newcomers are reported to be more alienated from China than were the Chinese who were part of an earlier migration.

The second Chinese association interviewed was a large, well-established family association. It started over eighty years ago as a self-help group for Chinese in New York. The founding members were roommates in an apartment house in the Lower East Side, and they came together in the spirit of mutual aid. The early emphasis was on providing translation services, financial help, employment referrals, and meals for immigrants. The association has not changed its original purpose, but the services it provides have been diminished because of changes in the availability of public social service funds and the recent growth of ethnic services in the community. This association has a membership base of several hundred who are all Chinese men over 18 years old with the same surname. Most of the members have little education, with less than half at the high-school level, and they work mainly in factories and restaurants in Chinatown. The association does not rely on public funds but supports itself with endowments, dues, and donations. It owns a seven-story building in Chinatown, which is used for social functions.

As a contrast to the associations that represent earlier immigrants, the third Chinese association interviewed was less than two years old, having been established in 1983. It was organized by a group of Overseas Chinese from Indochina to enhance self-help and mutual aid among other like immigrants. Its establishment was an expression of its separate identity, distinct from both the Chinese from China and refugees who are ethnic Indochinese. The association is made up of about five hundred families; about 95 percent are newcomers. Reported occupations include entreprenuers, bankers, factory owners, insurance brokers, travel agents, and restauranteurs. The group is self-supporting with membership and contributions.

KOREANS

Korean immigration to the United States accelerated sharply after the 1965 change in the laws on Asian quotas, and those Koreans who have since migrated tend to be self-supporting and closeknit. One Korean association interviewed was founded in 1960, with the original purpose of promoting fraternity and solidarity among Koreans in the New York area. As the Korean population increased rapidly in the 1970s, so did the needs of the newcomers, and the association became a coordinating body to facilitate communication and promote fraternity among 120 separate Korean community groups. This association has a board of directors and a paid staff of two. Its main activities include the celebration of ethnic holidays, relating to city officials and the Korean Consulate on the needs of resident Koreans, and adjudicating areas of dispute within the Korean community.

A second Korean association interviewed, a group of Korean greengrocers, was established to give its members "a sense of belonging . . . of community." However, as the membership gradually increased, a strong need was felt to protect the group from external constraints, including the pressures against Korean grocers entering into the wholesale market. Anyone who owns a vegetable stand is an automatic member, and presently there are 830 active dues-paying participants, all Korean, about half of whom came to New York in the past few years. They were said to differ from earlier arrivals, who used to "play golf on weekends." The newcomers work an average of twenty hours a day, seven days a week. The association, supported by dues and contributions, speaks for members to the three levels of government, city, state, and federal, and deals with non-Korean ethnic groups in cultural and community activities. It tries to improve relationships with both black and Italian grocers, and to counteract prevailing resentment against Koreans taking over the greengrocer business.

Although the new Korean immigrants are primarily self-supporting, direct social service needs have emerged for Korean newcomers. In 1973 a Korean service center, the third Korean association interviewed, was established to serve Korean immigrants, particularly with regard to housing, health care, education, and social services. In the last decade, problems with Korean teenagers, runaways, and school dropouts grew, and a direct-service organization on the model of an ethnic agency was developed with support from both public and voluntary sources. This service center reached over 2,000 Koreans in 1983, about three-fourths of whom were newcomers. Whereas the earlier immigrants were concerned with such problems as family discord, downward mobility, and a sense of alienation, these immigrants seek information and referral on problems of daily survival.

INDIAN

Indian associations have proliferated with recent immigration from the subcontinent, and they follow the multiethnic pattern of their homeland, being organized by language, religion, and geographical origin. One association interviewed began in 1965, when a few people got together and formed an organization to unite the Hindu community and cultivate its heritage. Since then the purpose has broadened, with emphasis on the education of children, maintaining a sense of heritage, language, and religion. As part of this effort the organization has a priest (*Swamiji*) brought from India, who attends to functions such as weddings and funerals; a musician has also been brought from India. This is a membership organization of about three hundred families who pay $150 per year in dues, but nonmembers are also involved and about 1,200 to 1,400 people may attend the various functions. Mostly urban and well educated, the majority are in business, the professions, or white-collar work, and the twenty-five board members, mostly professionals, generally give a minimum contribution (of about $10,000) to be on the board. The group relates to several other Indian associations, as well as to temples and ashrams, and engages in joint festivities. Its present goal is to build a temple and a separate community center for such festive occasions as weddings, where alcoholic beverages and meat can be consumed. This marks a change in practice, since such consumption would not have been customary for this group in its native country in the past.

The second association of Indian newcomers interviewed were the Gujaratis. This group was founded in 1974, to meet the needs of the large numbers of Gujaratis who came to this country between 1970 and 1974, and who initially had a hard time getting jobs, getting accustomed to the new foods, finding places to celebrate holidays, and adjusting to their new environment. The immigrants who formed this group were also mainly educated people, and the association, which started in the home of one of its members, has as its main purpose the preservation of its native culture. Activities are social, religious, and cultural. About 6,000 Gujarati-speaking people are involved, 80 percent of whom reside in New York. Whereas in the past primarily single men immigrated, today there are increasing family units, whose needs are different from those of the earlier population.

INDOCHINESE

In contrast to the cultural and social associations of the Korean and Indian immigrants are the two Mutual Assistance Associations of the Indochinese—Vietnamese and Cambodians. These two groups of newcomers are refugees, most of whom were in camps in Asia before arrival. They are survivors of war and unrest in Southeast Asia, and their movement to the United States was part of the international refugee resettlement strategy. An early elite group of Indochinese with resources arrived first, but the large numbers who followed and the "boat people" who came from the camps were destitute. In response to the needs of these populations Mutual Assistance Associations were set up with state help, using federal monies to channel support to specific refugee groups.

The Cambodian society interviewed was established in 1979, when eight well-educated Cambodians came together to try to upgrade refugee life and "help get the refugees off welfare." Now about 250 families belong. New arrivals have little education; about 80 percent were farmers. Here they lived in the inner-city areas of New York City. Most work at unskilled jobs and many are unemployed. The association helps Cambodians to obtain public assistance and food stamps, and helps with tenant problems and hospital referrals. It is seeking to establish a temple, and has a refugee monk who is not paid, but is fed and housed, and whose job is to teach Buddhism.

For refugees from Indochina, another Mutual Assistance

Association was established in 1976 under the leadership of a Vietnamese priest. Among its members were an earlier group of Vietnamese students, who were already in the United States when the refugees started to arrive. Its purpose was to serve Indochinese refugees with mental-health and health-related services as well as a range of other supports. The association's director reports that about 2,000 individual members belong, and about 4,000 clients are served, with no fees. Vietnamese make up about 65 percent of members, Cambodians 25 percent, and Laotians 10 percent. There is a director and nine full-time salaried workers, supported mainly by public funds. About one-half of the members came to the United States in the 1975 migration, and the rest since that time. The earlier arrivals include more single, urban males, but later arrivals are characteristically from rural areas and are more likely to be family groups with children. There is also some secondary migration to New York from other cities.

Central and South American Associations

There are ten associations with newcomers from countries in Central and South America in the study. Collectively, people from these regions constitute the largest newcomer group in New York City. Several languages are spoken: Spanish, English, French, and Haitian Creole. Included in the study sample are three associations of Dominicans, one of Colombians, three of Haitians, one of Jamaicans, and two of Cubans. These newcomers entered a city with a substantial black and Hispanic population, most of the latter being Puerto Rican. Their ethnic association activities generally follow the pattern of earlier community organizations already established in areas of large minority populations. Some of the Hispanic organizations experienced a changing membership of first one, then another, immigrant group, with language as the unifying force enabling the transition to occur.

DOMINICANS

One of the associations serving Dominicans illlustrates such a transition. It started in 1952 when a group of Hispanic social clubs founded at a neighborhood church decided to become independent. The original purpose was to provide referrals for housing and jobs for Puerto Rican migrants, but the changing composition of the community meant first a shift to serving Cubans and then to serving Dominicans. More recently the association has become more focused on education, but it is still concerned with social services, and, with a paid staff of thirty, has come to resemble an ethnic agency. This association is heavily dependent on the public sector for funding, but also does private fund raising. It serves over 400 persons, approximately 70 percent of whom are Dominican, the rest being Cuban and other Central and South Americans. Over half of all people served are newcomers, and they are different from earlier arrivals in the larger numbers who are more educated. They work closely with religious migration services and college and university programs around social policy issues including housing, immigration, and education.

The second Dominican association interviewed began in 1974, because of the concern of the Dominican community with what was perceived as the social and economic neglect of the newcomers. It is not a membership group, but is community based and publicly funded, and serves about 12,000 people at numerous sites, including schools, day care centers, and youth programs. Dominicans are the largest groups served (40 percent), followed by Puerto Ricans (30 percent), other South and Central Americans (23 percent), and blacks and others (about 7 percent).

A third Dominican group interviewed was founded in 1980, also to deal with the needs of the Dominican community. This is a membership organization of about thirty active members and ninety nonactive ones. About 20 percent are recent arrivals, and almost all are Dominican with from 70 to 80 percent from rural areas. There is public money for a summer youth program. The association works with a coalition of other groups, mainly to get a new public school built. They try to create an awareness in the community regarding not only Dominican but also Hispanic problems in general.

COLOMBIAN

The Colombian immigration to New York has a substantial middle-class base, and a membership association of about two hundred was started in 1974 to bring together Colombian professionals from various areas in New York. About 15 percent of its members are not Colombians, but they too, are primarily Hispanic. Most adults are in professional work. They are doctors, nurses, social workers, business administrators, and some paraprofessionals; about 10 percent are recent arrivals. Newcomers are said to be more at ease and more sure of their identity than were earlier immigrants, demanding more in the way of general services and assistance. Some of the current activities of this association are conferences on cultural matters, parties for adults and children, scholarships, and the sponsorship of an annual health fair. It receives no public funds.

CUBANS

The other Hispanics interviewed were in two Cuban associations, one of earlier and one of later origin. The former was founded in 1962, and the major purpose was reported to be to help Christian Cubans to "keep their faith while in exile." According to the respondents, they sought to maintain religious values, recognize changing times, and maintain cultural ties with their homeland. Over the years their emphasis changed from education and job finding to service referral and advocacy. This is a membership organization with about 250 active members and 1,500 others who are involved, about 98 percent of whom are Cuban. The more educated members work in banking, social service, and other professional jobs; those with less education work in office jobs. They do not receive any public funding, but support themselves by raising funds from such special events as feasts, raffles, and bingo games.

The second Cuban group interviewed was formed in 1980 for the purpose of assisting new arrivals, the "Marielistas," to adjust in the United States. It is specifically concerned with health, mental health, employment and other social-service needs. This is a membership organization of about forty professional people, all Cubans, who are mainly earlier immigrants. They do not get public money. They view the newcomers as different from themselves, accustomed to a paternalistic state where the government provides everything. Marielistas, they report, are often hostile, not socially adaptable, and not trusting of anyone. The respondent said, "They have to learn that they are responsible for themselves."

HAITIANS

The oldest of the three Haitian groups interviewed was started in 1967, in order to help work for a better life for the Haitians in New York. The goals were to help Haitians find jobs, adapt to the city, and gain access to social services. The group was also committed to helping bring family members to the United States. This association operates a center sponsored by a community development agency and is not a membership organization; it functions more as an ethnic agency. In 1983 it served about 2,600 clients, about 98 percent of whom were Haitian; its staff is Haitian. The educational background of its clients covers a broad range: about 25 percent completed college, 20 percent high school, and 30 percent elementary school; about 25 percent are illiterate. The men work mainly in maintenance jobs and in factories, the women in sewing and domestic work. About 15 percent of the clients are newcomers, and they differ from former immigrants in that many are illiterate with no prior education. The center has a five-person paid staff, including four professionals, has received public money specifically earmarked for entrants, and also has had subcontracts from a voluntary agency to carry out an employment training program, and from a national foundation to develop a literacy program.

The second Haitian association studied was organized in 1979, with the main purpose of providing a place where Haitians could come and feel at home, and where Haitian arrivals could be helped to get working permits and to adjust to American society. This is not a membership organization; it functions more as an ethnic agency, serving about twenty clients a day and running an after-school program for fifty boys and girls. Most of its adults have some high-school education, and work in factories or do domestic or farm work, the latter as migrant workers in the environs of New York. About 75 percent are newcomers. There are seven paid employees, including several professionals, and funding is provided from federal, state, and city grants as well as private sources, including contracts with voluntary social agencies.

The third Haitian group was incorporated in 1975, and its concerns were the social, cultural, and service needs of new Haitian immigrants. The purpose was to assist with the immigration and adjustment problems of the Haitians, and the focus was on those in poverty. Unlike the two previously described Haitian groups, this association is set up as a membership organization with about fifty-five official members, but it reports that 1,000 nonmembers are also involved in activities, although not in decision making. About 90 percent of all members are Haitian. The jobs they work at reflect their varied educational backgrounds: the most educated are in professions and business, many of the middle group are mechanics and work in warehouses, and the uneducated mainly do janitorial work and housekeeping. At least one-third arrived in the last few years, and they differ from earlier immigrants in three ways; their educational level is lower, more are undocumented, and more are from rural areas. There are four full-time salaried staff, including the director. The association's basic funding is public, but is also depends on philanthropic contributions and fund-raising activities.

JAMAICANS

The last association interviewed from the Americas was the Jamaican; it was officially established in 1938, with the political purpose of working for the independence of Jamaica from Great Britain. That was achieved in 1962, and the respondent states that it now seeks Jamaican economic independence from the United States. It also provides services to Jamaicans and other West Indians in New York City.

This is a membership organization, with about 2,000 members, of whom 400 to 500 are active and dues paying; about 50 to 60 nonmembers are also involved in activities. Of the total membership, about 98 percent are Jamaicans, and the rest are from Trinidad, Guyana, St. Vincent, and Martinique; there are also some North Americans. Many Jamaican women work as nurses and aides; the men work as artisans, plumbers, carpenters, fewer are professionals, managers, and computer operators. This association primarily represents an earlier immigrant group, and it serves, but is not heavily involved with, the needs of newcomers.

According to the respondent, older members feel that newcomers are militant, expect too much, are more aggressive, and want to see more things happen. The earlier immigrants were more realistic, more patient, and had a more "balanced" approach; they settled into jobs and education.

The leaders volunteer their time, and they do not receive any regular public money but conduct fund-raising activities. They sponsor a Caribbean education group, immigration and legal advice, cultural activities, employment referral, student advisement, and informal referrals for jobs and housing.

European Associations

Five associations representing new waves of earlier immigrant groups, with some recent arrivals, were included in the study. There were two Italian groups, and one each of Greeks, Poles, and Russians. The associations of Italians and Greeks, often labeled "white ethnics," came into being as an aftermath to the programs of the mid- and late 1960s in the United States, when public funds became available for services to designated minority or poverty groups.

ITALIANS

The Italian association with the most comprehensive program is actually a coalition of organizations, formally established in 1979 after the demise, because of organizational and fiscal difficulties, of another group serving the Italian community. Its original purpose was to fight discrimination and stereotyping; now the main purposes are described as educating Italians to receive social services and achieving justice for Italians. This association includes twenty-six organizations, as well as individuals of leadership status, 98 percent of whom are of Italian origin. The educational levels of members vary according to each affiliate; some have completed college, and others secondary school. Only about 5 percent of the individual members came here in the last few years, but among the twenty-six member affiliates are a few with an over 50 percent newcomer membership. According to the respondent, the lifestyle of the newcomers is cosmopolitan and they come from industrial centers, in contrast to earlier immigrants. Recent arrivals are more educated and prepared to deal with the American system than were earlier immigrants. This "umbrella" association has some paid staff, and receives public funds as well as support from a foundation and fund-raising activities. It works with many groups, including a community planning board, political clubs, church groups, government agencies, and other ethnic groups.

The second Italian organization interviewed came into existence in 1976 to meet a need in the Italian community for coordinated services, to breach language barriers, and to help the elderly. It sought to educate new Italians primarily on how to ask for help and how to attain citizenship. Today it is a federation of about twenty-five organizations or clubs serving Italian Americans, and each club has about 350 individual members. About 200 nonmembers are also involved. From 80 to 90 percent of the total membership is Italian. It was reported that the new immigrants tend to be more aggressive and demanding than earlier arrivals. There is a paid staff of three, and funds are obtained from the public sector and voluntary groups, and through fund raising.

GREEKS

The major organization serving Greek people in New York is properly described as an ethnic social agency, comparable to other voluntary agencies, rather than as an association or a self-help membership group. Its beginning was comparable to that of the Italian and Polish associations, since it grew out of the community efforts of the late 1960s. It was incorporated in 1972, and sought to meet the needs of new Greek immigrants for language and acculturation; of Greek youth with intergenerational conflicts; and of Greek elderly with social-service needs. The agency has six satellite branches, and is supported by grants, contracts with the city and state, donations, and some fees. It serves about 1,500 clients a year, some of whom are referred elsewhere for appropriate services. The percent of newcomers served varies by program; in information and referral about 85 to 90 percent are recent immigrants, as is the case for about 95 percent of families in the children's counseling service. As a group, Greek immigrants tend to be varied in educational background, including some with graduate degrees and some who are illiterate. There are many working mothers, some of whom are single parents, and more elderly. Many men work in Greek restaurants and in other ethnic enterprises. The newcomers are said to be different from old-timers in being more urban and more heterogeneous in their educational backgrounds. Among its many activities the agency is a sponsor for a new community housing development, has a biweekly radio program on a local station, has published a research report on the Greek community, and has sponsored educational conferences.

POLES

A center to serve Polish and Slavic people in New York was established in 1972. Initially the center's purpose was to operate a home attendant program and a community action program. In 1983, the center became a provider of services to a new Polish refugee group, and this meant the development of new programs, with an emphasis on language, training, and job placement. Most of the refugee population is young and it varies from college-educated professionals to a small group of high school—educated unskilled workers. The newcomers are different from earlier groups, and several overlapping populations are served, since each wave of arrivals has a different point of reference. The descendants of the early turn-of-the-century immigrants have a relationship to the pre—World War I Poland; there is a post—World War II group, some of whom were veterans who fought with the Allies; there are the small numbers who came in the 1950s and '60s; and finally there are recent political refugees. In addition there are undocumented Poles, who come as tourists and stay. Tensions exist between the latter group and the refugees, since the undocumented are legally at risk whereas the refugees have entitlements to a range of public programs. The center has a paid staff and a director of refugee assistance, and the latter program receives public funds. The center works with community planning boards, the civic council, and secular and sectarian social agencies. A sister organization, a credit union, was organized out of this center to help people save and manage money.

RUSSIANS

Recent Jewish refugees from the Soviet Union were resettled in the United States under the auspices of established Jewish voluntary social service agencies, but have been slow to develop self-help associations of their own. One effort was made to organize such a group in 1978 to help Soviet Jews adapt to their new situation. It is a membership association, with a reported two thousand-person membership of whom about two hundred are active; about ten thousand nonmembers are also reported to be involved. About 60 percent of the members came to New York after 1980. This association has no paid staff, but received some public money last year for professional education. It works with other Jewish groups, and with an engineering association that helps Russian engineers learn American standards. Like the Poles, there have been different waves of Russian immigrants. This group identifies with recent political defectors, and with Jewish refugees. According to the respondent they related to sectors of the American Jewish community, rather than to other Russian emigreés.

Middle Eastern Associations

There has been an acceleration in immigration from the Middle East since 1975, and this is reflected in the ethnic associations. Many of the newcomers are relatives of those already here, some coming for financial reasons and others because of political unrest. The three associations visited are organized for Arabic speaking, primarily Lebanese, Palestinians, and Israelis, respectively.

ARABIC SPEAKERS

A facility for the Arabic-speaking elderly, including many Lebanese, was begun in 1978 under church auspices, but it has since changed sponsorship and developed a nonsectarian board. It now includes a home for the aged as well as a service center for newcomers from the Middle East. The home provides a meeting place and support activities for a variety of Middle Eastern groups. There is a paid staff, but no public money is received; support comes from fund raising and payments from residents. The facility works with other organizations such as hospitals, churches, and senior centers, with other Arabic organizations, and with local political groups. Its main focus is serving senior citizens, preserving family ties, being a center for meetings and advocacy, and preserving culture and traditions, primarily of Arabic-speaking people.

PALESTINIANS

A different type of organization is an association of Palestinians, started in 1975 out of the concern of the community for "their brothers at home." This is an umbrella organization providing a framework for other groups: about 70 percent of its effort is helping people abroad, and 30 percent people in this country. They send medicines and doctors overseas and help get medical training for Palestinians. This is a membership organization, with an estimated 250 members, and with nonmembers, including students, estimated at about 800 persons. The association is particularly popular with newcomers, who need help with housing and the law. It was reported that earlier immigrants had less education, and that they followed "old ways"; newcomers have more education, they know English, and can adapt more easily to American life. The association receives no public money, but is supported by contributions and fund-raising activities. It works with other groups, in particular other Arab associations, black organizations, and solidarity and antidiscrimination groups. Its domestic activities are mainly social and cultural, and two schools are maintained for teaching Arabic.

ISRAELIS

Many Israelis in New York have an ambiguous status—they retain the right to go back to Israel under the "law of return," applicable to all Jewish people, and they tend to adopt a "sojourner" status in New York. They reject the finality of classification as immigrants, yet they remain for extended periods. One common concern is for the education of their children. An effort was started in 1983 by a major Jewish agency to assess the needs of New York City's Israeli communities, and to recommend ways to enhance their Jewish identity and encourage self-help groups. The main focus of this work has been to set up a school for Israeli children, with a cultural rather than religious emphasis. There are about two hundred people involved in the various projects, and this includes the parents of both Israeli and Jewish American children.

African Associations

ETHIOPIANS

Until recently the Ethiopians who immigrated were urban, educated, single, and young—from their late teens to their early 20's. Now families are coming, some from rural areas. Many recent refugees lived in camps for several years, and suffered severe deprivation.

Two groups concerned with the needs of refugees from Ethiopia were interviewed. The first was established in 1979 by an Ethiopian in New York and is concerned primarily with the international goal of assisting refugees still in camps. In addition, it helps newcomers with orientation, English classes, counseling, housing, and other needs. It tends to operate in an informal manner, often helping on a person-to-person basis. It serves about 250 Ethiopians in New York, from very varied educational backgrounds, from the illiterate to the university educated. Most are newcomers. It does not get public money, but conducts fund raising and solicits contributions. A large church in the city provides meeting space.

A second organization of Ethiopians is set up as a Mutual Assistance Association. This group was chartered in 1981, mainly to identify common needs of Ethiopians and provide assistance in the areas of immigration, civil rights, and welfare. There are about five hundred persons involved in this association, approximately one hundred of whom are dues-paying members and the rest simply participants. The larger proportion are newcomers. Funds are obtained through fund raising, donations, and, for those with refugee status, public support. This second Ethiopian association sees its immigration activities as its most important work. As the respondent stated, when people are unsettled it is difficult to motivate them in programs for social adjustment.

Differentiating Factors and Typology

Can systematic data be derived from this heterogeneous set of associations? That they are different from each other is evident, but there are also commonalities. The analysis will examine patterns of associations, including their forms and functions, will summarize what can be quantified, and develop a typology for use in working with these groups.

DATE OF ORIGIN

Information on the dates of origin of the associations studied shows that eight began before 1970, seventeen between 1970 and 1979, and five after 1980. Thus twenty-two of the thirty associations originated after 1970. This reflects the influence of three main factors. The first was the change in immigration law which occurred in 1965. Second, there were the community development programs of "The Great Society," prevalent in the late 1960s, which generated funds for neighborhood services for ethnic groups. Finally, the Refugee Assistance Act of 1980 regularized the entry of refugees and clarified their entitlements.

MEMBERSHIP AND PERSONS SERVED

Of the thirty associations, twenty-one are membership organizations, and nine are not. Exact figures on persons served are hard to come by. Where family membership was reported, a multiplier of four was used for estimation of the total number of individuals. The small membership groups reported on the basis of dues paid, but many membership associations ran classes and conducted programs for nonmembers, and could not produce unduplicated counts. In a few cases umbrella groups were interviewed, where membership included other associations, and sometimes also included individuals. The goal in compiling the data, was to get some approximation of the number of persons reached, whether members or nonmembers.

In this way it was found that one-third (ten) of the associations studied reached between 1,000 and 5,000 people, and one-fifth (six) of the associations, mostly umbrella organizations, reported over 10,000 constituents or clients. Only two reported reaching fewer than one-hundred persons. A minimum total estimate shows that the ethnic associations studied reached well over 100,000 people. With regard to ethnic homogeneity almost half of the respondents (thirteen) reported that their constituents were all of one ethnic group; another seven reported that over 95 percent were of one group. Thus two-thirds of all associations reported at least 95 percent of members to be from one ethnic group. Only three associations had as few as from 30 to 40 percent membership from their own ethnic group, and none had less. In some cases, where an association had government contracts for service programs, the requirement was that these be available to all residents of the catchment area. Thus the membership of the association might be mainly one ethnic group, but clients of many groups could be served.

The study was primarily concerned with "new" immigrants, defined as those who arrived within the past five years. About two-thirds of the associations reported that over half of their members or clients were recent arrivals, and over one-third said that was the case for over 75 percent of those involved. Four of the associations said all members came in the last five years.

Since most respondents differentiated between earlier and more recent immigrants, they were asked if the new were different than the old. Of the total, twenty-three respondents said yes, six said no, and one could not answer. Of those who reported differences, eight respondents said the new arrivals represented a "higher" or more desireable group, whereas fourteen said they represented a "lower" or less desirable group. One respondent could not answer. Since almost half of all respondents felt the new immigrants to be less desirable than the old, the reasons for this response were explored. A number said they were less well educated, less stable, poorer workers, and less ready to accept life as it is. For those who said the newcomers were "more desirable" the reverse explanations were used.

An analysis of the responses in terms of whether newcomers are perceived to be of "higher" or "lower" status shows a sharp differentiation by nationality group. Nine of the ten Asian associations perceived new arrivals of their groups—Cambodians,

Chinese, Indians, Koreans, and Vietnamese—to be of a "lower status" than immigrants of an earlier period. Before 1965, Asian immigration was largely restricted to professionals and persons with jobs in specialized occupations. The change in immigration legislation meant that working people and poorer people from Asia were admitted as resident aliens in large numbers for the first time. Entry was further extended through the refugee programs, with the admission of the second wave from Indochina, the "boat people." The reaction that new immigrants were of a lower status than earlier ones was also given by Cuban and Haitian respondents, where political events resulted in class differences between earlier and more recent arrivals.

On the other hand, four of the five associations of Europeans said that new arrivals were of a higher status than earlier members of the same groups. This did not apply to each individual, but was a perception of the respondents based on the generally higher educational and professional level of the arriving Europeans, including refugees, as compared to the earlier waves of immigrants. Immigration from Europe was becoming more selective, while at the same time immigration from Asia was more open.

ADMINISTRATIVE FACTORS

Two factors that could be tabulated across all thirty associations are whether the association was in receipt of public money, and whether it had paid staff. Of the thirty, half received public money, and half did not. Seventeen had paid staff, thirteen did not. There was a strong relationship between getting public money and having paid staff, but two associations that received public money but did not have paid staff had professionals who were assigned from other agencies to give support services. The four associations with no public money who did have paid staff had business or sectarian funding.

The question of whether or not ethnic associations are actively involved in relation to their country of origin was determined by reference to actual program activity. This could be organized travel, scholarship or relief funds, advocacy, political action, or other efforts. The responses were almost evenly divided; fourteen associations reported such involvement, sixteen did not.

There was no discernible pattern here; some immigrant groups expressed disinterest, others retained political advocacy roles.

In general, it should be noted that in some ethnic groups where more than one association was interviewed, respondents often took different positions on a variety of issues, indicating that personal or political orientation, rather than ethnic origin, was the critical factor.

Patterns of Associations

In addition to summarizing the data, the various association interviews have been scanned to see what differentiates one association from another, and if there are discernible patterns of associations.

ASIAN ASSOCIATIONS

The review of ten Asian associations shows four different patterns of responding to needs, based on different historical and social factors. The first pattern reflects the situations of recent Chinese immigrants who entered a society where there was a long-established ethnic population, and who settled in communities where there already was an ethnic service's system, with funded programs for Chinese services in established settlement houses and a community planning organization with well-articulated Chinese ethnic concerns. Thus there was little need for new associations to set up social-service programs, because there was access to ethnic services in the community. Where there was a particular concern for identity, however, as in the case of a group of Overseas Chinese from Indochina, they broke away to set up their own association.

A second pattern was seen among the people served by the Korean associations. They were mainly self-supporting, and began by establishing cultural support and advocacy groups. Emerging problems of adjustment, however, in particular the language differences, meant that the special ethnic needs of people with problems could not be denied, and a Korean service center was established.

The third pattern is seen among Indian immigrants, who

use their ethnic associations for cultural, identity, and mutual self-interest purposes. Although there are problems of acculturation, the fact that most Indian immigrants speak English may make their need for special ethnic services less acute than that of other Asians.

Finally, the fourth pattern describes the refugees who enter with entitlements to support and services, and who come under the protection of the resettlement agencies. The goal is to move refugees to be self-supporting. Mutual Assistance Associations are encouraged to develop a community base and offer social services.

From this review of the ten Asian groups with their diversity of situations and backgrounds four questions emerge as considerations affecting service delivery. They are:

- What was the previous immigration pattern, and is there an already established ethnic-services base?
- What are the resources of the immigrant groups that allow for self-support and avoidance of dependency?
- What is the sociocultural gap between the newcomers and the host country, including language?
- What are the special legal status and entitlements of the entering group, and the administrative structures for their implementation?

CENTRAL AND SOUTH AMERICAN ASSOCIATIONS

The review of Central and South American associations suggests three additional differentiating questions to add to the four identified for the Asian groups:

- Is there a history of breaking away from an established agency, whether sectarian or secular, to set up an independent organization?
- Is there an organizational change from an association base to a more professional ethnic agency, usually supported by public funds?
- Does the association relate to a broader group than one single ethnic or national category?

Associated with the last question is the capacity of an organization to shift its population base from one group to another.

A membership association cannot as easily accommodate to changing neighborhood demographic patterns as can a social agency serving clients. Latin American associations were more flexible, often expressing concern for all Hispanics, not just their own nationals.

Analysis of the six Hispanic groups identified commonalities among them, as well as differences. Culture and language were unifying forces; class and special immigrant or entrant status were differentiating factors, for example for the Cubans.

The three Haitian association centers, each in a different borough, have some structural and operational differences, but they are basically functioning as ethnic agencies to meet distinct needs. The fact that their language is French Creole differentiates them from English-speaking blacks, and the immigrant issues add a particular dimension to their service needs which involve both legal and civil-rights issues.

EUROPEAN ASSOCIATIONS

The five associations of European newcomers, two Italian, one Greek, one Polish, and one Russian, have several factors in common. In all cases there was an earlier immigrant group, and some base of ethnic organizations and services. Many Europeans came with education and skills which, after an initial period of adjustment, facilitated self-support. There was interest in, but little involvement with, the country of origin. The newcomers in two of the European groups, Russians and Poles, came as refugees, whereas this was not the case for the Italians and Greeks. Except for the Russian group, these associations incorporated professionalized services within agency operations, using paid staff and receiving public funds.

A variety of types of ethnic associations are found in each national group. Within the Greek community, for example, there are strong fraternal organizations, there is a Greek Orthodox Church, and there are the so-called "outlaw" churches, set up by new immigrant groups who feel that the established church is "too American" an institution. These new churches reportedly take contributions but do not charge dues, and make day care available to working mothers. Finally, there are the Greek home town groups, which are men's clubs, primarily of new immigrants, who often meet in storefronts and serve an important socialization function.

The review of the agencies and associations serving immigrants and refugees from Europe suggests two additional differentiating questions particularly noted for the Greek and Italian agencies:

- Do they receive public money?
- Do they employ paid staff?

MIDDLE EASTERN AND AFRICAN ASSOCIATIONS

The three groups serving people from the Middle East are very different from one another. All of them, however, reflect the feeling that they occupy a marginal place in the host society. Israelis, for instance, see themselves as sojourners, unsure of their permanency, but having freedom of choice. A further differentiating factor among associations emerged particularly for the Palestinian and Ethiopian groups, namely, program activity in relation to the situations in their home countries. This suggests a further question for differentiating between associations:

- Is there involvement in a programatic way with the country of origin?

DIFFERENTIATING QUESTIONS

After reviewing the survey responses from the thirty associations, information related to the ten questions that appear to differentiate among associations was tabulated (see table 2.2). The first seven were yes or no answers, the next two were scored on a 1-2-3 continuum, and the last on a 1-2-3-4 scale.

Based on the categories of question 10, associations fall into four groups.

Group 1. This includes four associations, all European, where the organization functions largely as an ethnic social agency, rather than an association. They are professionalized, with trained social work staff, public funds, government contracts, and access to the traditional service system. The Greek group, for example functions as a voluntary social agency.

Table 2.2. Scores of Agencies on Differentiating Questions[a]

Question	Number of Responses	
	Yes	No
1. Was there a previous immigrant group and established ethnic services?	13	17
2. Are there special legislative entitlements or a special status for the newcomers (i.e., refugee or entrant)?	12	18
3. Is the ethnic association involved in some programatic way with the country of origin?	15	15
4. Did the association break away from the parent group?	5	25
5. Is membership or service broader than a single ethnic group?	11	19
6. Does the association receive public money?	16	14
7. Does the association have paid staff?	17	13

	Number of Responses
8. How close is the sociocultural background of the immigrant group to the host setting?	
1 = very close	9
2 = moderately close	15
3 = very different	6
9. What was the primary class or economic base on entry and shortly after?	
1 = independent, own resources	12
2 = skills, but needing employment	15
3 = dependent, welfare supported	3
10. How professionalized is the association in social-service delivery?	
1 = full gamut of social agency services	4
2 = association structure, members and/or clients, neighborhood based, varied service programs	6
3 = membership base with some ethnic service programs	12
4 = cultural and ethnic base with identity and self-interest goals, minimal interest in services	8

[a] Seven responses were in the yes/no category. For question 8 scoring judgments considered the language, technical development, and educational level of newcomers, and scores were by consensus of the investigators. For question 9 data on level of welfare and reports on economic functioning were used. Finally, for question 10, criteria for scoring included the comprehensiveness of the program, the training of staff, and the reported relationship to the formal service system.

Group 2. This includes six associations, all minority ethnic groups, with extensive service programs. These are primarily neighborhood based, but most are professionally run, with public money and paid staff. These are ethnic associations that have developed strong service components. The Haitian associations are a prototype of this group.

Group 3. This is the largest group, comprising twelve associations. They have mixed characteristics. All are associations with a strong ethnic identity and a service component. The services are not as extensive as in groups 1 and 2 however, and may be in only one or two areas, such as education, help for the elderly, or job training. Included in this group are some associations that may have been active in service delivery in the past, but are not at present. A long-established Chinese association is in this category.

Group 4. This group includes eight associations, primarily with cultural, social, and self-interest bases, with minimal or no participation in service delivery. The Indian associations fall into this category.

These classifications are not hard and fast, as the thrust of these groups may change and they may also be perceived in different ways by different investigators.

FACTOR ANALYSIS

A final approach to examining the separate associations was to undertake a factor analysis, a statistical procedure of deriving intercorrelations of data for the ten differentiating questions that have been identified. The purpose was to see which variables "went together" in a statistical sense, in being highly intercorrelated. When such intercorrelation variables are identified, they are named "factors," and a common element among them is designated with a factor name.

From this statistical analysis three distinct groupings or factors emerged, as follows:

Factor 1: *Professionalized services*

	Factor loadings
Use of public funds	.86
Employment of paid staff	.74
Professional services with full service base.	.89

It can be assumed that there is some crossover among the separate categories—for example, having public funds enables one to employ paid, professional staff. But there are also associations with public funds who do not employ such staff, and some with paid staff not giving professional social services.

Factor 2: *Special status from third world countries*

	Factor loadings
Special status: refugee or entrant	.81
Lack of program related to home country	.51
Sociocultural differences from host country, including language	.61
High dependency and/or lower-class base	.88

The refugee or special status in itself is not enough to define this factor. It describes a group of newcomers with special needs and problems of skills, training, language, and continuing economic dependency.

Factor 3: *Culturally related to host country and including other ethnic groups*

	Factor loadings
Program related to home country	.41
Multiethnic membership	.84
Socioculturally close to host country	.58

This factor describes associations that are neighborhood based and often involve people who may move back and forth from country of origin to host country.

The results of the factor analysis have sharpened the impressionistic review of the associations, since the factors are based on quantitative analysis of the differentiating questions. Factor 2 describes the group 1 organizations in that it identifies the professionalized arrangements and describes the end of the continuum where ethnic associations become ethnic agencies. This would be true of the Italian and Greek groups. In addition, it applies to some associations in group 2, where there are funded programs and extensive services. This describes the Haitian organizations.

Factor 2 essentially describes aspects of the refugee/entrant groups, where they are ethnic minorities with a dependent status.

The Cambodian group is in this category. Factor 3 tends to describe several Hispanic associations, some of whom fell into groups 2 and 3 in the agency classification. The difference is that they are less likely to have funded programs, but more likely to be neighborhood based and culturally closer to the host country. This describes the Dominican associations.

Both the classification into four groups and the factor analysis help in describing the pattern of ethnic associations. Since the factor analysis technique only relates to the ten differentiating questions that have been included, the results do not apply to some of the atypical groups studied, such as two of the Korean associations, or the Israeli group. There is no place for "other" in a factor analysis. Therefore the classification by groups may be more useful in bringing order to the large number of seemingly heterogeneous associations.

The four groups suggested by the descriptive classification has utility in planning service delivery. An association in group 4, for example, could probably utilize a needs assessment of its membership to see if there are unserved people; group 3 might need technical asssistance; associations in group 2 could probably utilize professional staff; and a group 1 association or agency could bid on contracts and implement programs. This analysis suggests a model with a differentiated approach to working with ethnic associations on the part of the established public and voluntary social service system.

Identity and Acculturation: Strategies for Coping

Ethnic associations, by definition, have a stake in the preservation of ethnic identity, if only because their membership is made up primarily of persons from one ethnic group. Once they are organized, however, they may be more or less active in encouraging members to retain their ethnic identity and transmit it to future generations.

Acculturation, on the other hand, may also be encouraged

by ethnic associations on the grounds that, to succeed in the new environment, adaptive skills should be developed, especially language. The concept of acculturation can be defined in different ways. It is used here to refer primarily to adaptations to the new society that enable the newcomer to function in terms of communication, self-support, and self-development. Issues of adaptation arise in both structural areas, such as employment and schooling, and in cultural and personal areas such as child rearing and marital relationships.

Most ethnic associations are in fact performing a dual role. Identity and acculturation, although they may appear to be opposite goals, are in fact both coping mechanisms leading to survival in the new society. Identity is a more acceptable political concept in the 1980s than it was in the 1940s, when the "melting pot" ideology prevailed, but acculturation may produce compensatory economic advantges, particularly in the job market. In any case, information on both processes is needed to plan service delivery appropriate to newcomers' needs.

Although both goals are often expressed by associations, they are often not explicit; the relationship between identity and acculturation is not apparent. In order to help explain the nature of each process, respondents were asked four questions:

1. What behavior and attitudes distinguish your group from North Americans?
1. What behavior and attitudes distinguish North Americans from your group?
3. What is your group doing to become more like North Americans?
4. What is your group doing to retain its own identity?

The responses to these questions give some sense of the perceptions of leaders of what is involved in defining both identity and acculturation.

Differentiation of Groups

The questions of what differentiates each ethnic group from North Americans, and conversely, what differentiates the latter from each ethnic group, drew slightly different responses, but were essentially like two sides of the same coin. The responses will be reported together. Because they showed substantial regional differences, especially for Asian and Hispanic respondents, the analysis will follow a regional pattern.

ASIAN RESPONSES

The Asians interviewed included persons who were Korean, Chinese, Cambodian, Vietnamese, and Indian—a varied grouping with substantial differences in their immigration status, class base, and history of earlier immigration. Yet the individual responses of leaders on what distinguished their particular group from North Americans were almost identical. They fell into two main categories, relating to interpersonal and family issues.

At the interpersonal level Asians reported that they were respectful of each other, had concern for the feelings of others, had patience, were polite, were reserved, passive, nonaggressive, unassertive, and "indirect communicators." Americans, on the other hand, were reported to act with more freedom, to be more selfish, not to care about hurting others, to be independent, materialistic, self-centered, assertive, practical, open, individualistic, and used to immediate observable rewards.

With regard to family life, it was reported that Asian children listen to their parents, respect their elders, put family interests above individual interests, are serious about marriage, think women should be submissive to men, and value the extended family. Americans were reported to lack control over children, not to respect elders or family, think women should work, and encourage the young to be independent.

CARIBBEAN AND SOUTH AMERICAN RESPONSES

The respondents from the Caribbean and South America reacted differently than the Asians on the interpersonal items. They agreed for the most part on the family variables, but they raised a number of cultural issues which were not mentioned by any of the Asians interviewed.

On interpersonal matters these respondents said they were more friendly than North Americans, made friends more easily, shared more, were not so individualistic, saw friendship as sacred, were not technically oriented, placed less emphasis on organization and responsibility, stuck together, and had pride. North Americans, they reported, were difficult to reach, distrustful, money oriented, believed success is money, were not concerned with others, based friendship on self-interest, were more open minded, promiscuous, acted superior to non-Americans, forgot they were once immigrants, had racial hangups, were more extroverted, more organized, more aggressive, and less sensitive.

On family issues respondents from the Caribbean and South America reacted similarly to Asians. They saw themselves as family oriented, having control of children, treating the elderly with respect, valuing the extended family, and having the man "king in the home." North Americans, on the other hand, were seen as having no strong family ties, only caring about the nuclear family, and allowing women more say at home.

Differences in culture and politics between their own groups and the North Americans were noted by all respondents from the Caribbean and South America. They noted that they had a different language, and different food, dance, music, and dress. They also said they were more tied to their country, honored their patriots, and had more fear of police and authority. The North Americans, they felt, had racial hangups, were not attached to their country, compromised too much, and were too pragmatic.

EUROPEAN RESPONSES

The respondents from the various European countries expressed yet other traits that they felt differentiated them from North Americans. Cultural differences were not stressed, nor was family. What were noted were personality traits and political differences.

Respondents from the associations with European immigrants felt themselves to be more expressive than Americans and more realistic. They also said they were more courteous, more fraternal, had a clearer demarcation of male-female roles, and were less trusting of outsiders. Politically, some respondents felt they were less ready for the democratic process, and those from socialist countries were more used to having basic needs met by the state. On the other hand, they felt that North Americans were more spoiled, more used to the good life, had more of a sense of freedom, and had the political discipline to function in a democracy.

MIDDLE EASTERN AND AFRICAN RESPONSES

The Middle Eastern associations were too dissimilar to be aggregated regionally. Each represented a different point of view. The respondent speaking for a primarily Lebanese group said they differed from North Americans in their desire to hold to tradition and maintain continuity, whereas the North Americans wanted diversity of choice and personal freedom. The Palestinian respondent also spoke of tradition and conservativism, but stressed the family aspect. Although close family relations were reported, there was no display of affection in public. The young men, the respondent said, "don't have girl friends, they get married." The major difference was that North Americans were thought to have weaker family ties.

The Israeli respondent took American Jews to be the comparative group, when asked how Israelis differed from Americans. She said that Israelis were more nationalistic, and linked religion with nation and Jewish identity with Israeli identity. Americans, on the other hand, express their Jewish identity through synagogues and through making contributions to Jewish causes.

Finally, the two Ethiopian groups interviewed responded very much like the Asians, in terms of personality and family differences. They said they were more shy than assertive, more cooperative than competitive, had respect for law and order, and were used to a traditional society with strong social supports. With regard to family, they had respect for the elderly, and had an intact and extended family system. North Americans, they said, on the other hand, have a stronger notion of private property, are competitive, have little respect for others (as when the youth carry loud radios), and will not get up in the subway for pregnant women or older people.

How can these responses be interpreted? A hasty reading sounds like a litany of stereotypes, cliches, and prejudgments which may or may not be valid. The responses are only useful in terms of their sources. They are not the stereotypes of Americans about newcomers, they are the perceptions of ethnic leaders of their own groups and of others. The correspondence among Asian respondents when each reported on his own group suggests a regional self-perception which transcends class, status, and national differences. The Asian, Hispanic, and African leaders emphasized family values, which were not mentioned by the European respondents. This suggests that "North-South" differences exist, and that industrialized and Western societies are seen by third world countries as undervaluing the family. These perceived differences should be known by workers who are formulating a service strategy to approach newcomers from non-Western backgrounds.

Adaptation vs. Preservation of Identity

The next two questions on the study instrument explored the leaders' perceptions of differences, and asked what, if anything, the group was doing to be more like North Americans, and what, if anything, they were doing to preserve their own culture and identity.

ADAPTATION

One thread that ran through the responses was that the adult immigrants did not themselves want to be like Americans, but that their children needed to learn new ways. Some Indians, for example, were telling their children to eat meat; Koreans said their youth were copying the music and food of American teenagers. Cambodians said their association was trying to make their people more American, but also trying to see that they did not abandon their culture. Several respondents said the learning of English was what was needed; others said they were learning technology to be more scientific.

Several Hispanic respondents just answered no to the question of whether they were doing anything to be more like North Americans, as did the Jamaican respondent. A Haitian said their young people were trying to walk, dress, and talk like Americans, that they play their radios in the street, and that some refused to speak Creole. A Cuban respondent said they accepted the idea of the United States Constitution when they became citizens, but resented the fact that many North Americans did not follow it.

The most affirmative response came from the European groups, presumably those who were already culturally close to their new environment. Italian respondents spoke of acculturating, associating, intermarrying, becoming citizens, voting, and getting more education; the Russian respondent spoke of learning business, the Pole of learning to accept the free-enterprise system, and the Greek of watching children move away from parents.

The Middle Eastern groups did not differ much among themselves in responses; they spoke of getting used to American food and dress, and "getting used to freedom." The Israeli respondent said that their children try to be like Americans, but that their parents hold them back. The Palestinians said that some let their daughters go out without chaperones, that there was less socializing with neighbors than before, and that they did jobs they would not do at home and were adjusting to seeing their wives shop, work, and take on more responsibility. The Ethiopians said they were becoming business wise as they had to learn American life-styles.

Overall, the responses to this question were minimal. There was no sense of what may have characterized earlier waves of immigrants—the concept of a "melting pot" which would lead to Americanization. Since respondents were leaders of ethnic associations they had a vested interest in fostering identity. But they had been asked to respond in terms of their membership, and the general attitude was clear. English was encouraged because it is needed, enterprise was important to get along, but acculturation was primarily for the young.

IDENTITY

The second question was what the group was doing to preserve its own culture, and here the responses were much fuller and more diverse.

There were a variety of ways in which ethnic associations were working to preserve their own cultures. There were more references, for example, to teaching native languages than to the teaching of English. Asian groups sponsor classes for children, in particular, and the goal is for youngsters born here to learn the language of the country or group of origin. All groups celebrated special holidays, supported cultural affairs, and participated in ethnic fairs, parades, and events. Where possible, contact was maintained with the country of origin, and there was travel help for visiting relatives. A further area where it was reported that ethnic members sought to preserve culture was in family relations. One Korean respondent said the new immigrants tried to teach filial piety, family solidarity, and decorum. A Vietnamese respondent said that children were taught at home to keep the customs of the people. Others reported efforts to maintain family centeredness and respect for parents.

Respondents from Central and South America also expressed a range of efforts to maintain identity. When asked what they were doing to preserve their culture, one Dominican interviewed said, "everything possible." A Cuban respondent said, "We are trying to recreate the way of life we had in Cuba. When we come home, we want a Cuban home." Native language was a major way to preserve identity. Associations sponsored Spanish classes, supported bilingual education in schools, showed films, gave plays and folklore presentations, and taught the children the history of their countries. Jamaicans had a Miss Jamaica U.S.A. contest; Haitians encouraged their members to speak Creole.

The response from the associations of Europeans cited such aspects of traditional culture as: food, dance, music, religion, language, celebrating holidays, and belonging to ethnic fraternal organizations. The Polish respondent said the Poles try to "take their own principles and values seriously while moving into the main stream." The Middle Eastern response emphasized language and education for the children. One group sought to unify Lebanese, Syrians, Jordanians, and Egyptians "under the umbrella of Arabic culture." Both Palestinians and Israelis expressed a desire to have their own schools, and each tried to develop classes for their own children. Finally, the Ethiopian associations emphasized group cohesion; one respondent reported advising members "to stick together, to help each other, to share what they have."

To sum up, the ethnic associations expressed far more interest in preserving their own culture than in "becoming like North

Americans." There were three responses to whether the latter was a goal: an outright no; an indication that accommodation in language and technology was necessary in order to get along; and an expression of reluctant acceptance of the movement of children and youth to the prevailing norms. The preservation of culture was stressed through family values, language, and life-styles.

One aspect of this new wave of immigration is that the newcomers enter a highly pluralistic society, and many perceive acculturation not to some abstract "American" lifestyle, but to the earlier arrivals culturally closest to their own group.

Among the Hispanic association leaders, one Dominican respondent spoke of the need to preserve the unique Dominican culture, as distinct from that of the existing Hispanic groups such as the Puerto Ricans who are their "American" reference group. Jamaicans and Haitians in the interviews referred to American blacks as people with comparable problems, and both Russians and Israelis compared themselves not to "Americans" but to American Jews. Thus the pluralistic aspect of the host country has altered the acculturation issue, at least for the adult immigrant. In terms of culture, the newcomers seek first to preserve their own identities and second, to relate to the ethnic component in the resident society that is most comparable to their own.

There are two further contexts affecting identity and acculturation issues: the "jet age" and the "electronic age." The turn-of-the-century immigrant was less likely to return to his home country; the weeks in steerage were bought with a one-way ticket. Today's immigrant knows that in less than twenty-four hours he or she can return home, and for many the cost is not necessarily prohibitive. Political considerations stand in the way of return for refugees, but for others there may be relative visits and trips back and forth. Long-distance telephone calls can be directly dialed. Even where personal contact is not possible, television provides live views of familiar places, and news coverage keeps memories fresh. The impact of these factors on the process of assimilation has not been documented, but it seems reasonable to hypothesize that they probably lessen the finality of the separation experience for the recent waves of immigrants and refugees.

The Scale Scores: An Empirical Approach

In order to secure comparable responses on identity and acculturation issues from the thirty associations and develop scores for each, a list of twenty fixed items was included in the interview. It consisted of ten items presumably related to the preservation of ethnic identity, and ten items presumably related to acculturation, scrambled in order on the list. Respondents were asked to check on a Likert-type scale from 1 to 5 how important they felt each item was for their members. The items were developed by the investigators and pretested on members of the various ethnic groups. Examples of items to be scored for importance are: retaining the native language; speaking English at home; marrying someone from the same ethnic group; studying for citizenship papers.

For analysis, the twenty items were separated into two scales of ten items each, and labeled "identity scale" and "acculturation scale." The legend in response to the items was 1 = not at all; 2 = slightly; 3 = moderately; 4 = substantially; and 5 = absolutely. The scores were examined for level of agreement, and item intercorrelations were computed to test the reliability of each scale.

IDENTITY RESPONSES

The item scores reinforced the open-ended responses. On the ten identity items the mean scores ranged from 3.9 to 4.5, and the overall mean on the identity items was 3.94, just a fraction below "substantially." The item pulling the strongest response referred to the importance of retaining the native language, which had a mean agreement score 4.5 from the thirty associations, between "substantially" and "absolutely" necessary.

When the correlations were computed, however, several items did not show intercorrelations as high as others, reflecting the diversity of the respondents' situations. For example, the item on the importance of living in a neighborhood with one's own group drew a varied response, and would be affected by established patterns of residential segregation. It was decided to eliminate four items with low reliability, and thus reduce the scale to six items, with an overall mean score of 3.97. Item intercorrelations ranged from .33 to .76, and the alpha coefficient of the reliability analysis was .85, indicating a high level of confidence in the reliability of the scale.

The six items in the revised identity scale are as follows:

Respondents are asked to rank, on a scale from 1 to 5, the importance of:

1. Retaining the native language.
2. Teaching children the customs and language of the native country.
3. Celebrating the holidays of the country of birth.
4. Preparing foods of the old country.
5. Belonging to an association of people of the same ethnic group.
6. Marrying someone of the same ethnic group.

ACCULTURATION RESPONSES

As would be expected from the responses to the other parts of the interview, there was a much lower level of agreement with the acculturation items than with the identity items. On the initial ten-item instrument individual mean scores ranged from 2.14 to 4.14, or just over "slightly" to "substantially" important, with an overall mean of 2.87, a score just below "moderately." Furthermore, the correlation matrix showed low reliability. Some of the items, such as celebration of traditional American holidays, getting to like hamburgers and hot dogs, and letting teenagers date, had generally low responses. It was decided to drop six items with low scores. The item with the highest score, 4.03, "substantially" important, related to learning to compete. The revised acculturation scale is as follows:

Respondents are asked to rank on a scale from 1 to 5 the importance of

1. Making new American friends.
2. Studying for citizenship papers.
3. Learning to compete in order to be successful.
4. Getting involved in American organizations with all kinds of people.

In further analysis, scores on identity items and acculturation items were assigned to each association and a correlation coefficient computed. A low but negative correlation of $-.21$ between identity and acculturation scores (p = .13) was found. This suggests that identity and acculturation goals were somewhat negatively related, according to the respondents.

This hypothesis was strengthened when identity and acculturation scores were incorporated into the factor analysis of ten characteristics of associations, reported earlier. Those data show the relationship of identity and acculturation scores to the ten differentiating factors. On the rotated factor matrix, factor loading for the identity score was $-.25$ on the first factor, correlating negatively with the use of public money, the hiring of paid staff, and the offering of a broad spectrum of professionalized services. For the third factor, the groups culturally close to the host country, factor loading for the identity score was low but positive at .17. Acculturation scores loadings were too low for any significance, but the signs were reversed: positive for factor 1; negative for factor 3. Factor 2 was not related to either of the scores.

Although the scores are not high, the direction of the scores supports anticipated responses. The perceptions of leaders in the professionalized settings, the factor 1–type associations, were that members were less concerned with identity issues and more ready for acculturation. In the broader multiethnic community-based associations, culturally close to the host as well as to the home country, as described in factor 3, identity was perceived as a more positive goal by association leaders.

The discussion of scale scores on identity and acculturation has a number of limitations. The sample is small, and the leaders are expressing perceptions of members' attitudes. Most seriuos, particularly in relation to the acculturation items, is the fact that the items did not arise from the immigrant group itself, but from a pretest survey of the attitudes of ethnic professionals. They were based, therefore, on imperfect guesses of what it is to be "American," and traditional markers such as baseball and hot dogs did not appeal to many of the newcomers. This may be, in part, because the reference groups for these newcomers were the earlier arrivals. Recent immigrants from Jamaica, for example, may be more enthusiastic about a West Indian soccer league playing in New York than about either Yankee or Met baseball. For further research, it would be useful to ask the new immigrants themselves what they specifically think about the markers of the American culture, and then to construct a scale based on those items. Identity items, however, worked well and seemed to be more stable.

In summary, it was found that ethnic associations give priority to maintaining ethnic identity, and appear to be much less involved in the acculturation process. In comparing respondents' views of the behaviors and attitudes of their own groups and those of North Americans, the findings were rarely flattering to the citizens of the host country. Americanization was not the reported goal for the new immigrants, except possibly for the youth.

A further response relevant to this analysis is that the pluralism of American society was reflected in the reference groups for the immigrant association members. Where there was an ethnically or racially comparable resident group, they tended to represent "Americans," an understandable assumption on the part of the newcomers. Haitians observed American blacks, Hispanic newcomers observed Puerto Ricans and Chicanos; Israelis and Russian refugees observed American Jews. Minority movements, sparked by the black efforts of the 1960s and subsequent affirmative-action activities, appear to have had a substantial effect on the situations in which newcomers find themselves. These findings indicate what has shaped the programs of ethnic associations. The relationships among groups have altered somewhat, to the advantage of ethnic newcomers who enter a more pluralistic society where there may be increasing acceptance of those who retain their identity and preserve their culture.

Ethnic Associations and Human Services

A key focus of the study interview was the ethnic associations' responses to the human-services needs of the newcomers among them. Specific questions related to housing, employment and training, family supports (with special attention to the needs of youth, the elderly, and women), income maintenance, health and mental health, education, and legal-service provision. In each area, ethnic leaders were asked to identify needs as they saw them and describe association responses, if any, including their use of available community resources. In presenting this area of interview result, there is a shift in the analysis from looking at individual associations to looking at specific problem areas.

Housing

Like most older urban areas, New York City has suffered a severe decline in available low- and moderate-cost housing. Old buildings badly in need of repair have been abandoned. New buildings, which have been expensive to construct and maintain, have been designed and priced for high-income luxury tenants. Compounding the picture has been a total halt in the construction of federally subsidized low-income housing of all types. Into this very tight housing market have come thousands of new immigrants, often without resources. And those newcomers who are marked by their language and often by their skin color come into a city that has many segregated neighborhoods. Finally, real estate is largely a private, for-profit industry where competition and autonomy prevail. Housing that has been publicly constructed and maintained and operated by the New York City Housing Authority has always had long waiting lists. It is within this context that questions were raised about the experience of newcomers in locating housing, and about the availability of housing, its cost, and space requirements. Did the association help, and how? Was public housing viewed as a resource, and if not, why not? If referrals were made, what were the results?

Ethnic associations are keenly aware of the housing needs among their constituents. The lack of available housing, high housing costs, and, to a lesser extent, space and location, were almost universally reported to be problems. Discrimination was a major issue, identified particularly by those from the Caribbean. Haitians were said to suffer triple discrimination—for being black, being foreign born with a different language, and being seen as potential carriers of the Acquired Immune Deficiency Syndrome (AIDS). Dominicans spoke of anti-Hispanic discrimination and, in one case, of discrimination against newcomers by resident Hispanics.

Proximity to others from the home country and to work and shopping areas, were stressed by the Chinese associations whose leaders said housing was one of the greatest needs of newcomers. They added that the priority is to be in Chinatown so they can speak Chinese and eat Chinese food. Yet rents are high in Chinatown, and many newcomers cannot afford to live there. One Korean association spoke specifically of landlord exploitation of Koreans "and probably all Asians." An Indian respondent said that newcomers stay at Indian temples, with relatives or friends, or at the YMCA. Another said: "It is easier now than in 1971 since there are many Indians in real estate." In speaking of discrimination in housing, one Gujarati association leader said it was not really a problem because they live in areas with other Gujarati; another said it depends on skin color: "While they can usually pass as Italian or Spanish, South Indians have a more difficult time since their skin is dark." Another respondent said: "For those who are westernized and professional, it is easier adjusting. For those who aren't, it is more important to live among people from the same background."

Refugees, such as Poles, Cambodians, and Vietnamese, have different initial experiences because they are assigned housing by the resettlement agency responsible for them upon arrival. The problems usually come later when entitlements run out. Family size, as among the Vietnamese whose extended families live together, compounds the problem. And, as an Ethiopian leader pointed out, newcomers "have the same problems as all third world people and blacks."

In response to these housing needs, some ethnic associations provide concrete aid as members or staff help locate housing, intervene with landlords, advance a month's rent, and in one case directly provide housing. In about half of the associations help is provided in a range of less formal ways, e.g., by keeping lists of vacancies, maintaining a bulletin board with housing information, providing names of landlords they know, working through their informal networks, and acting as translators and interpreters—all on a relatively ad hoc basis.

The Palestinian association said "People's homes are open. One can't say no. One must pick up newcomers from the airport, get them apartments, share the rent if they can't manage themselves." In the case of the association for Arabic-speaking people, the leadership said "we call our contacts, for example, board members, real-estate agents, and churches, and often get apartments and rooms in the parishioners' houses." Respondents from the European associations reported working with a senior citizen housing complex, making referrals for public housing, and working with the community to help its members locate suitable housing. All three Haitian associations were active in giving housing help. Assistance ranged from keeping lists, making referrals to shelters and hotels, and describing the need for housing on a Haitian radio show, to having the social worker actually locate housing and assist with the first month's rent.

Although associations of refugees are not immediately faced with finding housing for newcomers, they are involved in helping them deal with housing-related problems. Tenant organizing, for example, is a major activity for the Cambodian association, whose housing problems are said to be severe. Ethiopian associations report help by friends, using newspapers, and contacting landlords. They say that racism and the vulnerability of their members to crime in ghetto areas are both problems.

Public housing was not found to be a significant resource for newcomers. Only two of the nine Caribbean and South American associations said they referred members for public housing. Among the remaining seven associations that did not refer were two that did not think their people were eligible because they were not citizens, and one where the respondent said "the new immigrant should start a life being responsible." None of the three Chinese associations refers to public housing. One gave its reason that "public housing is for the poor." Waiting lists for public housing were also cited as problems by two European associations and by the Vietnamese. The location of public housing was also a deterrent; for example, one Korean respondent reported that the desire of his members to live near other Koreans operated against referrals for public housing.

Employment and Training

New York has undergone a major shift in its economy—a shift from being primarily a manufacturing city with an abundance of low-skill, entry-level jobs, to a center of finance, insurance, and other high-level service businesses, requiring skilled technical and managerial employees. Some of the types of jobs available to earlier waves of immigrants are no longer readily available for today's newcomers, and in a shrinking job market they compete with low-skilled minority Americans. Governmental response to unemployment in general, and to this type of job dislocation specifically, has been severely curtailed. Public service employment has been eliminated altogether.

Immigrants arriving as refugees/entrants, however, could at the time of this study exercise their entitlements to vocational counseling, orientation and job placement, and other services under the Targeted Assistance Program of the New York City Department of Employment, or participate in the Refugee Urban Skills Project sponsored by the VOLAGs (voluntary resettlement agencies).

The need for jobs—any jobs or better jobs—was mentioned by nearly every ethnic association head when asked: "What do you see as some of the major problems of newcomers in your group?"

Almost uniformly, language was identified as the key problem or barrier to employment. Some specifically mentioned that certain jobs required competence in English. Others linked language problems with the ability to communicate that is required in employment. The associations of European immigrants mentioned language limitations as a major reason for many working below their skill levels.

The second most common problem identified was the absence of skills. This referred both to the lack of basic skills (including basic education), as well as the need to adapt any existing skills to the American workplace. Dominicans, for example, were said to need both basic education and technical training as well as help in understanding "the system," or the American way of working. Many who did find employment worked in nonunionized jobs that do not provide employment-related benefits. All three Haitian associations reported the problem of lack of skills. Job training and employment were considered major needs for Ethiopians; for the better-educated Ethiopians, the problem was having to take transitional jobs far below their capabilities.

Discrimination was another frequently mentioned barrier to employment. Koreans who came with education, often having had clerical and white-collar jobs in Korea, were said to be unable to find similar jobs here not only because of language problems, but because of discrimination. Discrimination was also identified as a barrier to employment by Jamaicans and Haitians, and legal status was said to be a barrier for Haitians.

Service provision is relatively high with regard to employment. Over half (seventeen) of the associations provide direct service (i.e., help with finding a job through job placement), and thirteen associations help informally through providing information on jobs that they have learned about through informal networks and contacts. Referrals are also an important practice: nineteen associations make referrals to nonprofit agencies, sixteen to the private sector, and thirteen to the public sector.

Even though many newcomers want employment, but lack marketable skills, at the time of the study only nine associations had training programs with courses aimed at helping the participant develop or upgrade employability skills. A much larger number of associations (twenty) know about training facilities in the community and make referrals to them. Three associations help informally by having members of the association or volunteers go to homes to teach English, which would help the newcomer find a job at a later time.

The Dominican associations illustrated the range of efforts: one works to locate jobs directly and follows up; another keeps job lists, helps with job histories, and has a volunteer teacher of English and a summer youth job program; the third offers classroom training with supportive services including day care, and refers to employment and training programs in a network of agencies. All three Haitian associations provide direct training in such skills as housekeeping, building maintenance, typing, word processing, and carpentry. In addition, they do job development and placement, may pay private employment agency fees, advocate with employers, and maintain contact with key people in companies. One Haitian association also has an ESL (English as a second language) program; another helps with work permits. Among Cuban associations, one mentioned efforts to help Cubans get building maintenance and construction jobs.

The associations of newcomers from Europe also had a variety of program responses to the employment needs of their members. One has a job developer who links workers with jobs, another has arrangements with a professional association (engineers) to do orientation and teach American standards to those with skills.

Both Ethiopian associations interviewed were active in helping members in relation to employment. One monitors newspaper ads, provides information, and refers mainly to Ethiopian enterprises (i.e., Ethiopian restaurants). The other helps people to do well on interviews—as stated—"to Americanize their interview-taking skills." This association relates to special programs in both industry and academia.

The Palestinian respondent said that although getting work was the major problem for his people, this was not a problem that was brought to the association for formal help. Young women work, but married women are expected to stay at home and care for their families. In general, however, Palestinians get jobs through friends and relatives and from their countrymen who have businesses.

Asian associations also provide employment help in a variety of ways, such as posting advertisements and teaching resume writing. None of the Asian associations currently provide job training, although one—a Korean association—used to teach mechanical skills, typing, and computer technology, but had to discontinue these programs due to lack of funds. The Vietnamese association has an extensive referral program, and volunteers who teach English to home-bound women. They have referred people for social work and computer training, as well as to the Job Corps. Aware of potential problems, they only sent people whose language ability had been assessed. Unlike the Koreans or the Vietnamese association, the Cambodian association has not been involved in job training but focuses on teaching English.

Financial Assistance

When the income required for daily living expenses cannot be obtained through employment, or is otherwise not available, newcomers may need financial assistance. They may turn to relatives or friends or to a community resource for help. In New York City the primary community resource is the Human Resources Administration (HRA) which, under specific rules and regulations flowing from federal, state, and local funding sources, provides income assistance to eligible individuals and families.

To determine the place of ethnic associations in helping to meet the basic income needs of newcomers, questions were asked about how newcomers managed financially, what direct aid, if any, the association provided, and what the association's experience was with the Human Resources Administration.

Financial need as such was spontaneously identified as a problem for newcomers by only two of the thirty associations interviewed. When the interviewer explored in more depth how newcomers without resources managed, and the ways in which the associations helped meet such a crisis, the responses varied widely, reflecting both the immigration status of the newcomers and the socioeconomic class of the group. About half of the associations (twelve) provide some temporary financial aid in case of need, and nearly twice that number (twenty-three) know of sources of such help in the community. Seventeen associations refer their members to voluntary agencies, and sixteen to the public agency, for financial help.

The ten Asian association leaders had various responses to the financial problems of their members, especially newcomers. One said that up to $100 was available as a loan in an emergency, another said that it helped its members get loans from loan companies or banks, and a third said that special fund-raising events or collections helped meet an individual need. On the whole the Asian associations interviewed did not stress financial problems, and when members had refugee status, public assistance was a resource when needed.

Of the ten associations with newcomers from the Caribbean and South America, six said they referred needy members for public assistance, usually helping by providing escorts, translators, and advocates. One provided carfare for these referrals, and others provided emergency food or clothing, held a fund raiser or took up a collection for a particular family.

The five European ethnic associations include two that are refugee groups and three that are not. Although one refugee group (Polish) provided no direct financial assistance, it made referrals for public assistance, and had established a credit union for members. The other refugee association (Russian) had a small special fund to help its members and also referred them to a voluntary agency. The three nonrefugee associations helped members obtain public assistance when necessary by serving as translators and advocates, and they referred to voluntary and church groups for emergency aid. None gave direct financial help.

None of the five African or Middle Eastern associations interviewed had a formal financial aid program. Rather, referrals are made to churches, members "chip in" when necessary or lend each other money, and the associations collect donations. One respondent said, "People should not go to seek help from any formal agency. They don't need it since everybody helps everybody else."

Public Assistance

When specifically asked if they made referrals to public assistance, sixteen of the thirty associations said that they did; twelve said they did not, and two said the question was not applicable to their group. Utilization or not of public assistance, and the reasons for it, varied from one ethnic group to another. Among the comments made by an Asian asociation that did not make referrals to public assistance were: "As these programs seem to be geared to English and Hispanics, utilization by Koreans is low"; "Our people would not be eligible"; "Members will seek help on their own if they need it." Asian associations that did make referrals to public assistance said they sometimes accompanied the member to the welfare office and acted as translators. One Asian association described how the public agency had stationed a worker at the association's office, and said that this was a good arrangement. A special income maintenance office has been established for the Indochinese which handles not only applications but continues to be responsible for cases while they remain open.

Seven of the ten Caribbean and South American associations said it was their practice to refer needy persons in their groups for public assistance. As one respondent put it, "Our persistence aids in getting service. We have people with experience in using government agencies. The agencies know and respect our help." Another said, "We refer to public assistance only as a last resort," and added, "One problem is that public assistance won't help unless there is an apartment address. This creates a problem." Reasons given by the three associations that did not refer members to public assistance include; "This is not our objective; we deal with the struggle of the people"; "People should start with work and not public dollars"; and "They are not eligible."

Haitians are not described as heavy users of public assistance. The reluctance to apply for assistance may reflect their strong feeling about independence, and also they struggle to bring their families here—and the fear that if they apply for public assistance they may not be able to sponsor a relative's immigration. In an interview with an official in the public sector, one comment was, "Haitians seem to be allergic to public assistance."

It should be noted that the HRA has designated one of its income maintenance (IM) centers to handle public-assistance applications from all non-Indochinese refugees. Unlike the arrangement for the Indochinese, the Cuban, Haitian and other non-Indochinese refugees, once found to be eligible, are transferred to the appropriate district office.

All five European associations made referrals for public assistance, acting as advocates, escorts, and translators, and helping to complete required information and application forms. Three spoke of the language problem involved and of the slowness of the "system." In contrast, none of the five Middle Eastern and African associations reported referring members to public assistance. As a reason, one Ethiopian association said, "First we give what we have, then we urgently try to find employment, then we send them to church groups where there is an emergency fund—public assistance is a last option."

The response of New York City's HRA to the financial needs of newcomers shows a readiness to recognize special needs: for some groups (refugees and entrants) two specific IM centers have been designated to handle applications; a significant percentage of staff must be Hispanic; Creole-speaking staff are reported to be present at the IM center designated for Haitian applications; outreach efforts have included promotional materials in a range of different languages; social workers have been outstationed in the offices of a few ethnic associations while at the same time having translators/interpreters in some of their own offices. The HRA official interviewed saw ethnic associations as having the potential for improving the delivery of assistance to newcomers, and welcomed linkages with the associations to achieve mutual goals.

Family Needs: The Personal Social Services

Newcomers' needs for—and knowledge and use of—personal social services, as well as the ethnic associations' role as provider or facilitator, were areas explored in some depth in the interviews. Ethnic-association leaders were asked what, if any, problems families were experiencing in settling here, and what, if anything, the association was doing to help. In addition to general questions about family needs and problems, the elderly, youth, and women were selected for special attention.

Among the problems affecting the family life of newcomers, the two mentioned most frequently—cutting across almost all ethnic groups—are the problems of adjustment and of communication/language. A key element in the "culture shock" referred to by all three Dominican associations, for example, is the strain on parent-child relations with children and youth "talking back" to their parents and, in general, challenging parental authority. A Cuban association spoke of separated families as an added adjustment problem. They also said there was a problem with newcomers from Cuba not being welcomed by many of the resident Cuban population from an earlier migration.

Although the three Haitian associations said there were language and adjustment problems, equally pervasive among the family needs identified were those associated with the changed roles of men and women (husband and wife) which attended the migration of the family to New York. Here the wife is likely to be working. One respondent said that in Haiti men "possess the wife" and therefore find it difficult to let their wives go to work. Traditional forms of control over women and children in Haiti would not be acceptable here. Parent-child conflicts leave Haitians in the United States with a feeling of powerlessness, as children "have keys" and can come and go as they wish, imitating American youngsters.

Respondents from all ten Asian assocations, when asked about the family problems members of their association face, refer to one or more of the following: communication, intergenerational conflict, marital discord, loneliness, and isolation. The Indian associations, noting culture shock, the problems of raising children, and the particular loneliness of women, said that families talk to one another about their problems but seldom seek outside help. Family problems "are a stigma and they won't talk about it." Sometimes they will seek out a priest "who solves all kinds of problems" or go to an Indian psychiatrist. A Korean association, in describing the parent-child conflict and intergenerational problems, said there was poor communication between parents and children, as both parents have to work long hours away from home.

One Italian association respondent said wives are often forced to work because living costs are high and men cannot find jobs. Yet many women are unqualified for skilled employment, and many have children who need care. To this, the Greek association added the problem of male/female role changes which attend the employment of wives outside the home.

Problems associated with immigration status and exile leading to the separation of family members and to quarrels, divorce, and trauma were noted by both the Polish and Russian associations. Not all family members could immigrate and "singles" often were isolated: many divorce and remarry. Strains in parent-child relationships, especially as children mature, were also identified by the Greek and Russian associations, the latter saying that "since it is easier to make a living here, children become financially independent earlier and don't want to be with their parents."

Ethiopian associations spoke of family breakup, the unacceptability in the United States of "hands-on" punishment of children and wives, loneliness, adjustment and mental health, and living and health care costs as problems for families. One of the Middle Eastern associations pointed out that war and deaths from bombings in the homeland have left their marks on the families who have migrated here.

In the area of assistance with family needs, more than in any other area, ethnic associations were actively engaged in providing some form of direct help. Twenty-two of the thirty associations interviewed provided counseling, sponsored special activities for youth, women, and the elderly, gave ad hoc financial help and other types of family support services, and made referrals to community agencies with which they were familiar.

All three Haitian associations work with families around their needs. Services provided include family counseling and escort services, and less formal help such as, for example, providing information on "how to use the subway; how to cope with American society."

Each of the Cuban agencies responded differently to family needs. One has a special committee on refugee Marielistas, provides direct help, and refers clients to a nearby church for food assistance. The other has a volunteer counselor who helps with reorientation. As for other associations of Caribbean and South American peoples, the Dominicans provide little direct help, but all three of their associations interviewed know about and refer to a wide network of agencies, including both neighborhood-based organizations and established social agencies that provide family counseling services. The Jamaican association, which identified early pregnancy, drugs, and the adjustment of children as problems, has volunteers who help and know about and use community resources. In contrast, the Colombian association disclaimed special knowledge of family problems in its group, but said families sought help in the community for "problems that other groups share with them such as housing, jobs, and language.''

Of the Asian associations, the Koreans said their group did not seek help from outsiders. As one respondent put it, ''As far as I know they would not seek help from outsiders unless they were forced to do so by schools or police.'' Yet these Korean associations do try to help others of their own group. One said, ''A referral service to other agencies would be totally ineffective because of the language difficulty on the part of Korean immigrants.'' Although one Chinese association said they were never asked for help, the two others said they tried to help with marital and family conflict and made referrals to agencies they know. One said, ''Very few Chinese use services by such professionals. They do not trust them.'' The two other Asian associations (Vietnamese and Cambodian), because of the refugee status of their members, have recourse to sponsoring agencies which help with a range of family services including counseling, job referral, translation, outreach, adjustment, and conflict resolution. Referrals are also made to other agencies.

Of the five European associations, the Greek agency has the most comprehensive direct service program to help families. Attention is given to counseling around child and spouse abuse. Referrals are made to Greek psychiatrists, and the association knows about and refers to a wide range of community agencies for help with specific problems. An Italian association spoke of making referrals to Italian therapists as well as to generic family counseling programs. Although the Polish association also made referrals, they said that ''those with serious problems are those who don't speak English and wouldn't get help.'' The Russian association, which neither helped directly nor knew about places to which to refer members, added, ''Also, people won't go for help. Who can help if there is a problem between husband and wife?''

One of the Ethiopian associations said it tried to work on the problem of physical violence in the family, saying, ''We tell them we are outside our country; we have to stick together. Life is short, and there is no need to fight.'' They spoke of referrals to "the elders." The elders go to the people, intervene and mediate, and are reported to be "very effective."

One of the three Middle Eastern associations attempts to help with family problems, which they say derive from the separation of families because of war and death from bombings. The association provides counseling and referrals for psychiatric services. Making such referrals is only feasible for those who have a command of the English languge. Of the other two associations, one focuses on the education of children and youth; the other said, "People don't like to talk about family problems at all. If anything, they would talk to relatives. The association would be willing to be helpful but would never interfere."

WOMEN

To explore the special needs of women and how they were met, the question asked was: "Often the women who come as newcomers have different and special problems from those of men. Is this the case among women of your ethnic group?" From the replies, two predominant problems emerge: the care of children and how that ties women to their homes, and the changed roles—and thus the changed relationships—between men and women.

One of the Dominican associations said that the problem was that most women were single parents who had to stay home and care for children, and this confinement to the home meant that they could not go to school, work, or become leaders. The Haitian associations said the changed roles of husbands and wives after the families migrate here may result in separation and divorce, as well as in wife abuse. Compounding the situation is the fact that the wife often works (and the husband may not), since, as one respondent said, "Women have a better chance of getting a job than men." To help Haitian women who are victims of abuse, one association keeps a list of persons who will take women in, and the other provides counseling services and refers to a coalition of Haitian women. Except for the latter, community resources that help women were not known to these Haitian associations. Cubans spoke of single women as often being "stereotyped as prostitutes," and said that alcoholism and the loneliness asociated with the separation of families were problems for women in their group. Both Cuban associations make referrals, but one noted that this does not always help because their members do not trust people." Another respondent said, "This is a complex problem. We don't know of agencies to refer them to." The Jamaican respondent, in contrast, said, "Our women have been very fortunate. They usually come in and pave the way for the men."

A number of Asian associations had similar responses, but some did not. To the problem of child care, the Vietnamese association added not only inadequate education but the factor of cultural change. Greater equality between men and women and adopting a new way of life causes conflict. The fact that some women brought home a salary changed relationships in the homes. This association tries to help directly with family conflict. It also knows about and uses a network of community services. In contrast, three other Asian associations (two Chinese and one Indian), when asked about the special needs of women, said there were none. One Indian association said there were no needs because women are economically dependent and "they follow their husbands," noting also that many had relatives here. The other Indian association described its women as being mainly housewives who spoke no English. Their pride prevents these women from speaking openly about their problems, and this inability to express their feelings may cause depression. Although the association has no program for these women, it tries to help informally and tries to break through their isolation and loneliness. One Chinese association respondent spoke of the need for day care but said, "Most of the families can find day care service on their own." To them the bigger problem was that it had been difficult to "neutralize teenage women from negative peer influence."

All three Korean associations linked the special problems their women were facing with the dual roles of these women. Problems included: excessive work, both at home and outside (long hours at the stores leave no time for social life); the lack of child care; and the changed roles of women, from a traditional submissive role to that of a self-assertive one, resulting in more marital disputes and conflicts than prior to the emigration. The Cambodian association stressed the problems of widowhood and caring for children alone, situations faced by many of their women as the result of wartime conflicts in Indochina.

Among European associations, the problems identified for Italian women related more to concrete needs (education, day care, employment) than to the stresses of a changed culture. One association, although not providing direct services, knows about and refers to community resources, but a barrier to utilization has been language, especially for the more recently arrived Italian women. Language was also cited as a deterrent to community referrals by both the Polish and Greek associations. The latter, however, had its own counseling program which helps with single parenthood and some of the other problems faced by women. Such direct help was not provided by the Polish association, although they described frequent psychological stress, especially among middle-aged and older women.

Two of the five other associations interviewed (Palestinian, Ethiopian) said they had no information about the special problems of women, but the three others emphasized child care needs. The Israeli association drew a contrast between child care resources in New York City and the wide availability of child care in Israel. Although referrals are made to two day-care centers in Queens, the respondent said "people don't feel comfortable going to social service programs. It is synonymous with welfare and welfare offices." The problem identified by the Arab association was that sometimes just the women migrate here, and the husbands stay behind. The women have skills and get jobs as medical technicians and nurses, but they need child care. The association, although not helping directly, does refer to churches and tries to get housekeepers for these women. One Ethiopian association said inadequate education limits the employability of their women and child care ties them to their homes. They help them join classes in English, jewelry making and clerical skills.

THE ELDERLY

A second special group given attention in the interview was the elderly. The definition of "elderly" varies among different cultures, and many newcomer groups have relatively few elderly.

The interviews with ethnic-association leaders, however, pointed to a number of problems of the elderly. Language handicaps, low income, loneliness, and problems of "negotiating the systems" were mentioned repeatedly. Although these problems are not unlike those of other newcomers, they are exacerbated because of the difficulties of adjustment for this age group. For some groups, for example Indians and Palestinians, it was reported that some of the elderly prefer to return home rather than try to cope with the adjustment problems.

Association responses to the needs of the elderly varied. The Haitian associations try to arrange friendly visits, and provide help with financial planning, an escort service, and translators. One Haitian association recruits and trains home attendants both for its own community and for the community at large. The Dominican associations saw fewer needs among the elderly, and they said that the needs of the elderly were met by their own families. The Cuban elderly were said to suffer from depression, linked, in part, to the stress of family relationships and the generation gap. One Cuban association actively assists the elderly, through "consciousness raising," making referrals to a senior center, and arranging theatrical activities. The other neither helps directly nor makes referrals. In reference to the elderly, the Colombian respondent said, "This is a delicate subject. The values are different and the family concept is to help one another. Even if there are problems, we don't use social services since the family is supposed to take care of them." The Jamaican association also said that it is the childrens' responsibility to care for the elderly.

All European associations expressed some concern about the needs of the elderly and all were involved in one way or another in addressing these needs. The Greek agency provides transportation, home attendants, and "meals on wheels," operates a senior center, makes referrals to community agencies for health needs, and works with the family, including making contacts with relatives in Greece. The Italian associations also help with locating and placing home attendants and help the elderly to accept these services. The need for Italian-speaking attendants and the lack of money to pay for home care were cited. These associations know about community programs and make referrals and advocate for them. The Polish association has a home attendant program but said, "There are hardly any Polish refugees who are aged." The Russian association also helps with home attendants, keeping a list of Russian-speaking ones.

One problem identified by the Asian associations was that of the elderly who speak no English, and are thus totally dependent on their children. The children, however, must leave them and go to work. Among the Chinese, the chief problem identified was the need for housing—not just any housing but housing in Chinatown. The Hong Ling House for the Elderly was known to one association, but no referrals were made because of waiting lists. Social agency services for the elderly in Chinatown are said to be known to the community, and association members use them; thus neither assocation referrals nor direct help were considered to be necessary.

The Vietnamese association has an active program for the elderly. It brings them together at a center, teaches them how to use public transportation, provides counseling on aged-adult–child relationships, and refers to appropriate community resources as needed. The problem in using these services, however, is that the elderly lack English-language competency and transportation. One Indian association said that it works to combat loneliness among the elderly by sponsoring cultural events. The other said it was considering establishing a condominium so that elderly Indians could live together. To combat social isolation and loneliness, two Korean associations sponsor special activities for the elderly and help those who are seeking food stamps, Medicaid, and other services.

The association of Arabic-speaking people was founded in 1978 in recognition of the need for a facility for the elderly. The respondent said, "Now it is not just a home for the aged. It has become a place of service for the community. Many who have come from the Middle East have found a haven here." Currently all age groups are involved, with service to senior citizens still one of the association's main programs. Except for this association, other associations from the Middle East and Ethiopia said the elderly were not a problem. There are relatively few older people among the newcomers, and those who do come often do not stay but return to their homeland. One Ethiopian association, however, did describe their elderly as still being very active, adding,

"The elderly are asked to intervene with advice. There is a great respect for the elderly."

YOUTH

In a further attempt to gain an understanding of some of the problems families of newcomers face, the interview included a subset of questions focused on youth. In discussing the problems of youth one Dominican respondent said, "They turn the schools upside down. . . . The schools do not know what to do about their large numbers and problems." Truancy is widespread. He added that the uneducated families could not help. Both Cuban associations stressed the impact of culture shock on youth. Youth are "not prepared to live in the system." One noted that the family had come to lack cohesion and that youth had lost touch with the Cuban culture. The Colombian association that is oriented primarily toward professionals said that youths "don't come to the association for help," but added: "They have the same problems that adults have—jobs and language barriers." The Jamaican association spoke of the problems of drugs, teenage pregnancy, and parent-child clashes among their youth.

The Chinese associations interviewed said they were not concerned with special youth issues. In contrast, the seven other Asian associations described a range of youth problems: language; school placement at the wrong grade level for age, truancy, and school suspension; runaways; alienation; premature parenthood; choosing a field of work; and dating and courtship i.e., "who will make the decision regarding marriage."

There were four associations of European immigrants who also spoke of the special problems and needs of youth. Italian youth were said to have employment needs and unrealistic expectations, and generally to be bored. The independence of the young, their rebelliousness, and, in one response, crime and narcotics were listed by the Greek and Russian associations. One Ethiopian interviewed spoke of the problems of alcohol and suicide among young adults. The association of Arabic people identified language and employment as key youth problems, and the Israeli associations described parental fear "of the corrupting influence" of the Americanization of their youth.

Responding to these concerns, many of the Caribbean and

South American associations reported that they had activities to help. Cuban associations, for example, organize youth activities, son and daughter encounters, and meetings for parents. One Haitian association has films for parents and teens on how to cope with problems of adolescence, and another has teen and children's clubs run by a social worker. Among Asian associations the response to youth needs ranges from none to consultation, the provision of classes in English, and efforts to serve as mediators among the schools, the parents, and the youth.

Three of the five associations of European immigrants were also actively involved in helping with youth problems. Both Italian associations make referrals to community organizations serving youth. In addition, one has a government contract which supports an after-school remedial and tutorial program. The Greek agency sponsors a number of special year-round and summer activities in athletics, arts and crafts, job training, and other programs, and makes referrals to youth programs in the community, including those sponsored by the Youth Bureau, schools, and churches. Neither the Russian nor the Polish association had youth programs.

One Ethiopian association said that it brings youths together to talk about common problems and how to overcome them; no use is made of community agencies. The Arabic association said they try to help get young people to the appropriate licensing examiners and help physicians get residencies so they can practice. To combat what they describe as the Americanization of their youth, the Israeli association said it is initiating special youth programs: one a post–Bar Mitzvah group, and one for youths who are going back to Israel to study.

CHILDREN IN SCHOOL

For families with children, education is almost as universal a need as housing and employment. In New York City the Board of Education has responded to the changing makeup in a number of ways. It currently provides English as a second language (ESL) programs and has bilingual teachers in Spanish, Chinese, Vietnamese, Creole, Arabic, and a number of other tongues. It has been the board's policy to work with parent and community groups including those that involve immigrants, and there are formal arrangements with several ethnic agencies.

In reporting responses on school problems, it is difficult to separate out those that are specific to newcomers from those that are endemic to the entire school system. Nine out of ten respondents from Hispanic, Jamaican, and Haitian groups felt that their children had problems in school. None of them, however, felt that the problems were specific to their particular ethnic group, but rather were related to all newcomers. The main problem, stressed by all respondents, was language. Children were handicapped by not understanding English. This was true for Hispanics and Haitians, and even extended to Jamaicans, who said the teachers send their children to a psychologist because they say they "talk funny." The children's lack of English facility had yet another negative outcome: Hispanic and Jamaican respondents all complained that their children were improperly evaluated and placed, and often labeled retarded, because they were not fluent in English. The Jamaican respondent said that guidance counselors often steered their youth to service jobs, rather than training for the professions. Elements of racial discrimination were also noted. Another problem related to language, but in a different way. Several respondents said that the fact that parents did not know English was a real handicap for children, since they could not help with homework or talk to teachers.

Of those associations for whom bilingual education was relevant, only three responded positively on the quality of bilingual programs in the schools. The Haitian respondents said that the availability of bilingual programs (French/Creole) depended on where people lived. For this group they only existed where there was a concentration of Haitian children.

Associations that included new immigrants from Europe responded differently than Hispanics and other Caribbeans. They minimized the problems of children in school, were generally positive about school performance, and were not unanimous in support of bilingual education. It was reported, for example, that immigrant Greek children have language problems at first, but in general they do well in school where there is good language instruction. Bilingual programs are provided, depending on the neighborhood and the concentration of need. Polish students were not reported to have problems in school. According to the respondent "they tend to be quicker learners and better students than the others." Some are in parochial schools where they may be placed below their grade level in English, and some are in public schools where they are in special language classes.

It was reported that the school problems of Russian immigrant children were not academic, but social. The respondent said, "Our children don't tell other children that they are from Russia because there will be difficulty. This is due to the attitude of the American population which is now worse because of the American press." This respondent spoke against bilingual education, saying "The bilingual schools are not helpful." He gave an example of one high school where the Russian children are in a bilingual program and the graduates are very weak in English. Respondents of both Italian associations said their children sometimes have school problems related to language, to a lack of communication between school and family, and to high parental expectations. They did favor special classes in English as a second language.

Most of the Asian respondents felt their children had problems in school associated with language. This included problems parents had with helping their children. Most of the Asian respondents, however, saw the language difficulty as temporary and were interested only in transitional programs. One Chinese respondent said, "Our children have limited English in the beginning but after a while they are O.K., and then they excel." Eight of ten Asian respondents stressed the importance of retaining the native language, but all eight said this was the responsibility of the parents, who should speak the native language at home. All saw bilinguilism not as a necessary policy for the state, but as only a temporary expedient.

Another problem noted by associations was that though in school Asian children were generally perceived to be passive, meek, and submissive, there is concurrently a high dropout rate. Cambodian children were reported to be suffering from their war experiences, some had hearing losses, many had no previous formal education, and some were considered by teachers to have emotional difficulties. Lack of understanding or appreciation of these problems was mentioned, and in some cases problems were incorrectly diagnosed as language problems when, in fact, they were due to physical disabilities resulting from war. It was reported that many Southeast Asian children were not placed with their age group, causing problems in social adjustment.

The Palestinian group did not report any special problems of their children in school, but stressed the different customs and traditions, saying, "We don't like children in bars, gambling, taking drugs, or dating." Arabic was felt to be very important to the group and they run a special school to teach it. It is felt that knowledge of the language can best be retained by speaking it at home.

Almost all associations of Caribbean and South American peoples had programs involving education. Eight of ten provided some kind of direct educational services, and of the remaining two, one had a scholarhip program and one participated in educational conferences and policy discussions. The active associations had classes for members, after-school educational and recreational programs for children (i.e., tutoring, arts and crafts, music, and dance), psychological and vocational counseling, and programs to prepare adults for citizenship. One association had volunteer teachers who help the children in school. Another reported that it acted as a mediator between school and family, and helped with interethnic conflicts. In one case where there was serious conflict between Haitian and Puerto Rican youths, the association called together community leaders of both groups to negotiate the differences.

Only three of these ten associations said parents did not participate in children's school activities, two because the associations' concerns were with adults, and one because members had no formal education. The other seven associations, however, said members go to parent-teacher association (PTA) meetings, sit on advisory committees, and participate in raffles, fund raising, health fairs, and school board and community board elections. One Haitian association made the point that almost all Haitian mothers work, so they are pressed for time and this limits their participation.

Among Asian associations some said that parents attend PTA meetings, but that their participation in school activities is severly limited because of the language barrier. Korean and Indian respondents both mentioned long hours of work which left little free time. A Chinese respondent reported that "Chinese parents tend to rely on school teachers to educate their kids." The Vietnamese association respondent said, "we focus on education very much, just like the Jews."

The European associations interviewed were less involved with the schools and the educational activities of their children. One exception was the Greek agency, which had a full range of classes and youth programs. The Polish group advised parents about school and made referrals for scholarships, while the Russian group reported that parents tended to seek Jewish or private schools, which they could hardly afford. After-school reading and math tutorials were sponsored by the Italian groups. For Israeli families in New York, a major issue has been an attempt to set up their own school. Parents of Ethiopian children are reported to be involved in their children's education, and to go to school when called in by the teacher. Members of the association accompany them to the school. The Palestinian association runs two special language schools for the youth in its group.

Health and Mental Health

The health needs of immigrants, refugees, and entrants are affected by a combination of factors, including the conditions from which they came, the particular situation they find on arriving in the United States, the nature of the service system, and their relationship to it. These needs are expressed in terms of both physical and mental health problems. Health, however, is defined differently in different cultures. The prevalence of health problems is exacerbated by culture shock, differences in traditions and relationships, different perceptions of "normal" behavior, and differences in acceptable treatment modalities in the homelands of the newcomers and in their new settings.

Haitians are said to suffer a range of health problems including malaria and bronchitis, as well as mental health problems that are not clearly defined. Many of the health problems result from the lack of such basic necessities as warm clothes. The Cubans, for the most part, have different health problems than the Haitians, citing mental health, alcoholism, and drug abuse as the main problems. Jamaicans report the problems of teenage drug abuse and the mental health problems of the older people in their group.

Among recent European immigrants, one main problem for Greeks was said to be a lack of health insurance coverage. In addition, Greek families resist applying for Medicaid. When they are referred for health care, language is a problem and the attitude of personnel at clinics and hospitals is not always responsive. The respondent said that many Greek women do not use pre-and postnatal and child health facilities services since "they are not used to preventive care and only use services when clearly needed." One Italian association mentioned cancer and leukemia as health problems, and said that financial coverage of hospital and health care for the incapacitated elderly was inadequate. Except for alcoholism among the undocumented, reported by the Polish associations, the three other European associations did not report any special health problems for their groups. There is said to be a lack of awareness of mental health problems among the Polish immigrants, who come from a society where the need for mental health services is viewed as shameful. For newcomers, however, mental health is not seen as a widespread immediate problem, but rather as an issue that may arise and needs to be dealt with in the future. Such problems, according to one respondent, only develop after immigrants have been here for some time.

Among the Asian associations, at one extreme are those that deal with refugees and entrants who have the most pressing and drastic problems, coming from situations of warfare and extreme hardship, while at the other extreme are Asian immigrants who come from relatively comfortable economic situations, yet who seek a better way of life.

Respondents from Asian refugee associations reported many mental health problems. Many of the Overseas Chinese have experienced the hardships of flight and the traumas of war, and witnessed killing, violence, and rape. A number of Cambodian youths had war-created deafness; some suffer from paranoia and many are emotionally unstable, making it difficult for them to concentrate and function in school. The Chinese in New York City who work largely in the garment industry and in restaurants are said to suffer from health problems that are related to their class and occupational status. The older immigrants suffer from exhaustion and lethargy. Newcomers are said to have special health problems, in particular a high incidence of lung disease made worse by poor living conditions. The major physical problems reported by the Cambodians were lead poisoning and conditions of cold exacerbated by below-standard housing.

There are mental health problems for Indian women, but in their culture many consider mental problems to be a stigma, to be hidden and suppressed as long as possible. Many Indians feel that American practices in mental health do not work; social and cultural factors are not considered. In discussing alcoholism and suicide among Ethiopian youths, one respondent said, "People don't know what to do or where to go. They come with high expectations which are not fulfilled."

Different concepts of what constitutes direct service apply to health and to mental health. Associations that help with filling out Medicaid forms, provide escort services to clinics and hospitals, and act as translators and interpreters in health care settings could be considered to help directly with health care needs. For mental health, on the other hand, direct service usually means that the association has counseling services. Altogether ten associations were found to provide some form of direct physical-health services, even more made referrals, and twenty-four of the thirty associations gave evidence of their knowledge of health care resources. Furthermore, nine asociations provide mental health services directly, and ten know of mental health resources available in the community, and make referrals to them.

The Caribbean and South American associations, who deal with the largest numbers of undocumented aliens, face the greatest problems with regard to health care because of issues of eligibility. This affects referrals to the public sector as well as the availability of reimbursements for services. None of the Haitian associations deals with health care directly, although they do so indirectly through referrals, counseling, and the organization of health fairs at which information is given and referrals are made. For those referred to Medicaid, according to one respondent, it is "hard for them to get into the office, and they want a lot of papers clients don't have." One Haitian center makes such referrals, but reports that many are rejected. On the other hand, all three associations refer to public hospitals, and clients are said to make use of the WIC (Women, Infants and Children), MIC (Maternal and Infant Care) family planning clinics and well-baby clinics. Although two Haitian association leaders interviewed reported no problems with referrals, one said there were problems when no interpreter was present. Referrals are also made to Haitian doctors. Mental health problems may be treated through counseling, but few Haitians would themselves seek help from mental health professionals because, according to one response, there are no therapists in Haiti. Many Haitians make use of their own health professionals and of *brujos*, traditional native healers. Since mental health problems are considered to be often related to the interference of spirits it is felt that American mental health practitioners must understand voodoo in order to help.

Both Cuban associations make referrals in the health area, including referrals to Medicaid and to public health facilities for prenatal, postnatal and child health care. Many Cubans seek help from priests. In addition Hispanic people use indigenous helpers who are variously called *santeros* and *espiritistas* who may practice spiritualism or utilize herbs or other native medicines. The Dominican associations emphasized problems in the health care systems. They stressed inability to pay, long waits in clinics and hospital waiting rooms, the need for translators and the inadequacy of service. One association prescreens children through a child development program and refers them for help if necessary. Language problems are a barrier to obtaining adequate care and, according to one respondent, "The services are seen as services for blacks." Another Dominican association sees its role more in terms of advocacy, holding conferences on alcoholism and women's problems and participating in health fairs. Wide use of native healers was reported. The reason for the lack of recourse to mental health professionals was because "they can't evaluate the situation because they lack knowledge about the community."

The Jamaican and Colombian associations both have members who are well educated, English speaking, and middle class. Neither association provides health services, although the Colombian association does refer people to doctors and hospitals. Medicaid referrals are not made. The Jamaican association, however, said that its members do utilize the city's prenatal, postnatal, and child health care facilities in a hospital in their neighborhood. The Jamaican association has volunteer child psychologists and social workers who make referrals to counseling services, especially in response to the problem of teenage drug abuse. Commenting on Western practices of mental health, the Jamaican respondent said, "It's an American phenomenon. We don't give much credence to these things."

The Chinese associations interviewed do not directly provide health care, although one does make referrals to Medicaid, and a staff social worker from the public agency (HRA) comes to the association on a regular basis several days a week to review all of the Medicaid referrals. Chinese are said to use prenatal, postnatal, and child health care facilities in Chinatown, as well as the public hospitals. One problem is the need for insurance coverage by the elderly.

It was reported that the Chinese continue to make wide use of the traditional acupuncturists and herbalists. With regard to mental health, one Chinese association leader said his members "do not believe in psychotherapy, group therapy, or that any mental health practice can help." The association of Overseas Chinese said that they have "experienced severe losses that most of the American mental health professionals cannot understand." Another Chinese respondent pointed out the difficulty of diagnosis when dealing with a cross-cultural situation. In an interview with a representative of the New York City Health and Hospitals Corporation, the view was expressed that the opening of a special Asian clinic in a city hospital, with Asian staff and a concern for Asian practice and culture, had helped bring many Asians to the clinic for needed services.

The Cambodian and Vietnamese associations provide an escort service to hospitals and clinics, give background information on patients, and provide translation services at health facilities. One reported that people did not go for prenatal care due to lack of knowledge, and another said that people do not go "since most people think they do not need care until the delivery date."

There were several references in the interviews with Asian associations to the use of native healers. For example, the Cambodian association has a monk to whom people have access when they need to talk. The Vietnamese association spoke of the use of herbs. Mental health problems are not discussed as such, since diagnosed mental health is viewed as a stigma.

The Indian associations reported going to physicians of their own ethnic background, of making extensive use of traditional home remedies, and of taking mental-health problems to their spiritual leaders.

Only one of the three Korean associations said that it provided help with health care, and it did so through referrals. The first line of recourse for Koreans when ill would be a private, preferably Korean, physician rather than a clinic or public health center. The Koreans, like the Chinese, use traditional medical practitioners such as acupuncturists and herbalists, and Koreans were said to have negative attitudes toward Western health methods.

The Greek and Italian associations are very knowledgeable about health services, and refer to Medicaid, to public and private hospitals, and to clinics. The Greek association sends translators along with clients to help those with language problems. Because there is a stigma attached, problems of mental health are not dealt with as such, but are dealt with as family health problems for which only Greek-speaking professionals are used. One Italian association provides help with Medicaid forms as well as counseling and follow-up education concerning health services. The other Italian association does family counseling but finds that "families do not open up." The respondent said that mental-health practitioners at agencies are not successful because they do not tap family members as resources; also, there is a lack of Italian-speaking therapists.

The two Eastern European associations function in a similar manner with regard to health care. Both help with establishing Medicaid eligibility, filling out forms, and escorting people when necessary to health care services. The Russian group refers primarily to a single public hospital whereas the Polish association has an extensive referral network which includes a number of public and voluntary hospitals as well as private clinics. The respondent from the Polish association spoke of the difficulty of using private doctors because of their unwillingness to take Medicaid cases, and they make special efforts to secure health care for their members, regardless of their ability to pay full fees. Problems with Medicaid eligibility were also mentioned, especially the low-income eligibility. Both the Russian and Polish groups utilized prenatal, postnatal, and child health care clinics, and they encountered problems of communication both in obtaining these services and establishing Medicaid eligibility. Both Russians and Poles are said to use medications and remedies used in the country of birth, and the Polish respondent said that Poles feel more comfortable with Polish doctors who "approach treatment in a way more familiar to the people."

A preference for doctors of the same ethnic group was expressed by the Palestinian respondent. Although his group was not involved in health care he reported that there were Palestinian doctors to whom they refer patients. They, in turn, arrange any necessary hospital admissions. The association of Arabic-speaking people, except as it cares for the older people in its residence, does not provide direct health care services to others, but it does make referrals to Medicaid.

Legal Needs and Services

Newcomers may be faced with a variety of legal service needs, some of which they have in common with other families (e.g., housing and other contracts, domestic relations), others of which arise because they are newcomers (i.e., legal immigrant status). Legal service providers in the community include private attorneys, organized not-for-profit legal services, and legal units in some public departments.

Nine of the ten associations of Caribbeans and South Americans reported that immigration problems were the main but not the only legal issue. A Cuban association which serves only the Marielistas said crime was a problem; a Colombian group mentioned police arrests and "maybe drugs," and a Jamaican group mentioned "young people in trouble with the law." A Dominican association leader said that obtaining legal services is a severe problem, and that people seek services from individuals who have very little knowledge about what they are doing, in particular on immigration issues.

Immigration-related problems were also mentioned by all but one of the European associations interviewed. The Russian respondent, for example, complained of service at the immigration office which "is like a wall" in terms of the time it takes to get a green card, citizenship, or other papers.

Among the Asian associations, legal services were not one of the major issues, but nine reported problems relating to immigrant status, and an equal number spoke of problems related to business, either dispute settlements or contracts. Legal needs related to marriage and divorce, wills, real estate and housing, landlord-tenant relations, claims for car accidents, and, in one case, to interethnic fights between youths.

One or another form of direct legal assistance is provided by twelve of the thirty associations interviewed, and an even larger number make referrals. Seven of the ten associations of Caribbeans and South Americans know about legal services in the community and make referrals to them, although some do so only informally. All three of the other associations have private lawyers of their own ethnic group who can be called on when necessary. Five of the associations make referrals to the Legal Aid Society, and that experience was reported as being fair to very good. One association said that when there is trouble, the police may contact the association which then interprets and advocates for the person.

European associations also mentioned referrals to the Legal Aid Society, with which their experiences were reported as generally good. Other types of legal help include sending interpreters to court with clients where necessary, making referrals to lawyers of the same ethnic group, and hiring lawyers for individual cases. The Polish association, for example, makes referrals to the People's Firehouse, and the Legal Aid Society; in landlord-tenant–related cases; to the Catholic Charities for immigration problems; to the Legal Aid Society for cases of divorce; and to the Worker's Compensation Board for work-related legal claims.

All of Asian associations but one (Chinese) provided some

form of legal-related services, mainly referrals to community agencies which provide legal services or to practicing lawyers, many of whom were of their own ethnic group. Interpreters and translators are also provided.

Patterns of Service and Referrals

This analysis has assumed that the pattern of service and referrals will vary because the needs of groups differ, and the associations have a range of programs. But the overview of needs and services shows that there is an additional differentiating factor, the type of service category. Associations tend to offer direct help when the needs relate to education and job training. This is especially true for associations whose members have severe language handicaps. Direct help was also more likely to be provided around family problems where cultural conflicts between the old country and the new have strained family relationships. Associations, through their own staff, provided counseling services sensitive to these cultural issues.

Where there are large public programs addressed to the needs of all New Yorkers, the associations' role was more likely to be that of facilitator and advocate. Service referrals were made and association members acted as escorts and interpreters, assisted with the application process, and advocated for members.

A pattern also emerged with respect to the use of referrals by ethnic associations. Referrals were made to public agencies and programs when the need was related to health, financial assistance, or other family support. The largest number of referrals to voluntary agencies were for help with employment, family and legal problems, and financial needs. Referrals to proprietary providers were for employment, health, and legal services. Relatively few referrals were made for housing, probably reflecting the tight market and limited opportunities. One overall finding is that the area that engages the largest number of ethnic associations is family support, and here they are probably unique in filling a need which the established formal human service systems are not prepared to service.

Summary of Findings

The existence of a new wave of immigration in New York City, which differs from earlier waves in that the newcomers are mainly of Hispanic and Asian backgrounds rather than European, is clearly reflected in the data. The study also found that there is a proliferation of ethnic associations, involving almost all groups among the recent arrivals.

The selection process for the sample chose its cases from a broad band of associations with varied levels of social service activities. As expected, the interview results reflected this range; associations varied from groups that were mainly fraternal to those that functioned as ethnic agencies. But even those associations least concerned with service needs, and least knowledgeable about service opportunities, reported that their members were experiencing problems, and they saw potential if not current unmet needs.

One major finding of the study was the list of ten differentiating questions, which can be used to classify ethnic agencies. A quantitative analysis, based on variables associated with ethnic associations, yielded a second important finding. Three factors emerged which provided a base for classifying most, but not all, of the associations. The groupings are:

1. The professionalized, full-service operation, usually conceived of as an ethnic agency.
2. The association serving members with special status, including refugees and entrants, from developing or third world countries.
3. The community-based associations serving persons culturally related to people in the host country, and often open to nationals of different countries, with a continuing interest and investment in their country of origin.

The perceptions of leaders of the ethnic associations with regard to both identity and acculturation issues were reported. Most leaders differentiated their groups from North Americans in interpersonal, familial, and cultural areas. Of interest is the finding that although there was substantial agreement about what North Americans were like, there were strong regional differences in self-perceptions among groups of associations. In three cases regional groupings (i.e., Asian, European, and Caribbean and South American) superseded distinctive ethnic differences within each region.

Two scales developed to secure comparable responses to identity and acculturation issues, which might be related to coping in the new environment, indicated that the six identity items with the strongest reliability were related to retaining the native language, teaching children the old customs, celebrating traditional holidays, preparing traditional foods, belonging to an ethnic association, and marrying in one's own ethnic group. Acculturation items were weak; the only item that showed real strength was "learning to compete in order to be successful." There was a low but negative correlation between identity and acculturation scores.

The ethnic associations' role in service delivery was at the core of the study hypothesis, which relates to their potential for linkages with the formal service system. The detailed reporting by association leaders, of a whole range of activities undertaken by ethnic associations is sufficient to document their important role in serving the families of newcomers. Having said this, it is also necessary to report the factors that affect the degree of involvement by associations in service activities. There are associations interviewed who were not active in this area, either because they felt that there was no need for it, or because they felt that it was not their role. In the latter category a few respondents pointed to other groups, mainly ethnic agencies or social agencies with ethnic programs who were providing services. At the other end of the continuum a few of the respondents did not view themselves as ethnic associations but saw their role as ethnic social agencies, comparable to the voluntary agencies in the formal service system.

The discussion of the continuum of services should in no way minimize the importance of the informal support provided by many of the less professionalized associations. Such support often takes forms not easily recognizable in terms of standard service delivery categories, yet allows the newcomer to cope with the circumstances faced. Both recognition and appreciation of these informal supports are necessary for an effective liaison between associations and the formal provider system.

Special note should be made of the particular positions of groups that are designated as MAAs (mutual assistance associations) and used by the state governments as conduits of services for refugees and entrants. These organizations are often noted in the literature in the category of "self-help" groups, but this is a misnomer. The "self-help" applies only to the fact that they are of the same ethnic group as their members or service recipients, but the analogy ends there. Characteristic of the MAAs at the present time is that they function as liaisons between newcomers and the formal service providers. The New York State Department of Social Services, for example, has contracts with MAAs for the delivery of services which are seen as filling gaps in existing programs directed at promoting the successful resettlement and acculturation of refugees and entrants. This may be a model, however, that only works when there are funding programs to back it up. Still to be determined is whether the MAAs have the cohesion and community support to function when, or if, the specialized entitlements expire. This will be the test of whether they are viable as ethnic associations, or whether they are primarily extensions of federal programming. In the meantime they are important providers of services, which is to be expected since that is what they are mandated to do.

The study set out to explore linkages between ethnic associations and the formal service structure. It concluded that such linkages not only exist, but are seen by responsible persons in the public sector as essential for appropriate access by newcomers to services. Such access, however, varies with the legal status of newcomers, and is more likely to be available to refugees and entrants organized in MAAs, or related to the resettlement agencies, than to other immigrant groups.

The situation is different for new immigrant groups who are not refugees. Some are served by existing ethnic agencies or programs established by earlier immigrants of their group, for example the Greeks and Italians, and to some extent the Chinese. Others do not see the need for special services since their people are self-supporting on arrival, like the Indians and Koreans. As these newcomers cope with the problems of living in New York, however, needs are emerging, in particular for youth and the elderly, and association leaders are exploring new ways to meet the needs of their members.

Many of the new immigrants are outside the major sectarian groups and uninformed about the public and voluntary agencies, seeing them as primarily for welfare recipients. At the same time, the current availability of HRA outreach workers, special ethnic health clinics in public hospitals (for Asians and Hispanics), and welfare centers for specified immigrant groups indicate that the public sector has begun to accept the need for ethnic-related services. The ethnic association route is one way to reach many otherwise inaccessible populations who would not be in touch with established, traditional social-service agencies.

Any such support to special groups needs to have adequate justification for ethnic sponsorship, however, and provide a strong accountability component. The element of ethnic-sensitive practice is not the only important factor in service delivery; others are quality of service, competent management, and concern for both efficiency and effectiveness.

Ethnic associations need more visibility in the social-welfare community, and more knowledge of programs, services, and funding sources. Currently, interface with the formal provider system tends to be formalized for the refugee groups with their special entitlements, but is sporadic for other groups of immigrants. Yet in the schools, the hospitals, and on the streets both groups are newcomers, and all face problems of coping in the new environment. Although there are differences in entitlements as between refugees and other immigrants, institutional arrangements which exclude some groups from the system can only reinforce interethnic hostility, which could move to interethnic conflict. Furthermore, special refugee entitlements are time limited, and when they expire, all groups will compete for the same limited service resources.

When support for ethnic associations is discussed, not infrequently the question is raised whether public money should be used for separate services. The other side of the coin, however, is that if specialized, mainly separate services are not offered, with language and cultural appropriateness, it is unlikely that needy people will have access to entitlements. Furthermore, New York City, in particular, has traditionally had sectarian-based services, supported primarily with public funds. The model might be just as viable for ethnic minorities as for sectarian groups.

Whether ethnic association will seek interethnic coalitions, or continue as separate enterprises, they have established a place for themselves in the dissemination of services that help newcomers in adapting to their new environments. As this effort is increasingly recognized in the social welfare community, the issue arises of whether or not there will be a shift in the traditional pattern of service delivery as between public/voluntary/proprietary services, and secular/sectarian services. Where do the ethnic agencies and associations' services fit? Are they a special type of public service? Or are they a categorical service for a defined population? These are all questions for the attention of the social welfare community.

Newcomers come to New York as immigrants, refugees, entrants, or undocumented aliens. Once here, however, they are all New Yorkers, and their human service needs cut across these status categories. Ethnic associations can play an important role in identifying those needs and responding to them.

References

Bryce-LaPorte, R. S. 1977. "Visibility of the New Immigrants." *Society.* Washington, D.C.:(September-October), 14(6):18–22. Smithsonian Institution.

Levine, D. B., K. Hill and R. Warren, eds. 1985. *Immigration Statistics: A Story of Neglect.* Washington, D.C.: National Academy Press.

Passel, J. and K. Woodrow. 1984. "Geographic Distribution of Undocumented Immigrants: Estimates of Undocumented Aliens Counted in the 1980 Census by State." *International Migration Review,* (Fall), 18(3):642–75.

Tobier, E. 1982. "Foreign Immigration." In C. Brecher and R. D. Horton, eds., *Setting Municipal Priorities, 1983.* New York: New York University Press.

3.

Ethnic Associations in Britain

Juliet Cheetham

Ethnic associations in Britain have been little studied. The reasons for this are worth examination because they introduce major themes that will facilitate a later analysis of their roles, contributions, and structures.

Traditions in British Social Policy

The first reason for this neglect is the long-standing expectation in Britain, now waning but still strong, that newcomers will, by choice, force of circumstance, or by the simple passage of time be assimilated into mainstream British society (Jones 1977; Cheetham 1981, 1982). In a long imperial history generations of British people have been brought face to face with different cul-

Professor Juliet Cheetham is director of the Social Work Research Center of Stirling University, Scotland. This paper was written when she was lecturer in Applied Social Studies and Fellow of Green College at Oxford University. The study was carried out in conjunction with the Refugee Studies Programme at Queen Elizabeth House, Oxford University. Professor Cheetham is grateful to Dr. Barbara Bond, the director of the program; Apophia Kibedi, Diana Pritchard, and Maria Salinas, who conducted many of the interviews; Rai Patterson, who interviewed members of Afro-Caribbean organizations; and the Commission for Racial Equality for a grant toward the expenses of the study.

tures, races, and religions. In spite of this, convictions of superiority (an essential ingredient of imperialism), reinforced by expectations of assimilation, have not encouraged enthusiasm for the continuity of difference and the retention of "old" cultures. Indeed, such continuities are often resisted lest diversity should mean division and the undesirable perpetuation of groups presumed to have an inferior life-style. When it suits them the British will claim that they are a nation of immigrants, referring to Celtic and Norman occupations and thence to the arrival of persecuted minorities in the eighteenth and nineteenth centuries. But the realities, the riches and the conflicts of a more pluralistic multiracial Britain, have only been slowly and somewhat resentfully grasped. Given such context, this study could expect to find ethnic associations having to struggle for existence and recognition.

A second, more benign, reason for a lack of interest in ethnic associations is the product of a long tradition in British social policy that, insofar as immigrants need welfare provisions, these should be provided by mainstream services. In the 1960s it was argued that there would in any case be little need or demand for services from the young, single men who were the majority of newcomers. The large-scale settlement of families was not anticipated; not were the ravages of disadvantage, discrimination, and economic recession. When problems were identified it was observed that there were no problems that ethnic minorities did not share with the numerous poor and disadvantaged white people.

The doctrine of increasing equality between classes, a principal objective of the welfare state, distracted attention from racial or ethnic inequalities, and a colorblind approach has been encouraged as the best route to fairness and equality. Class, not race, has been seen as the main divider of society. The belief that public education, health, income maintenance, and welfare services, which are intended to have universal application, should, could, and would cater satisfactorily to people on the basis of their needs, without regard to sex or ethnic differences, does not encourage support for the ethnic associations' welfare role. These expectations, combined with the attitudes outlined earlier, can lead to the view that "different" may be a synonym for "deficient." Hence it has been conventional wisdom that ethnic associations that aim to provide welfare services should be discouraged as being certainly divisive and probably inferior in the services they offer.

The third reason for ignoring ethnic associations is connected with the increasing resistance, since the 1950s, to further immigration to Britain by those nationalities or groups unfamiliar with British society, who have a strong wish to affirm their own cultural identity in an alien world. Every postimperial country faces problems about what to do when citizens, or half-citizens, who having been encouraged from afar to believe in one nation, one commonwealth, and one mother country, decide they will avail themselves of these ideals through migration. When this means the arrival of distinctive groups with largely unfamiliar backgrounds, in a chauvinistic and racist society which is facing and then engulfed in economic recession, major and continuous efforts are made to stem the flow of aspiring settlers. Successive legislation from the 1960s has dramatically curbed the flow of those who wish to settle, save those from the European Economic Community (EEC), unless they can claim British citizenship through their parents or prove that they are the close dependents of those already settled in Britain.

In an earlier paper Jenkins has produced a vivid image in which the Statue of Liberty with her welcoming message for the poor, the oppressed, and the seekers of freedom is cloned and placed at the new entry points for contemporary migrants to the United States. Britain's welcome for newcomers has always been more grudging and at times plainly hostile. In the nineteenth century she may have accepted the poor and the persecuted but she never invited them. Jewish and Irish enclaves of big cities were described as "smouldering fires eating away the very vitals of the metropolis" and "scum washed to our shores in the dirty water flowing from foreign drainpipes." Then, as now, members of Parliament complained, "there are some streets you may go through and hardly know you are in England" (Nicholson 1974). There has never been any equivalent to the symbol of the Statue of Liberty; aspiring settlers are more familiar with legislation and bureaucracy designed to obstruct them (Dummett 1973; CRE 1985).

The increasingly hostile atmosphere of the 1960s and 1970s

was also manifest in the politics of social services as their capacity to exacerbate as well as solve problems was recognized (Jones 1977). In the competition for eligibility for scarce resources and the struggle of the most deprived citizens for their definition of fair shares, certain groups became scapegoats, perceived as the causes of social and economic deprivation rather than its most vulnerable victims. In this potentially explosive climate it is tempting to obscure real estimates of need or to argue that meeting it will heighten racial tension by provoking hostility toward receivers and providers. In such a context a "race relations paralysis" can affect social policy; doing nothing is safer than doing something, especially for an identifiable minority whose rights are contentious. This was not a climate that encouraged active support for ethnic associations.

Contemporary Approaches

Paradoxically, it is the immigration of the last thirty years which, although it has been so strongly resisted, has forced the British to question assimilationist assumptions and politics and aroused a grudging acknowledgment of some forms of pluralism in a country that has, most reluctantly, had to realize that it is multiracial. Asians and West Indians may well hope for some integration into social and economic life, but not at the price of losing their ethnic identity. Public services are increasingly having to abandon a colorblind approach because, contrary to expectation, it is not proving a satisfactory basis for recognizing let alone serving adequately the needs of newcomers and their families. This change in attitude has not come easily. While great differences in history and interests among the countries of the EEC are expected and accepted, British administrators and policymakers still find it tiresome to encounter the wider divergence of culture and opinion among black and brown groups in Britain. They have been easily deflected from the task of making contact with many associations. One excuse for failing to provide ethnic-sensitive services has been that "they," i.e., the Pakistanis, Chinese, Indians, and West Indians, could not agree on what they wanted. The fairest and most sensible policy was, therefore, to treat everyone the same. This would, it was argued, at least avoid encouraging the undesirable continuation of separate cultures and traditions which could impede the process of integration. Equality would be best achieved by providing the same services in the same manner for all (Jones 1977; ADSS 1978; Cheetham 1981; Young and Connelly 1981).

In the last few years pressure from minority groups and growing political sensitivity, especially in local authorities, has meant substantial changes in this unitary approach (Connelly 1984). Nevertheless, most British administrators would still be amazed and probably baffled by the astonishing diversity of cultures and interests revealed in this study. Most would not easily be able to imagine how ethnic associations could be the means of delivering, perhaps in conjunction with statutory services, more appropriate and effective services for minorities. A few, were they convinced of the vitality and efficiency of the associations, might be tempted to divert to them total responsibility for meeting minority needs. This would demand less effort and adaptation on the part of statutory agencies. Can this bafflement and inertia of administrations be negotiated? This study suggests that behind the dazzling diversity of the ethnic associations' cultural traditions there are needs common to all their members and some common methods of meeting these which, in the experience of associations, have proved reasonably effective. If these approaches can be identified, and it will be argued later that they are neither extraordinary nor far removed from the traditions of mainstream social work, then the road to collaboration between ethnic associations and statutory agencies may not seem too hazardous. Further encouragement could come from the rekindled interest in voluntary and self-help programs which is the consequence of increasing demands on public services and reduced government investment in them.

The time is therefore ripe to look seriously at the ethnic associations and to explore the questions that lie at the heart of the different national studies reported in this volume. For newcomers and their families in Britain, do ethnic associations act as a bridge between the old life and the new or are they primarily focused on the preservation of links with immigrants' original countries, with the continuity of ethnic traditions? Can ethnic associations assist in the problems of settlement by giving services directly or through help in negotiating the labyrinth of the British public services? In terms of more general social policy, can they assist public agencies to develop services more sensitive to the enthically heterogeneous populations of many parts of Britain? What contribution can they make to the politics of a country which has made some gestures toward the promotion of racial equality, but in which direct and institutional discrimination are still rampant and relations between white and black people are at best distant and often tense?

These questions can only be explored, and comparisons made with the United States, Israel, the Netherlands, and Australia, with some understanding of the population and demography of Britain, particularly of its black and brown minorities. Special attention is focused on them in this study because the major questions of ethnicity in the last thirty years have concerned immigrants and their descendants from the New Commonwealth, that is, all those countries of the British Commonwealth excluding Australia, Canada, and New Zealand. It is these minorities and other smaller groups readily identified as black or brown that are subject to all the disadvantages arising from differential treatment based on color and, in some cases, on cultures regarded as alien and inferior.

The largest numbers of New Commonwealth immigrants have come from the West Indies and from India, Bangladesh, Africa, and Pakistan, which used to be but are no longer part of the British Commonwealth. These populations include substantial numbers of people who have lived in Britain for twenty or more years, and their children who were born here. Among recent settlers are the wives and children of men from the Indian subcontinent, who may have lived in Britain for several years before being in a position to reunite their families. Other recent arrivals include refugees from many countries, including 30,000 Ugandan Asians in 1972 and 16,000 refugees from Vietnam in 1979–1980. In terms of the whole population these newcomers are numerically insignificant, yet Britain has tried to severely limit the number of refugees entering the country; however, they continue to arrive.

Three thousand people applied for political asylum in 1980, and over four thousand in 1982; this was granted in 47 and 57 percent of cases respectively. The position and problems of refugees raise particularly interesting questions for a study of the role of ethnic associations.

The People of Britain

The population of Britain (England, Wales, and Scotland) is about 54 million. Estimates of the size of the black population (which, following common practice in Britain, means both Afro-Caribbean, African, and Asian people) are not entirely reliable because they are based on various relatively small-scale surveys and not on the 1981 national census which did not include a question on ethnic origins but only on birthplace. Thus the children of immigrants who were born in Britain are excluded from national ethnic enumeration. The most recent and comprehensive analysis of the black population of Britain was carried out in 1982 by the Policy Studies Institute (Brown 1984). Over four-fifths of these people have their origins in the Caribbean, the Indian sub-continent, or Africa. The black population is estimated to be about 3.3 percent of the whole population. The projection for 1991 is that there will be 2.5 million people in Britain with origins, that is parents born, in the Commonwealth, approximately 5 percent of the total British population. Table 3.1 indicates the ethnic origin and birthplace of the population of Britain in 1983.

The period of actual immigration of any scale began after World War II. An initially small migration from the West Indies, India, and Pakistan increased to a substantial flow during the 1950s. This peaked sharply in the years before the introduction of immigration control in 1962. Since then there has been an overall downward trend in black immigration, although this has been punctuated by two important fluctuations: a peak in 1972 when people of Asian origin were expelled from Uganda, and an increase between 1974 and 1976 as a result of changes in the rules and procedures regarding the immigration of spouses and dependents.

Within these broad changes in the level of New Commonwealth immigration there have been substantial changes in the

Table 3.1. Population by Ethnic Origin and Birthplace, 1983 (in thousands)

Ethnic Origin	United Kingdom	Outside United Kingdom	Not Stated	Total
White	48,728	1,792	254	50,774
West Indian or Guyanese	248	257	4	510
Indian	263	513	14	789
Pakistani	139	210	4	353
Bangladeshi	26	55	1	83
Chinese	21	83	—	105
African	32	58	2	92
Arab	10	58	1	69
Mixed	149	47	1	198
Other	24	86	—	110
Not stated	656	34	261	952
All origins[a]	50,297	3,196	541	54,035

(Birthplace spans United Kingdom, Outside United Kingdom, Not Stated columns)

SOURCE: Office of Population Censuses and Surveys, *Labour Force Survey* (1983).
[a]Totals not exact because of rounding.

composition of that immigration. First, the peak period of West Indian immigration was before the first immigration controls. Since then, and throughout the 1960s and 1970s, migrants from the Indian subcontinent have been in the majority. Second, the earlier stages of the migration were characterized by a predominance of adult males. These were later to be outnumbered by women and children; more than 90 percent of New Commonwealth citizens accepted for settlement on arrival in 1979 were women, children, or elderly men. These numbers, however, were small, approximately 20,000. The huge shift from "primary" immigration to the immigration of dependents has been particularly marked among Asians. Nevertheless, in recent years overall numbers have been very small (see table 3.2), and in terms of the size of the whole population far more people have left Britain than have settled there.

Population figures include considerable numbers of people born in Britain; estimates suggest that in 1982 over 40 percent of the population with New Commonwealth ancestry were born there, and that the proportion will rise to about half by 1991 (Brown 1984). Because of the differences in the timing of the migration, this process is more advanced for people of West Indian origin than for those of Asian origin.

Table 3.2. Immigration from the New Commonwealth and Pakistan: Acceptance for Settlement, 1971–1983 (in thousands)

Year of Acceptance	On Arrival			
	Men	Women	Children	Total
1971	6.8	12.0	16.4	35.2
1976	6.9	13.9	16.1	36.9
1981	1.8	7.1	9.6	18.5
1983	1.7	6.3	7.1	15.1

SOURCE: Home Office, Control of Immigration Statistics, United Kingdom, 1983 HMSO 1984, Cmnd. 9246, pp. 50–51.

Table 3.3. Regional Distribution of Whites, Asians, and West Indians in England and Wales

Region	Population in Households with Heads Born in:		
	United Kingdom (Percent)	Caribbean (Percent[a])	Indian Subcontinent, East Africa (Percent[a])
Greater London	11	56	33
Other Southeast	21	9	14
East Midlands	8	5	8
West Midlands	10	16	19
North West	14	5	10
Yorks/Humberside	10	5	9
Rest of England and Wales	26	5	6

SOURCE: *1981 United Kingdom Census: Regional Tables*. London: HMSO.
[a] Does not add up to 100 because of rounding.

Ethnic Minority Concentration and Needs

The black population of Britain is concentrated in certain areas, in particular Greater London, in which one-third of all Asians and one-half of West Indians live, as opposed to 11 percent of all whites. The Midlands, too, contain substantial proportions of immigrants. Within these relatively large geographical regions there are further concentrations. This means that black people, although a tiny proportion of the national population, have been seen to be relatively numerous in some localities. In one or two London boroughs nearly one-quarter of the population is black. Because of the young age of this population, at or reaching the family-building stage of life, and their concentration in areas otherwise largely inhabited by middle-aged or elderly white people, there are several boroughs in which the majority of births are to black mothers. A few local authorities in Britain have therefore relatively large black populations, but even within these concentrations the numbers are small. There are few adjoining streets in which black households predominate. The Policy Studies Institute study (Brown 1984) confirmed that in the vast majority of enumeration districts white people are in the majority and all live in the local authorities where they are the overwhelming majority. Although in one or two boroughs in the Greater London Council (GLC) 40 percent of school children are black, they make up only 3.5 percent of the total school population in the GLC; and in only twelve out of forty secondary GLC schools are black pupils the majority. This demography means that in local and national politics in most areas issues of importance to ethnic minorities are not likely to be high on the agenda.

The major locations of settlement of black minorities include the poorest and most disadvantaged areas in Britain. Within the general context of the stress associated with migration come the problems of life in boroughs with some of the highest indices of social deprivation. Overcrowding, poor amenities, high rates of unemployment and, in some areas, racial harassment are the daily experience of black people. Their need for public services is therefore great and there are likely to be disproportionate needs for specific services. First, there are the services commonly needed by families with preschool children. Forty percent of Asians and 30 percent of West Indians are under sixteen, compared with 22 percent of the whole population. While about 12 percent of the general population fall into the nine-and-under age group, 27 percent of Asian-origin children are in this age band (Brown 1984). Three-quarters of West Indian and nearly one-third of Asian mothers are employed outside the home at some time during their children's preschool years, many for substantial periods, compared with 45 percent of mothers in the general population (Osborn, Butler, and Morris 1984). A higher proportion of ethnic minority than white mothers say they work from economic necessity. Nearly one-third of West Indian households with children under sixteen, compared with one-tenth of similar white households, are headed by a single parent, usually a woman. Black mothers therefore have a disproportionate need for day care, much of which is probably met, because of the gap between demand and supply, by the poorest-quality, lowest-paid child minders (Jackson and Jackson 1979; Mayall and Petrie 1983). The pressures of disadvantages and discrimination in education and employment bear hard on all black people and particularly on young school leavers (Brown 1984; Swann Committee 1985). In some boroughs well over half of the black male population is unemployed (Scarman 1981). Many live a hand-to-mouth existence, more or less homeless and at the center of considerable family tension. They are liable to be harassed or arrested by the police out of all proportion to their numbers or criminality (Smith et al. 1983). Young blacks are disproportionately overrepresented in penal institutions.

At the other end of the age range are the small but increasing numbers of black elderly people almost totally neglected by social-service departments despite their comparatively high level of need (Glendenning 1979, 1982). Bhalla and Blakemore's (1981) careful study of elderly black people's perception of their needs and their use of voluntary and statutory provisions within inner-city areas found language barriers and ignorance about services in the general context of cultural isolation and great loneliness. This was particularly so for Asians, contrary to traditional expectations of the place of elderly Asian people within the extended family. The respondents also showed substantial interest in such services as home help and "meals on wheels" and in attendance at day centers. Practically none anticipated a return to their native countries.

With rare exceptions the response of social services departments and the probation service has been inadequate (Young and Connelly 1981; Taylor 1981), although in some authorities substantial efforts are being made to work toward the elimination of racial inequalities and for the provision of services that take account of ethnic heterogenity (Cheetham 1982; Connelly 1985).

Diversity Among the Ethnic Minorities

Considering that black people are only a tiny proportion of the general population, the diversity of ethnic and geographical origins, languages, and religions to be found among them is dazzling. The largest of the Caribbean groups originates from Jamaica, but the migrants from the West Indies include substantial numbers from Barbados, Trinidad and Tobago, Guyana and the Windward Islands, and the Virgin Islands. Asian migrants can be divided into principal groups by area of origin: those from Gujarat, a western state of India near Pakistan; those from the Punjab area of Northern India and Pakistan and the areas of Pakistan to the northwest of the Punjab; those from Sylhet and the maritime areas of Bangladesh; and those from East Africa, whose family origins were in various parts of India, mainly Gujarat and the Punjab. The majority of Asians originate from rural areas, although the "African Asians" generally come from towns and cities.

The first language of most Caribbean immigrants was English. Although there are differences of dialect and patois among the islands, and these have been preserved to an extent within the different communities in Britain, their fundamental closeness to standard English, and the use of English as the official language in the islands, have meant that West Indian immigrants have not encountered language problems on the scale experienced by the Asians. On arrival most of the Asians had as their first language Punjabi, Urdu, Gujarati, Bengali, Kutchi, or Pashto. Most additionally spoke at least one other of these languages or Hindi, but their knowledge of English varied a great deal. Table 3.4 shows Asians' fluency in English. The sample was not confined to recent arrivals, but was a general survey of the ethnic minority population. It can be seen that women are particularly likely to have

Table 3.4. Fluency in English Among Asian Adults

	All Asians (Percent)	Men (Percent[a])	Women (Percent[a])
Immigrant speaks English			
Fluently	41	48	32
Fairly well	23	27	18
Slightly	21	19	27
Not at all	11	4	20
Not recorded	4	4	4
Total	100	100	100

SOURCE: Brown (1984).
[a] Does not add up to 100 because of rounding.

poor or no English, and refugees are also likely to be handicapped in this way. There are studies that show a similar pattern among Chinese immigrants.

There are several different religions among the Asians in Britain. Although no strict delineation can be made according to areas of origin it is possible to generalize: most of those from the Punjab are Sikhs; most from Gujarat are Hindus; and most Pakistanis and Bengalis are Muslims. Among West Indians some of the most evangelistic Christian sects have a wide following, and the adoption of Rastafarianism by some young West Indian men is very visible. Religious affiliations and observance have very prominent roles in British Asian culture, far more so than among white people or many people of West Indian origin. There are few minority social workers and, outside the health service, very few, if any, minority staff in any of the public welfare agencies. Teaching for work with minorities has been extremely limited (CCETSW 1983). Understanding of different cultural backgrounds, languages, and religions is likely to be minimal and business usually has to be conducted through an interpreter with all the complications of confusion in communication that role can bring.

In the context described there would seem to be a clear role for ethnic associations to promote the welfare of newcomers and their families, who are often ill served by public agencies which find it difficult to respond adequately to diversity. Whether these ethnic associations want such functions or are able to perform them is a major question to be explored.

Field Study

The British study was planned to replicate the one carried out in New York, but was adapted to take account of the circumstances of ethnic minorities in Britain and the British welfare system. From what ethnic associations could the sample for the British study be drawn? A booklet compiled by the Commission for Racial Equality (CRE 1986) lists 230 ethnic associations of an extraordinarily varied nature. This number was known to be an underestimate because small new associations mushroom almost daily. The CRE list was also limited to the associations established by black (including Asian) people. There are also large numbers of European associations, some of which date back to before World War II and were founded to help immigrants to Britain who were fleeing the various religious and political persecutions in Russia and large parts of Europe in the last century. Some of these organizations have found new life and meaning in assisting new waves of European immigrants and refugees. But what kind of associations are relevant for the present study?

There were limited resources available for the research and it had to be completed quickly to run in parallel with the other studies. Furthermore, there was no homogeneous sampling frame from which to make a systematic or random selection of ethnic associations. Approaches were made to organizations that were known to have welfare interests in areas of high minority concentration, particularly London and the Midlands. These were selected on recommendation from the Commission for Racial Equality, or because they were already known to the author and her colleagues. African, Asian (including Chinese and Vietnamese), West Indian (sometimes known as Afro-Caribbean), and European associations were included in an attempt to illustrate and compare the predicament of the major minority groups and refugees in Britain and their relationship to ethnic associations.

Selection was complicated because there are virtually no ethnic agencies that deliver services as an alternative to or in conjunction with the public agencies. It has been shown that, despite its many inadequacies, the supposed universality and dominance of the public welfare system does not allow or encourage ethnic associations to develop alternative structures. There are, however, many associations which, with their own resources or through public funding, include in their various activities welfare functions such as information giving, advice, support groups, and help with the very old or young. There are a few that specialize in referral and advocacy and that may act as centers of information about the circumstances of minorities and as pressure groups for improvement in public services. Some of these have paid and qualified staff. There are others, perhaps the majority, whose original function was to preserve and promote cultural traditions and identity, which find that, at least implicitly, these activities have their own, usually unintended, welfare implications. Mother-tongue classes for children and English classes for mothers can rarely be free-standing discrete activities. They may provide their own support for lonely isolated people. Some associations have built on this so that apparently cultural activities may also act as a forum for advice and discussion, for example, about coping with the uncertainties and conflicts of parents and children whose lives straddle two cultures. Legal and welfare rights advice may be an obvious need for unemployed people whose citizenship status is in question. And so almost without noticing it associations whose original objectives were primarily cultural or concerned with the politics of the native country became caught up in the daily vicissitudes of their members. Some may deliberately exploit this to gain credibility for their cultural or political aspirations; others see little conflict and much satisfaction in preserving cultural traditions and creating bridges with the new society, with all the tensions that involves. Several such associations were included in the study and they illustrate well the difficulty, indeed the futility, of precise definition and division into different groups.

The questionnaire used by the New York study was adapted in minor ways for the British associations. The alternatives were largely to items on the grid determining organizations' priorities in preserving ethnic identity or working toward acculturation, which in Britain would most usually be described as integration. The questionnaire proved in large measure to be an appropriate instrument although the sections dealing with welfare were often briefly answered because of the associations' limited involvement in direct services. These sections did, however, confirm in sadly predictable ways the endemic deprivation and disadvantage minorities experience.

The data were not subjected to statistical analysis because the wide range of organizations and their differing objectives and structures would have meant subsamples too small to reveal significant differences. The small size of many organizations in terms of employed staff and committee structures also meant that such analysis would be inappropriate.

The interviews were conducted by the author, three researchers attached to the Refugee Studies Programme at Queen Elizabeth House, Oxford University, and a recently qualified black graduate social worker. The respondents were all fluent in English although a few interviews were conducted in Spanish. After the completion of the questionnaires a summary report was written drawing attention to particularly unusual or interesting features of the association and commenting on the shape of its welfare interests and its commitment to cultural activities and to building bridges to help its members become accustomed to British society. There were regular meetings between the interviewers and the author to focus on issues of particular significance.

The British study, like others in this volume, was limited to obtaining the views of the leaders and staff of the associations. Their constituencies and clientele may well have different perspectives. Some understanding of the satisfaction of people receiving direct services from the associations, which would almost certainly not have been available as readily or effectively in statutory agencies, was apparent to me in some interviews I conducted in associations' premises where I was able to watch, question, and comment on the problems being presented and the services provided. If ethnic associations are to be taken seriously by policymakers as one instrument of delivering and improving services for minorities, as this paper argues should be the case, then comparative studies of consumers' experiences in these and in statutory agencies would be well worthwhile.

Contact was made with thirty-seven organizations. A few, despite initial indications, turned out to have such limited welfare functions that they were inappropriate for the study. Others were too small, with, for example, only one spokesman, an uncertain number of members, and no clear organizational structure. One or two proved to have very specific but limited objectives, for example, providing legal advice to newly arrived refugees. Some were interested only in promoting religious observance. For all of these reasons eight associations were eliminated. The remaining twenty-nine associations all yielded information useful for the study although several, especially those concerned with recent refugees, were very small and so recently established that they were still rather poorly organized and inexperienced. Although the associations are identified below by group, they are not noted by name. Many respondents requested anonymity in the interviews, a usual convention in social science studies. Thus specific citations to association programs or quoted documents are not given, since that would violate the guarantee of anonymity.

Although there is something to be learned from grouping associations according to their geographical origins it must not be assumed that these groups are in other respects homogeneous. The African associations, for example, included some from nations with deep and lasting rivalries. Likewise, the European associations to some extent still reflected the divisions and hostilities which were the origin and legacy of two world wars. The Asian and Middle Eastern associations included such contrasting groups as Chinese, Bangladeshis, and Iranians. The crude nature of geographical groupings should not be seen as implying homogeneity and consensus among vastly differing nationalities.

The Associations' Histories

The history of associations largely reflects the history of major immigrations to Britain. The European associations are the oldest, with one dating from the Russian revolution and the others being established shortly after World War II as refugees from various parts of Europe were allowed to stay in Britain. Some of these associations have extended their responsibility to help new immigrants from, for example, Poland or Czechoslovakia who are fleeing the political regimes of these countries. The most recent associations, some of which are only two or three years old, have been established to help refugees from countries experiencing revolution or dramatic political upheaval: for example, Iran, Uganda, Vietnam, and the Sudan.

Associations established for about a decade are largely those of the immigrant groups who came from the New Commonwealth in the 1960s and 1970s. Some, like the West Indians who had been reared in a colonial culture, saw Britain as the mother land and expected a far warmer welcome and speedier integration than actually awaited them. They met ignorance, racism, and a set of institutions that were very different from those

Table 3.5. Associations Included in the Study

Region	Number
African	6
Afro-Caribbean (West Indian)	4
Asian and Middle Eastern	11
European	5
Latin American	3
Total	29

in their native countries, remote from the needs of immigrants, and unwilling to adapt (Cheetham 1972; Jones 1977). Desperate needs, disillusion with statutory agencies, and an increasing wish not to lose ethnic roots and identity, the common experience of immigrants (Kahn 1979), drove these citizens of the New Commonwealth, for whom British citizenship was in so much doubt, to form their own cultural and welfare associations. Initially these received little or no support from central government and local authorities which were, at best, lukewarm in their response to minority self-help. What little initiative there was from these sources was largely devoted to community relations councils which were meant to represent the interests of all New Commonwealth and other newcomers and whose tasks were enormous and resources small (Hill and Issacharoff 1971). Over the years, as communities have become more established and the support of minorities and the acceptance of diversity at least partly on the agenda of public authorities, these associations have received more backing. Some now employ several people and are recognized as centers of information and expertise.

Table 3.6. Years Ethnic Associations Have Been Established

Years	Number
50 or more	1
40–49	5
30–39	1
20–29	0
10–19	5
5– 9	9
Less than 5	8

Membership and Funding

Fifteen of the associations reported that they had membership arrangements. Four others had strong links with associated organizations. The nature of membership varied greatly. Sometimes it was said to consist of fifty to one hundred actively involved people, some of whom would act as volunteer helpers with the association's various activities and most of whom strongly supported the association's objectives. A few organizations reported a membership of several thousand, and this usually seemed to be membership by mailing list as one means of keeping in touch with fellow compatriots scattered around Britain. Membership arrangements may also be a way of keeping an ill-funded, new, or struggling association afloat before it is able to employ staff; in a few cases of very recently established refugee associations it seemed to be a method of excluding political enemies or people potentially hostile to the association because of events in the mother country. However, no association said it would confine its services to members only.

Only fifteen of the twenty-nine organizations at the time of the study were receiving public funds, usually from the Greater London Council (abolished in 1986), which was politically radical and active in promoting antiracist and feminist policies and supporting minority groups. Some public money is also channeled through the British Refugee Council or through local authorities' education or social-services budgets. This public funding, which is not usually more than £30,000 per annum and often considerably less, is usually used to rent premises and hire staff. Of these fifteen publicly funded agencies five have been established for less than four years; nine have been in existence for less than ten years, and only one for longer than ten years. They received funds either because they were seen as meeting the major needs of newly arrived and ill-served refugees (the most recent associations), or because they were serving more established New Commonwealth immigrants and their dependents.

The remaining organizations survive on private donations, membership fees (which are usually small), and fund-raising events. Several of these, while they would like to be richer, were doubtful about the wisdom or propriety of receiving public money.

They feared both control via the benefactor and an image as public scroungers. One or two ideologically committed to the virtues of self-help and the giving of what they had, resources or simply the support of shared experience and survival, to their fellows in need. These beliefs were found in their most sophisticated form in the few associations that were committed to establishing small industrial cooperatives, for example, a bakery, the profits of which could be used to fund welfare projects. Economic independence was seen as an important goal. In the case of Afro-Caribbean organizations these industrial enterprises were also seen as an important means of demonstrating West Indian business acumen and of providing opportunities to challenge the stereotype of Asian dominance in this sphere. Following Jewish and Asian traditions, businesses established with a strong cultural base were seen as an important foundation for a flourishing Afro-Caribbean community. Associations with these aspirations often faced a dilemma: acceptance of the public money they needed to get going was at odds with their philosophy of economic independence and self-help.

Four associations established to cope with the refugees of World War II had at the outset received public funds, but as the need for their welfare services declined, and refugees became integrated into British society and catered for by mainstream services, that support had been withdrawn. All except three associations reported financial difficulties. Of these three, two were associations over forty years old which had a steady income from the sale of property acquired when their activities and services were at their height. The remaining association, with exclusively Islamic cultural and educational objectives, was well funded by various Muslim countries and by its publishing activities.

What determines the receipt of public funding? A first priority is knowledge of possible sources and experience in dealing with the bureaucracy of grant aid. The problems are numerous. Few funding bodies advertise the possibility of their largesse. There may be language problems and, although refugee groups include many middle-class people used in their own countries to negotiating successfully with officialdom, the British welfare state labyrinth will be unfamiliar. This study revealed some very small associations, often in their infancy, that had a definite needy clientele and a clear agenda. They had not yet been able to establish their creditability, sometimes because they lacked the very things that only money could buy: premises, some kind of secretariat, some indications that they were already functioning effectively. Other associations that had become more established and had the trappings of at least some administration and bureaucracy found it much easier to attract funds. Here, as elsewhere, the rule "To those that hath, yet more shall be given" applies. It was astonishing to see how many tiny associations were coping with the vicissitudes of no proper premises and no staff. They often seemed to be kept going by the charisma of a few passionate, energetic individuals, although their long-term future was in doubt. It is difficult for public authorities that are large, highly bureaucratic organizations to recognize as serious enterprises the tiny associations that have not yet acquired the resources to negotiate assertively with government bodies. They also have to be wary of funding individuals whose claims to be acting disinterestedly for a constituency may be false. Such people can certainly be found. But in this particular field, where ethnic associations may be reaching out to desperately needy, isolated small groups, well beyond the reach of statutory agencies, imagination and flexibility in assessment are crucial. There is a case too for giving small "pump priming" grants simply to enable new organizations to make an effective case for further and more substantial funding. If they do not succeed little will have been lost, but without such funding on trust what is at stake is the existence of associations that may be the only link between very isolated individuals and mainstream society.

Added to this are the complications of establishing legitimacy and filling the eligibility criteria for public funding. Money can be made available for specific education and welfare activities but it is extremely difficult to obtain significant, and sometimes any, funding for what appear to be predominantly cultural programs. As I will demonstrate this policy ignores the close and sometimes inseparable relationship within ethnic associations of cultural and welfare activities. Cultural programs may be ends in themselves but they are also an essential component of support and help and the means of settlement with the minimum of trauma in often totally unfamiliar cultures. Fund givers need, therefore, to be aware of the interactions among associations' objectives and realize that the wish to fund direct-assistance services may not be realized if these are seen as totally separate from educational and cultural activities.

A further complication may be an association's explicit or implicit political activities. Public funds are not usually available to support political activities and bodies that have recognized charitable status (with all the associated tax advantages) are not allowed to engage in political activities. This rule has, of course, proved a hornet's nest of difficult interpretations of the nature of politics. Furthermore, in some ethnic associations it was clear that political and cultural activities were closely intertwined. While, for example, a Kashmiri association's promotion of certain political and military groups in the motherland might obviously be excluded from public welfare funding, what stance should be adopted toward a Ghanaian association that includes in its program active help for refugees, many cultural activities, and a continuing interest in and support for the political party that might eventually bring about their return home? In this case the cultural program was the essential context for helping uprooted, frightened, and insecure people; it was also a means of ensuring continued faithfulness to the old country and a relatively easy return; and some cultural traditions were a component of political differences. This association did not manage to disentangle its affairs to the satisfaction of the funding bodies. Likewise an Eritrean organization was seen, probably accurately, as closely involved in the political struggles of the Horn of Africa. However, in this case its attempts to promote the welfare of Eritreans in Britain and to provide mother-tongue classes and other cultural activities were recognized as genuine and useful. Funding was, therefore, made available for specified welfare or educational projects. This limited support was welcomed by the association but it also entailed a constant series of applications for funds for individual projects.

It is possible that British public authorities find it particularly difficult to adopt a sensitive and subtle approach to the multifarious activities of associations whose cultural backgrounds and political interests seem totally alien or remote. In the aftermath of World War II, when many Polish groups were energetically combining welfare and political activities, sometimes under the auspices of the Polish Government in Exile, there seems to have been little if any squeamishness about the public support of their activities. While this was probably in part the consequence of loyalty to a wartime ally it may also reflect a greater willingness to be flexible with European than with other groups.

Another example of the difficulties of funding political activities is the attitude adopted to associations with a radical, usually socialist, political philosophy. There were few such examples in this study, which included an African group with housing interests and a consortium of Bangladeshi associations. The Greater London Council (GLC), a socialist authority, was alleged by its enemies, who included the present Conservative government, to be inappropriately funding groups that shared or would advance the council's political priorities. While there is probably some truth in this allegation, it is also true that radical socialist politics have in metropolitan areas been the most likely context for the advancement of the interests of minority groups and of women. The abolition of the GLC has been a major blow for the life of many voluntary groups and it is predicted that the public authorities that take its place may have neither the will nor the resources to continue support for groups with a radical political ideology. A way through this problem might be for public officials to have engraved on their minds and on their forms: "It is what they do, not what they think, that is important."

Given this insecure financial base it is not surprising that only sixteen of the twenty-nine associations employed paid staff. One Polish cultural association that was heavily involved in publishing claimed to have 100 paid employees, although the majority worked only part time. The association with the next largest number of paid staff, nineteen, was a thriving Islamic educational organization. The other associations employed five or six people, or fewer, sometimes with short-term funding from the Manpower Services Commission. These paid staff had a range of skills including administrative, secretarial, and social and community work. In many associations the achievements of a very small and highly professional staff were extraordinary, usually because of their passionate commitment to the objectives of their association. Virtually all of the associations relied on volunteer help and over half had to function exclusively with this. That they survived bears witness to the energy and expert knowledge of people who feel they have a mission to help their fellow exiled compatriots. For some of these volunteers their "employment" by an association was the means of their own psychological survival. It might also bring with it such welcome fringe benefits as free if spartan accommodation and meals.

It would be neither sensible nor proper for public authorities to expect the small and emerging associations with few or no staff to play a significant role, as they stand, in the delivery of services, but their potential could be more carefully scrutinized. They reflect a long tradition of voluntarism in British social policy (Titmuss 1970; Crossman 1976). It is a tradition that could be grossly exploited by public authorities under the respectable guise of the promotion of community care, or it could become woven into a strong collaborative program of public services and voluntary endeavor.

Ethnic Associations' Objectives

Analysis of the information provided by the associations in this study showed that they could roughly be divided into three types, according to their different objectives. There are those whose role was the promotion of cultural activities, in some cases combined with political interest in the country of origin; those that were committed to both cultural and welfare activities; and those with an exclusive welfare function. The organizations in this last category included some that combined direct help for individuals with various community and political activities designed to bring about changes in mainstream services or in the laws or regulations of, for example, immigration and social security, which have a special bearing on minorities. Also in this category were two associations that interpreted their welfare function almost exclusively as gathering information about needs and service inadequacies and making proposals for change. They had as well established some pilot demonstration projects.

This division is, however, not a precise one. We have already seen how difficult it can be to distinguish between cultural and welfare objectives, and several associations had framed their constitutions and their associations to allow for flexible use of their resources. There were also associations, particularly the European ones established in the 1940s, whose activities had become more cultural as the needs of their constituents, most of whom had been settled in Britain for more than forty years, diminished. The urgent need now was to keep alive cultural traditions among a generation who had probably never seen their parents' native country. The one exception to this pattern among European associations concerned the elderly. As the original immigrant population grows old many return to their cultural roots. Ukranian, Russian, and Polish organizations all reported major preoccupation with the care and support of elderly people, including the provision for residential care and home visiting. It has to be recognized that these services would be welcomed by public authorities not simply because of their sensitivity to cultural needs but because of the strain all services for elderly people are under, because of demographic trends. This means that in Britain, as elsewhere, there has been substantial resort to the voluntary sector.

Bearing in mind the need not to make rigid distinctions, how may the activities of the associations be grouped?

First, there are those eight associations whose objectives are primarily cultural or religious. They were included in the study while other purely cultural associations were discarded because their cultural activities were often seen as having at least indirect welfare implications. For example, a well-funded and highly organized Islamic group spent much energy in interpreting Islam in a Western context, arguing that some more rigid rules and expectations were not true orthodoxy but the accretions of tangled political and national histories, and represented an inappropriate clinging to cultural and religious practices of a bygone age. Their quiet but persistent educational work with Muslims and non-Muslims had made it possible for some Muslim groups, families, and individuals to see, for example, the role of women and the relationship between parents and children in a new light, consistent, it was argued, with a true interpretation of Islam and with

life in a twentieth-century Western world. A particular priority
for this association was their youth, and an associated Muslim
youth movement had been established. They had estimated that
25 percent of the one and a half million Muslims in Britain were
aged between sixteen and twenty-four. Their plight was described
thus:

We are living in an era of crisis and transition, and, perhaps, also of
opportunities. Muslim children, adolescents and the young adults of the
80s may have to face some of the major changes and adjustments which
we still seem to manage to avoid and postpone. There are now, as there
were in the past generations and as there will be in coming years, young
people who feel that it is their responsibility to take a critical look at the
world, and to do something about what they see. There are many more
who are not angry and active, but apathetic and unassertive.

Even where a few try to offer a helping hand and assistance, a
deep-seated bigotry often bitterly obtrudes, as they seem to defend the
little they do possess. Far from challenging the world around them with
an insistent individuality, they seem personally and socially incarcerated,
their most personal modes of expression stifled. Each self-image they
have created for themselves has been repeatedly deflated, all futures
prematurely foreclosed.

It is to this great number of young people that the Association's
priorities will have to be assigned, and their number is indeed great: we
are told that nearly a third of the Muslim community are in the age range
of sixteen to twenty-nine years. As a result the focus of community
development must be upon these people if we wish to face the challenge
which besets us today. Those involved in working among Muslim youth
will only make a far-reaching contribution to individual and communal
development if their work with young people encompasses the physical
environment, the social situation of young Muslims, underpinned by
their Islamic aspirations, and if the participation of the community in
planning, provision, and management is the primary objective.

The task of the association was, therefore, as follows:

The foremost challenge to be met is the need to assist and support young
Muslims to adjust to their new environment, so that they are able to
make a significant contribution to the community from which they draw
their cultural beliefs, values and norms and at the same time to the wider
society where as British citizens they aspire to share in common objectives, resources and opportunities. By ignoring this dynamic and the two

forms of socialization experienced by the Muslim youth one will be forcing their identity, culture and language into illegitimate, personal and private spheres of life. The result will be that as the new generations are increasingly marginalized they will react indifferently or negatively, not only to the wider society but also to their own communities.

The Association sees itself as focusing upon the new generation of Muslims' creative attempts to participate in and contribute to society by providing support and services to Muslim youth groups which are emerging in British cities. Within this framework the principal forms of activity of the Association can be classified as centering around three functions: the identification of the special needs of the Muslim youth; the development of general or specialist initiatives in response to those needs; and [providing] liaison between Muslim youth organizations vis-á-vis their respective communities and formal state institutions. The overall aim, then, is to identify, promote and meet special needs, and the predominant forms of activity follow from the three categories of youth need identified above.

The activities of this association included training for youth workers and discussion and support groups for young Muslims. A particular objective, which many reared in a European culture would regard as probably hopeless, was to help the large numbers of young British Muslims who could expect to be unemployed find a meaning in their lives that was not determined solely by economic priorities and rewards. It was argued that according to a true interpretation of Islam, individuals are valued for what they are, not what they do; and there are many ways outside the formal economic system of serving God and one's fellow human beings.

An Afro-Caribbean association with a lively program of artistic activities gave opportunities for experience and employment to black people, but its dominant objective was the promotion of pan-African culture and identity. This was seen as combating a preoccupation among some West Indians with the politics and traditions of small islands, and a means of rejecting some of the laxness of British society. The attempt to promote the quintessence of a unified culture encompassing all Afro-Caribbeans may seem an odd or unreal enterprise to white people until they remember the various white European associations that have flourished in countries where they have been in a minority. A

European identity is as vague and heterogeneous as a pan-African one. Such cultural "unity," however, can promote feelings of confidence and equality without dominant groups and thus be an excellent base from which to negotiate with the more powerful.

These aspirations certainly do not escape criticism from black and white people alike who argue that, while Asians came to Britain with established culture, pan-Africanism represents a yearning for something that never was, a move "back into the future" which could divert collective activity from the issues that really do unite black people: their shared disadvantages and experience of racism. According to these arguments, being black and British is the reality and pan-Africanism a diversion.

Other associations that can most accurately be described as cultural saw their activities as being the springboard for the creation of other services. Cultural activities were welcome and unthreatening. They encouraged easy association between isolated and often stressed people. In this context common needs might be identified and this sometimes led to the establishment of a separate but related welfare project. The Latin American Refugee Association has grown out of a group established entirely to help Latin American children understand and to a limited extent recreate the diverse cultures of their parents' native countries. Through this project the problems and means of support of needy Latin Americans emerged.

The welfare aspirations of cultural organizations could be hard to fulfill because of lack of resources, but as has already been shown public authorities want to fund very specifically defined welfare programs.

"It's very hard to get money and support for simply cultural programs," said the secretary of a Bangladeshi organization. "But until we do we will have to stay primarily involved in cultural activities because we can lay these on ourselves. We would like, however, to free some of the time and energy this takes to help our fellows with their many urgent problems."

The second and largest group of associations are those that have both cultural and welfare objectives. The rationale for this has already been described and is well expressed by the leader of a Vietnamese association:

As refugees the Vietnamese feel that they have lost everything, in particular their social network. The organization is set up to provide support for each other; where people can come together in common brotherhood and share their culture. Only the Vietnamese can understand their own problems as well as their language. It is better that the Vietnamese try to solve the problems that arise in their own community. We allow refugees to come together without discrimination and to organize events during their traditional festivals. . . . People in Britain rely on social workers but this is not so with Vietnamese. Social workers face many difficulties when dealing with the Vietnamese. Language barriers are inhibiting and anyway the family does not traditionally speak of problems to a stranger.

Although this respondent spoke particularly of refugees his analysis extends to the needs and aspirations of other immigrant groups in Britain, particularly those from the New Commonwealth.

Eleven organizations had definite dual objectives and a further two hovered on the margins of the first and second groups because, for example, their welfare activities were a small part of the enterprise or were confined to serving a particular group such as the elderly.

Extracts from various constitutions illustrate these dual objectives as well as the wish shared by several associations to educate British people about their cultures. An Iranian association, for example, was established:

1. To promote any charitable purpose for the benefit of persons of Iranian origin and their dependents resident in the London area, including the relief of poverty or distress and the advancement of education and culture.
2. To educate the public about Iran, including its history, language and culture.
3. To preserve the good health of Iranian women and advance the education and culture of such women.

This last objective is an unusually explicit statement of women's needs which several associations mentioned without giving the impression that they are actively involved in alleviating them.

The chairman of a Chinese association said, almost wistfully, "The greatest day will be when we can be seen as a center of Chinese culture and so an asset to the local community. What we do now (providing practice advice and help) is not a source a pride. Pride comes when you can show off; when you can move out and invite the whole community to come and see you." These sentiments were echoed by a Vietnamese woman who said, "The Vietnamese are tired of being represented as uneducated peasants who batter their children. Give us a platform to present ourselves as a community, our identity as we are and what we can offer."

The constitution of an Afro-Caribbean association, now sixteen years old and formed to challenge the racism and disadvantage that oppress black people, demonstrates dual objectives very clearly. Its objectives are:

1. To help and educate young people particularly but not exclusively through leisure time activities so to develop their physical, mental and spiritual capacities that they may grow to full maturity as individuals and members of society.
2. To provide hostel facilities for young persons in necessitous circumstances.

The means of achieving these objectives include:

1. Arranging or providing for the holding of visits, exhibitions, meetings, lectures and classes for young persons.
2. Procuring, printing and publishing or otherwise [distributing] reports or periodicals, books, pamphlets, leaflets or other documents.
3. Procuring and providing information, advice and guidance.

A short history of the association spells out its ends and means forcefully:

The Association was formed mainly to combat and rectify the imbalance of pressures and stresses which the various institutions which make up this society were at the time (1960s) inflicting on "Black" people and their offspring and thus stifling and crippling their efforts to improve the quality of their lives and the lives of the community in which they live. We see as a fundamental and necessary precondition for any improvement in this direction, the eradication of . . . discrimination in society.

The association is particularly critical of schools that state that "you are no good and then produce an attitude and behavior for the realization of the concept. The teacher says the child is no good; this projection is then internalized and acted out to meet the teacher's expectation, thereby fulfilling the teacher's prophecy."

To counter these and other negative influences the association believes that black people should make a point of seeking out and availing themselves of all effective and powerful aids in education, medicine, finance, and law and apply them in our efforts to strengthen and promote the interest and welfare of individuals and ethnic minority groups, especially those whose mental, emotional, and physical energies are directed at meeting the particular needs of black people, both young and old, with a view to improving the quality of their lives and the lives of the peoples of the communities in which they live. The association likes to promote the use of West Indian patois and other forms of Afro-Caribbean culture.

Having started from such a modest enterprise as a youth club, the association now provides supplementary education, hospital visits, and accommodation for young people. Its long-term objectives are ambitious and include running a play group and nursery and offering trade training classes.

A Ugandan association included in its objectives:

1. The relief of poverty and sickness among civilians in Uganda and elsewhere, including the United Kingdom who are in need as a result of natural disaster or conflict in Uganda.
2. The maintenance of Ugandan cultural traditions.
3. Research into the conditions of Ugandans in Uganda and elsewhere and the publication of the findings of such research.

The last objective illustrates the campaigning and in some cases the political activities of some associations. An African housing association spells this out explicitly. Such an objective might put public funding at risk in local authorities that do not share the same political beliefs. The association was formed:

1. to promote the welfare of African refugees in housing, self-help community development programmes, education, health and employment.
2. to provide a forum, within a co-operative framework, where African refugees can commune in comfort and security of mind, body and

soul to encourage and facilitate the acquisition of essential vocational, technological, management and research skills in preparation for their eventual return home.

3. to support African refugee groups who promote the welfare of refugee communities by campaigning for human rights in their countries of origin.

4. to identify and align with immigrant, migrant and other refugee communities to campaign for equal rights, freedom of movement and expression against discrimination, racism and sexism.

The third group of associations were solely concerned with welfare activities. These took several forms. Two of them employed qualified social workers who were in touch with the local statutory agencies but who also helped families directly; one of these has established, among other services, a hostel for battered Asian women and their children. More common was the use of advice workers, paid or voluntary, who referred their clientele to available sources of help. This referral could include accompanying an individual, interpreting, and advocacy. It might steer someone toward doctors and organizations known to be sympathetic. Several associations provided specialist legal advice on immigration problems which were often said to be among the most pressing of all difficulties. Since personal security and the reunion of families is often at stake this is hardly surprising although it is little recognized by people unfamiliar, as most are, with the hazards of negotiating British immigration policy and practice (CRE 1985).

Another form of welfare activity is informed campaigning for better services from statutory agencies. The annual report of a consortium of Bangladeshi organizations described it thus:

On the whole, the Federation's main role is to campaign for equality and social justice with the support of affiliated groups. However the Federation, through the Youth Development Officer, also assists affiliated groups in setting up projects. . . . It gives administrative help and assists affiliated and other groups in a variety of other ways. It also helps new groups to establish themselves.

This association has been very effective in drawing the attention of local educational and welfare organizations to the needs of Bangladeshis. It also supports and works with youth and women's groups designed to alleviate intergenerational and cultural and religious conflicts.

An Afro-Caribbean association solely concerned with providing housing, especially in hostels, was clear that it also needed to campaign both for the housing of single homeless people in private, self-contained homes, and against herding them into hostels.

Problems Confronted

What problems confronted these associations' members and clientele? Twenty-one reported severe housing difficulties. As some of the newest and poorest people to join the housing market and the queues for local authority accommodation, they usually got the worst of what little was available. Particularly desperate is the plight of the large number of families who may for months and years have lived in bed and breakfast hotels and lodgings. For them community centers are a lifeline. Associations can do little to alleviate these problems apart from explaining and liaisoning with the bureaucracy of public housing and putting people on to what local minority network of private accommodation there might be.

Not surprisingly, in view of the high rate of unemployment in the nation as a whole, newcomers face particular difficulties in finding work, especially if they are unskilled or, as often happens, their qualifications and experience are not properly recognized. When minorities are black they also meet overt and indirect racism (Brown 1984) which further impedes their opportunities. Again, there is not much associations can do to solve unemployment problems, although four ran special training schemes and three had plans to establish work cooperatives.

The third most common problem, which has already been mentioned, was difficulties with immigration and legal status in Britain. There are few lawyers knowledgeable about such matters and no legal aid for representation at tribunals and appeals. Expertise in this area, which often includes personal experience of the immigration problems of these associations, is therefore particularly valuable.

Income maintenance was a further obvious problem and associations tried to help people steer their way through the intricacies of the British social-security system. This was, however, often done with some ambivalence, with the leaders of several associations expressing distaste for dependence on public money as being far from their own traditions and aspirations.

Surprisingly, only five associations thought that minorities had specific health needs that were not being met. These included proper treatment, psychological and physical, for people who had been the victims of torture. Depression as a consequence of uprooting and loss of family and familiar surroundings was frequently mentioned. Linking people with part of the old world via associations' cultural activities was seen as a major remedy. Most of the comments about health concerned the difficulties of negotiating a largely unicultural and monolingual public health system. Some limited resort to traditional methods was reported but on the whole the National Health Service was seen as functioning reasonably well. This is certainly not the experience of more established minority groups which are now campaigning for more ethnically sensitive and less racist health care (Cornwell and Gordon 1984; Rack 1982; Littlewood and Lipsedge 1982). It would be rare too to find health service personnel able to understand and work with the physical and psychological health problems of refugees (Krumperman 1983).

Education problems were mentioned by less than half of the associations. A major priority for some was learning English, especially for women. Some associations ran such classes and several put considerable energy into educational activities for young people, especially mother-tongue and religious and cultural teaching. There were few complaints about schools, which is surprising given the report of the Swann Committee (1985) on the problems faced by minorities within Britain's educational system. Nonetheless, some associations described schools as threatening cultural traditions, undermining parental authority, and thus increasing family conflict, a problem with which five associations said they were actively involved. These problems included parent-child and marital difficulties which were seen as one consequence of a change in male and female roles brought about by life in

Britain and the encouragement, and sometimes the necessity, for women to be more independent than they would have dreamed of some years previously.

Ethnic Associations and Refugees

The needs and experiences of refugees highlight ethnic associations' potential contribution to people in particularly difficult circumstances which may continue in different forms and over many years. Refugees in Britain are an extremely heterogeneous group and clearly their needs reflect their cultural background, the circumstances of their flight, and the arrangements made for their reception in Britain (Baker 1983). Some general points can, nevertheless, be made. First, refugees are likely to have, in particularly acute forms, all the practical problems of daily existence which are the common experience of recent immigrants to Britain. Unless special arrangements have been made for their arrival, and this usually occurs only for large groups of refugees, they will be dependent on the emergency arrangements of the social security system for the barest income. They will only be eligible for public housing if they have young dependents and this will nearly always take the form of bed and breakfast accommodations. Even these bare essentials will depend on application for political asylum being taken seriously by public officials. The process of being granted asylum, which allows access to employment and the wider social security system, can take many months. During this time, and after, many refugees turn for cultural support and practical help to the associations that have their interests at heart. The refugees for whom special arrangements have been made through the British Refugee Council have greater protection during their first months in Britain. However, the at least partial security of hostel life and orientation programs can bring their own problems of dependence, isolation, and feelings of uselessness associated with long-term unemployment and the inability to establish independent life and an individual or family identity in the new country (Whitlam 1983). There is evidence (Community Relations Commission 1974, 1976; Baker 1983) of continuing disproportionate unemployment, isolation, mental illness, and

general unhappiness among refugees allegedly successfully settled, or at least moved on from the resettlement camps and hostels
to which they were first directed. General policy has been to
transfer responsibility for refugees as soon as possible to the normal statutory agencies. In addition, the government has tried to
disperse refugees to areas where resources are assumed to be less
strained; thus concentrations have been avoided but the possibility
of mutual support is lessened.

It is not surprising that many such refugees have felt a
desperate need to associate with people with similar backgrounds
and in a similar predicament. Some have done this by physically
moving, others through belonging to associations established to
preserve the cultural identity and promote the interests of particular groups of refugees. Many of the most recently founded ethnic
associations have been formed by refugees, and they have had to
play a major role in trying to help other refugees with complicated
legal questions regarding their status in Britain and the possible
immigration of close relatives. They have also helped in meeting
their basic human needs, either directly or, more commonly, because of the structure of the British welfare system, by referral to
public agencies. These agencies, as we have seen, have difficulty
in meeting adequately the needs of larger minorities. They are
quite baffled by the refugees' predicament and there may be little
understanding of the problems they may have over and above
those of being an identifiable group of newcomers who, after the
initial burst of humanitarian goodwill that surrounded their arrival, are commonly regarded as an unwelcome source of demand
and difficulty.

The special problems refugees may experience include the
scars of the persecution or suffering that preceded their flight, the
trauma of departure, difficult journeys, and farewells, perhaps
forever, to close relatives and friends. Some feel guilty that they,
rather than others, survived. They may too be quite uncertain
about their long-term future in the new country. Many, even in
quite unrealistic circumstances, have their eyes fixed on a return
home. All of this can be at the root of depression, anxiety, and
feelings of persecution which can appear many months and years
after flight and settlement (Jagucki 1983; Braum 1983; Hitch

1983). These disturbances may not be well understood by people who have little experience of refugee affairs; and if they are understood they may be dismissed somewhat impatiently, with workers urging former refugees to let bygones be bygones, to congratulate themselves on and be thankful for their survival. There may well be a total lack of comprehension of refugees' continuing preoccupation with the political and social affairs of their own countries.

A further difficulty in the relationship between refugees and helpers can be differing perspectives on their predicament. Refugees may well be some of the most able citizens of their countries. They may have been victims of persecution because of their stalwart adherence to political or religious traditions. They are in their own eyes and the eyes of compatriots heroes and heroines, the flower of their nations. To the personnel of welfare agencies this history may not exist, refugees are simply the bearers of problems which seem to endure longer than they should. Suddenly refugees find themselves perceived as clients, and troublesome ones at that (Dorsh 1981). Benefactors who were willing to do much during the immediate aftermath of refugees' arrival feel used; refugees feel hopelessly misunderstood and trapped in a relationship they never sought.

The most effective help for refugees is likely to be that given by people who have themselves shared the same experience. This is now fairly well recognized by authorities that have experience in working with refugees. There have been some imaginative and well-organized, albeit small, projects to train refugees to give direct help, to make liaisons with public agencies, to negotiate appropriate help, and where necessary, as it often is, to act as forceful advocates on behalf of their fellows. Finlay and Reynolds (1985; 3–4), who worked with a training project for Vietnamese workers, write that "workers who are refugees can more easily step into their lives and go towards them." They bring a greater understanding of needs, and therefore can influence policies of organizations in a more appropriate way. In most circumstances they are more readily trusted, they can communicate in the mother tongue, which in turn helps the vital feelings of belonging and sharing, and they can reach out more effectively to their compatriots who are more isolated and vulnerable.

There are, however, problems for such workers if they work in isolation and without support or supervision. They can also do only what an individual worker can and the task may be immense. Ethnic associations are often the best context for these refugee workers and these associations may also provide specialist services and a supportive and familiar oasis in an alien and often unwelcoming world. That these functions continue to be necessary and valued can be seen from the activities of the oldest European associations in Britain which are still closely involved in work with elderly people. To perform these functions effectively refugee associations, like the others in this study, must be properly funded and supported, and linked closely with mainstream welfare agencies. There is no place for romantic and grandiose notions about the virtues and capabilities of self-help when this is left to flounder in tiny organizations neglected, for all practical purposes, by public authorities, while at the same time they are expected to cope with problems that are either not perceived or are neglected by mainstream services.

Ethnic Associations and Integration

The questions about acculturation and minorities' views concerning integration did not extract such precise data as the American study. However, it was interesting that the questions about the promotions of ethnic identity and identification with British society revealed some responses that might at first sight be contradictory. For example, associations might indicate as absolute priorities items that are clearly connected with the retention and promotion of ethnic identity, for example, retaining native language, keeping up with news in the country of birth, and teaching children the customs and language of the country of birth. At the same time they attached great importance to making new British friends, getting involved in British organizations, and moving to a community where most of the people are British. Twelve associations gave answers of this nature. They saw no contradiction or paradox in their responses, given their belief that comfortable settlement in British society and contributing to it come easiest and most effectively from a basis of firm ethnic identity.

Several associations' workers demonstrated with extraordinary insight and sensitivity the ways in which they worked to preserve cultural, family, and individual life, which reflected older traditions, while simultaneously helping people to as least come to terms and at best be associated with and contribute to an unfamiliar and often unwelcoming culture. A Chinese youth worker described his careful negotiations with conservative parents to allow their children to come to groups at the community center. The first meetings would have a strong Chinese flavor and take place in Chinese neighborhoods. An outing might then be arranged to a local sports center to introduce the idea of using public facilities at first by the group and then through individual or small group outings. Parents would accept this measure of independent activity because of their trust in the work that had gone before.

An Indian resource center with a radical socialist perspective accepted, worked with, and defended cultural traditions, providing immediate help in a familiar setting with an extraordinary diversity of problems. Observation confirmed the clientele's trust in the association which cared for them and met needs quickly. Nevertheless, conservative tradition did not go unchallenged by workers or by other users of the center who, gathered into the only meeting room available, would be asked to respond from their own experience to victims of the threat and conflict which are so much part of the life of newcomers who are seen as unwelcome in Britain. For me, a particularly refreshing and interesting aspect of the study was the ability of the workers of many ethnic associations to live in two worlds, the world of contemporary Britain and the older world of the mother country of their clientele. They demonstrated vividly the possibility of living with the tensions between these two worlds, the futility of making people choose between them, and the richness and the potential of drawing from two traditions. They showed that it is possible to identify with certain features of a culture while wanting to challenge or change parts of it. Several of these workers also combined

respect for and recognition of the strength of conservative political
ideologies with a commitment to socialism, often of a quite radical
nature. Avid ideological disputes had little place in their lives and
work; they devoted their energies to running discussion groups
on the shape of family life and its strengths and weaknesses outside
feudal society. For such workers, without losing the hope and
vision of their radical beliefs, politics was indeed the art of the
possible. As the secretary of an association with a radical socialist
perspective said:

We live in the real world. What we see must inform our feelings and
temper our ideologies. We see race and not simply class as being a major
determinant of life chances. We have to deal with life as it is and therefore
with the salience of race. We know how women should live, according
to our own beliefs; and we know how they do live and how their
oppression has become so much part of their psychology that it cannot
be touched by speeches and rhetoric but only by toying and tentatively
experimenting with alternative life-styles. It can be agonizingly slow, but
when change comes it is real and well founded. We see now that many
of our fellows, the old and the young, are very far from a revolutionary
view of the world. We see them too drawing strength from the ancient
traditions but when these are respected and not attacked they can recognize the adaptations that are needed in the world in which they live.
The orthodox and less orthodox cannot simply live together; they can
perceive their common interests and work together to reduce the multiple disadvantages they experience in Britain.

In a country where political ideologies and divisions are
becoming more extreme, the ability of associations to draw on,
without falling apart, the energy of old traditions and of radical
politics is inspiring. It might not survive in statutory agencies
where subtlety may be regarded as improper compromise and
where there may be little understanding or support for people to
negotiate the often acute tensions of working with radically different traditions. Statutory agencies are baffled and often antag-
onized by the traditions of minorities which they see as repressive.
Their understanding could be extended and their response modified through collaboration with ethnic association workers who
have proved in their own activities that absolute choices do not
have to be made between old and new worlds.

Questions about British and native characteristics and attempts to become more British did not reveal such precise data as in the American study. Few people were said to be consciously trying to be British, and several indicated that this was the last thing they would want to do and that the question was either ridiculous or insulting. This response is not surprising given the largely negative accounts of British characteristics: cold, unfeeling, not interested in family life, formal, racist, and so on. By contrast, respondents painted themselves in largely glowing terms as warm, friendly, loyal, spontaneous, hard working. With hindsight it might have been interesting to frame these questions so that respondents had to try to identify positive and negative features of both cultures. Being made to choose or differentiate may produce the false and extreme dichotomies that are so skillfully avoided by the ethnic association workers just described.

Conclusion

The Promotion of Ethnic Associations

Ethnic associations may now provide the only decent or nearly decent help available to some minority groups, especially those for whom there are serious language problems, or a great reluctance, for cultural reasons, to seek outside help. These associations can reach out to people when public authorities assume that lack of demand reflects a degree of self-help that renders state intervention unnecessary. They also have inevitable limitations, particularly in their present form. "Self-help groups lack power to change attitudes, partly because they are not yet recognized and lack the resources to build on their services. The people we saw expressed a wish for training in counseling, practical skills such as getting access to statutory services, learning more about social work and welfare benefits as well as all sorts of specialized services. They also wanted to find ways of . . . more effectively leading to a better working relationship with social services" (Finlay 1985; 6).

While wanting to improve their services, the associations in this study would prefer appropriately qualified workers to be employed by public welfare organizations to provide ethnically sensitive help. Despite the many inadequacies and rebuffs of the British system, without exception the associations wished to influence, change, and collaborate with it, and not establish alternative, separate structures. They worry about the long-term isolation of "ghettolike" services and fear that they could marginalize their members' interests. Will these associations, which now provide direct help, continue to campaign for mainstream provision as the long-term aim? Some consensus can be detected among state "providers" and ethnic association leaders that integrated services should be the goal. The position is different in the United States, where the dependence on voluntary but publicly funded agencies, plus the celebration of ethnic diversity, has contributed to a widely (but not universally) held belief that ethnic associations may well be the best equipped to provide some of the services for minorities (Jenkins 1981). If there is some move in Britain to contract out services to ethnic associations this is far more likely with respect to help for the elderly people than for children. Elderly people are regarded as having a right to their roots and to have cultural, social, and religious needs best catered for by the voluntary sector. By contrast there is a prevailing expectation that children would and should assimilate or integrate (Swann Commission 1985). Mistakenly, in the author's view, ethnic associations are seen as likely to be barriers to such processes (Cheetham 1982). Statutory agencies could learn much from the subtleties of approaches described earlier. If they do they could eschew the belief that ethnic associations have rigid or unitary objectives and accept the potential strengths of their work for children.

There are, of course, strong counterarguments against the substantial use of ethnic associations, particularly if they are seen as dividing communities that should be united, as uncritically espousing a form of pluralism which can easily be used against black people, and as attracting token but minimal funding. Patterson, writing about America in the 1970s, argues powerfully and bitterly against the danger of ethnic chauvinism. Having acknowledged the effectiveness of black ethnicity in ameliorating poor self-image and political and legal disabilities, Patterson condemns the contemporary substitution of a rhetorical celebration of the glories of the urban ghetto for an attack on the terrible economic problems of black people which are inextricably tied up with the American economy.

It was ridiculously easy for the establishment to respond by changing the color of a few faces in the ads for the "Pepsi generation," and by introducing a few network shows in which the traditional role of the blacks as clowns and maids was updated . . . by publishing a spate of third-rate books on the greatness of the African tradition, by the glorification of black roots, and, most cruel of all, by introducing into the curriculum of the nations' colleges that strange pack of organized self-delusion which goes by the name of Afro-American Studies. . . Black American ethnicity has encouraged an incapacity to distinguish the things that are worthwhile in black life from those that are just plain rotten . . . It is enough to know that all black problems are due to racism; that all whites are untrustworthy . . . that black folks must control their communities. (1977: 155–56)

This is not, of course, the whole story. "There were major although certainly not sufficient improvements in the social and economic conditions of American blacks during the nineteen sixties and early seventies. These achievements of positive discrimination were in part the product of successful ethnic politics. More recently, the legitimation of ethnicity in politics has meant that it can now be a respectable disguise for covert anti-black policies" (p. 156).

These risks must be recognized and guarded against but they are not, in my view, so great as to justify discouragement of ethnic associations. There is a tendency in Britain to seize on the failures of American social policy and in so doing to dismiss or ignore the successes. The heady optimism and the energy of ethnic commitment in the United States and now increasingly in Britain, in the face of enormous problems, provides a striking contrast with the failures of the attempted alliance of groups whose mutual discomfort undermines a weak belief in common interests.

Are there any unifying themes in this study? Are the aspirations and methods of ethnic associations far removed from mainstream social work, or are they in its best traditions and endeavors?

Language, Culture, and Integration

Given the kaleidoscope of diversity in this study, unifying themes may be an artificial concept. Nevertheless, two issues emerge. The first is the centrality of language and culture. At the most basic level a major role of associations is to interpret, to explain and simplify, to be a center for ordinary communication. By no means all started with this service orientation, and probably most had their origins in wishing to preserve and promote the mother tongue and other features of native culture. For political, religious, and personal survival reasons the retention of culture, starting with language, has been the central aim. This is easier when there is a common class, religious, or political background, and is more difficult for associations whose members or clientele may have one nationality but little else in common. Here the achievement of political unity may become the main goal and cultural activities seen as a trivial distraction. But this seems rare. Most common is the recognition of shared culture as a basis for political unity amidst diversity: "When you are clear what you are you can tolerate difference."

A second common theme may seem at first sight a paradox. It is the parallel commitment to retention of culture and to helping people accommodate, settle, and integrate in Britain. There is neither a cut-and-dried rejection of British society, nor an open-armed espousal. Over and over again criticism or fear of features of British life, for example, the alienation of children from parents, has been combined with an acceptance that length of stay will mean influence from the dominant culture, but that this could be incorporated into or blended with minority traditions, maybe to the advantage of both. The evidence also suggests that fears that focusing on ethnic identity and interest will lead to an unman-ageable degree of pluralism are ill founded. Almost without ex-ception the leaders of these ethnic associations argued that the speediest and most effective route to contented settlement and active contribution to the new society was via the fostering and promotion of ethnic identity. The apparent paradox of the association of strong individuality, ethnic roots, and security in the wider community was lucidly analyzed by Eistenstadt (1954) over thirty years ago. This old lesson needs to be relearned.

Both of these themes are consistent with social work's commitment to focus on individual need and background, to use the dynamic of groups of people with shared experience, to defend diversity and self-determination, to start where people are, to help them use their own resources and strengths. It may be more difficult for these values to permeate the services of large, bureaucratic statutory agencies, but they are the life blood and raison d'être of ethnic associations.

Although many associations seemed preoccupied with the politics of their original countries, there are a few where sophisticated and articulate leaders see their organizations in the wider context of race and class. The experience of respecting, negotiating with, and being fairly dependent for cultural continuity on often highly conservative older people may have forged an interesting blend of pragmatic, slow-moving conservatism and radical ideology. A very few left-wing associations put their ideology into practice in their organizations and, for example, espouse self-help and community control as the ideal forms of welfare. State services may then either be eschewed or exhorted to follow this model. Most of the more politically radical groups espouse state welfare in improved and strengthened forms. They also see beyond ethnic divisions and aim for unity with other minority organizations as part of the attack on racism and disadvantage which is one important political and practical goal. All this is a good example for community workers, in quite different contexts, who are struggling to find a common purpose in the heterogeneous and conflict-ridden areas that are their preoccupation.

A final observation must underline the extraordinary vitality, energy, and commitment of the ethnic associations in this study. This is a world far from the cautious, bureaucratic, and often impersonal style of the large statutory agencies, whose re-

sources and authority, together with ethnic associations' resource-
fulness and pride, would be a formidable combination in tackling
the problems of people who suffer some of the worst disadvantages
in society.

References

Association of Directors of Social Service (ADSS). 1978. *Multi-Racial Britain: A Social Services Response.* London: Commission for Racial Equality.

Baker, R., ed. 1983. *The Psycho-Social Problems of Refugees.* London: British Refugee Council.

Bhalla, A. and K. Blakemore. 1981. *Elders of the Minority Ethnic Groups.* Birmingham: All Faiths for One Race.

Braum, G. 1983. "Breakdown in Elderly Polish Refugees." In Baker, ed., *The Psycho-Social Problems of Refugees,* pp. 77–85.

Brown, C. 1984. *Black and White Britain: The Third Policy Studies Institute Survey.* London: Heinemann.

Central Council for Education and Training in Social Work (CCETSW). 1983. *Teaching Social Work in Multi-Racial Britain.* London: CCETSW.

Cheetham, J. 1972. *Social Work With Immigrants.* London: Routledge and Kegan Paul.

Cheetham, J. 1981. *The Development of Social Work Services for Ethnic Minorities in Britain and the USA.* London: Department of Health and Social Security.

Cheetham, J., ed. 1982. *Social Work and Ethnicity.* London: Allen and Unwin.

Commission for Racial Equality (CRE). 1985. *The Report of the Formal Investigation into the Immigration Service.* London: CRE.

Commission for Racial Equality (CRE). 1986 *A Directory of Ethnic Associations in Britain.* London: CRE.

Community Relations Commission (CRC) 1974. *One Year On: A Report on the Resettlement of Refugees from Uganda in Britain.* London: CRC.

Community Relations Commission (CRC) 1976. *Refuge or Home? A Policy Statement on the Resettlement of Refugees.* London: CRC.

Connelly, N. 1985. *"Social Services Department and Race: A Discussion Paper."* London: Policy Studies Institute.

Cornwell, J. and P. Gordon. 1984. *An Experiment in Advocacy: The Hackney Multi-Ethnic Women's Project.* London: The King's Fund.

Crossman, R. 1976. "The Role of the Volunteer in the Modern Social Service." In A. H. Halsey, ed., *Traditions in Social Policy,* pp. 259–285. Oxford: Blackwell.

Dorsh, M. D. 1981. "Reframing the Refugee as a Client." *International Migration Review*, vol. 15.

Dummett, A. 1973. *A Portrait of English Racism*. London: Penquin.

Eistenstadt, S. N. 1954. *The Absorption of Immigrants*. London: Routledge and Kegan Paul.

Finlay, R. and J. Reynolds. 1985. *Better Social Services for Refugees*. London: Refugee Action.

Glendenning, F. 1979. *The Elders of Ethnic Minorities*. Leicester: Beth Johnson Foundation.

Glendenning, F. 1982. "Elderly Ethnic Minority People: Some Issues of Social Policy." In J. Cheetham, ed. *Social Work and Ethnicity*. London: Allen and Unwin.

Hill, M. J. and R. M Issacharoff. 1971. *Community Action and Race Relations*. Oxford: Oxford University Press.

Hitch, P. 1983. "The Mental Health of Refugees: A Review of Research." In Baker, ed. *The Pscho-Social Problems of Refugees*, pp. 41–50.

Jackson, B. and S. Jackson. 1979. *Childminder: A Study of Action Research*. London: Routledge and Kegan Paul.

Jagucki, W. 1983. "The Polish Experience Forty Years On." In Baker, *The Psycho-Social Problems of Refugees*, pp. 361–66.

Jenkins, S. 1981. *The Ethnic Dilemma in Social Services*. New York: Free Press.

Jones, C. 1977. *Immigration and Social Policy in Britain*. London: Tavistock.

Kahn, V. S. 1979. *Minority Families in Britain: Support and Stress*. London: Macmillan.

Krumperman, A. 1983. "Psycho-Social Problems of Violence, Especially Its Effects on Refugees." In Baker, *The Psycho-Social Problems of Refugees*, pp. 21–28.

Littlewood, R. and M. Lipsedge. 1982. *Aliens and Alienists*. Middlesex, England: Pelican.

Mayall, B. and P. Petrie. 1983. *Childminding and Day Nurseries: What Kind of Care?* London: Heinemann.

Nicholson, C. 1974. *Strangers to England: Immigration to England 1910–1952*. London: Wayland.

Osborn, A. L., N. R. Butler and A. C. Morris. 1984. *The Social Life of Britain's Five-Year-Olds*. London: Routledge and Kegan Paul.

Patterson, O. 1977. *Ethnic Chauvinism: The Reactionary Impulse*. New York: Stein and Day.

Rack, P. 1982. *Race, Culture and Mental Disorder*. London: Tavistock.

Scarman, Lord. 1981. *The Brixton Disorders*. CMND 8427, HMSO.

Smith, D. J. et al. 1983. *Police and People in London*. Vols. 1–4. London: Policy Studies Institute.

Swann Committee. 1985. *Multi-Racial Education in Britain*. Leicester HMSO.

Taylor, N. 1981. *Probation and After Care in a Multi-Racial Society*. London: Commission for Racial Equality.

Titmuss, R. 1970. *The Gift Relationship? From Human Blood to Social Policy*. London: Allen and Unwin.

Whitlam, R. 1983. "A Health Visitor's View of the Reception and Resettlement of Indo-Chinese Refugees into the U.K." In Baker, *The Psycho-Social Problems of Refugees*, pp. 29–34.

Young, K. and N. Connelly. 1981. *Policy and Practice in the Multi-Racial City*. London: Policy Studies Institute.

4.
Immigrant Associations in Israel

Josef Korazim

In Israel, because of the special role played by the central government in the absorption of immigrants, ethnic associations are actually immigrant associations with a mix of public, semi-public, and voluntary support. In sociological terms, such organizations can be described as special structures between formal public bureaucracies and primary social networks, which help to absorb each group of immigrants according to its special socio-cultural characteristics. An immigrant association, with its strong ethnic dimensions, is thus simultaneously bureaucratized and nonbureaucratized, using different combinations of hired personnel and volunteers primarily of its own ethnic origin.

Ethnic associations started out in Palestine (pre-State Israel) on a totally voluntary basis. After the establishment of the State of Israel in 1948, the "melting pot" and social integration ideologies took hold, and the responsibilities of the ethnic asso-

Dr. Josef Korazim, at the time of writing this paper, was Lecturer at the Hebrew University, Baerwald School of Social Work, Jerusalem. He now serves on the planning unit of Project Renewal, The Jewish Agency, and lectures at Tel Aviv University's School of Social Work. Acknowledgment is made to Professor Eliezer Jaffee of the Hebrew University who commented on the paper, and Ora Morely of the Ministry of Absorption for assistance in reaching the key informants.

ciations went beyond the voluntary sector. Over time, several unplanned and uncoordinated divisions of labor evolved between immigrant associations and the more formal organizations of the government ministries, the Jewish Agency and, later on, the Ministry of Immigrant Absorption (MIA) with regard to the delivery of social services.

Currently, most immigrant organizations receive some degree of public funding from two sources: the Ministry of Absorption and the philanthropic/semipublic Jewish Agency. Immigrant organizations offer a sensitive understanding of cultural backgrounds and ethnic differences as they affect problems in absorption. These associations have the advantage of flexibility and freedom from government rigidity in terms of staffing and procurement, as well as the actual running of programs.

Public interest in ethnic associations in Israel developed when it was found that the existing immigrant organizations were more effective in helping their own groups become absorbed into Israeli culture and coping with problems of adjustment than were the general social services of the country. Their effectiveness was based on eased communication between worker and client, due to common cultural and language backgrounds. Because these organizations fulfilled an important social role, the government decided to help them with public funds. The roots of this decision, however, go far back in Israeli history. The complex relationship of ethnicity and religious and national origin needs to be examined to understand the roles and function of ethnic associations in modern Israeli society.

Historical Background

Israel, since the proclamation of its statehood, has accepted over 1.7 million (Jewish) immigrants on a nonselective basis. The semiconstitutional "law of return" established the national commitment for the rights of all Jews to immigrate and settle. Today, 83 percent of the country's slightly over 4 million citizens are Jewish, originating from some eighty different countries from all over the world. They represent almost one-third of the world's estimated 13 million Jews.

The history of the Israelis and of the Jewish people is both ethnically and psychosocially unique. As modern Israelis they have a short past. The State of Israel was established in 1948, after a thirty-year period of British mandatory government. Yet as Jews, Israelis have a past extending over thousands of years. Most modern Israelis have strong roots in the ideology of Zionism. It provides them a secularist, social-democratic basis for the return of the Jewish people to their historic homeland, and for their desire to build a new society on the ideas of justice, egalitarianism, and the revival of the Hebrew language as a means to support national integration. A minority of the Israelis (about 10 percent), however, have their roots in Jewish orthodoxy, many of them disregarding the centrality of modern Hebrew.

Another root of the Israelis relates to their ethnic origin. After the dispersion of Jews from Israel in the Roman times (70 C.E.) and their expulsion from Spain and Portugal at the time of the Inquisition, Jews resettled in Europe, in the Mediterranean and Middle Eastern countries (primarily Arab), and a minority went as far as the Far East. With the emergence of the Zionist ideologies and the "ingathering of exiles," two culturally different groups of immigrant Jews have met in Israel: the actively Zionist European Ashkenazi (with a minority of extremely orthodox Jews), and a more traditional Sephardi group (mostly from Arab countries). At the present, if the Sephardi group is defined as including all the foreign born from Asia and Africa (excluding South Africa) and their descendants, they would constitute about 52 percent of all Israeli Jews.

The question of whether or not these heterogeneous Jewish immigrant groups in Israel comprise in fact different ethnic groups is moot, depending on the definition of the concept of ethnicity and the relative emphasis on components such as national origin, religiousness, language, a sense of shared past, and consciousness of kind. Social status, however, frequently uses the Ashkenazi-Sephardi ethnic dichotomies as the basis for the definition of ethnicity in Israel.

The differences and the tensions between the Ashkenazi and the Sephardi go back to the first decade of Israel's existence. Those differences are political, socioeconomic, and cultural. Early

Ashkenazi immigrants established a ruling majority elite, which regulated many policies relevant to the lives of the subsequent flows of Sephardi immigrants. Those policies affected political leadership, settlement, labor, education, housing, and culture, and they left the Sephardi—not necessarily by intention—on the lower levels of the social ladder in most measures of standards of living and social opportunities.

In the area of social services, this unique history of Israel created allegiances at the same time to both strong and centralized governmental services and to voluntarism. The latter is strongly related to, though not identical with, the traditional idea of Jewish charity from outside the country to support "the poor Jews in Palestine." During that pre-State period, charity donations were designed for distribution to groups with particular geographic and ethnoreligious bases. Thus, being part of a community, emotionally and geographically, was required for participation in the distribution (Macarov 1978).

In modern Israel, the combination of centralized secular socialism with religious orthodoxy requires a compromise between these major sectors for service delivery. The government tries to maximize the efficiency of the public sector, while the Orthodox sector seeks to maximally address the special needs of its own group without direct government intervention. On the other hand, both the public and the Orthodox-voluntary sectors are aware that each sector needs the other to accomplish its mission. The public sector is looking for ways to provide basic services to all, and thus needs mechanisms to reach the Orthodox, whereas the Orthodox voluntary sector is aware of both the financial aid and the specialized tasks the public sector alone can provide.

Formalization and Transformation of Absorbing Institutions

The unique role of ethnic associations in Israel is best understood in terms of their historical origins. As part of the 1922 League of Nations action, which gave Great Britain the Mandate for Palestine, it was stated that, to implement the Balfour Declaration (1917), which viewed with favor the establishment of a national home for the Jewish people in Palestine, there should be established a "Jewish Agency." In 1929, the Jewish Agency for Palestine was founded as a partnership with the World Zionist Organization (WZO) and, until the establishment of the State of Israel, they were the world Jewry's organized involvement in the building of the national home. They were also directly responsible for the health, welfare, and educational institutions, called the *Yishuv*, serving the local Jewish community. (Elazar and Dortort 1984). Thus most social institutions in present-day Israel originated in the Yishuv. The Yishuv was characterized by a strong tradition of volunteerism and self-governing institutions, with political parties representing various labor, middle-class, Zionist, and religious interests. Each party organized its own projects for rural and urban development, social development and social services, education, medical care, culture, and defense (Eisenstadt 1956; Kramer 1976; Neipris 1981).

During that time, three distinct types of social service systems emerged. The first, involving residents of Palestine for many generations, was sponsored by the religious orthodoxy and depended almost entirely on charity from abroad. The second, created by the secular socialist-labor pioneers, who rejected all forms of philanthropy, consisted of several mutual aid societies. Finally, the Vaad Leumi (the National Council) evolved, made up of purely voluntary membership consisting of approximately 95 percent of the newer Jewish settlers. It was the Vaad Leumi that the British government recognized as "the government in waiting." It established the Social Welfare Department to aid families and children regardless of religious, labor, or ethnic affiliations, laying the foundation for universal social services, which also included all Arab minorities. This department formed the basis for the Ministry of Social Welfare, organized by the government in 1950.

In the years following the establishment of the State of Israel, it was widely assumed that the Jewish Agency for Palestine would wither away by transferring its leadership and its bureaucracy to the new state. Nevertheless, the Jewish Agency survived as the arm of the WZO in Israel, and as a political platform and power base for certain sectors. It functioned in part because there was a need for a way to channel philanthropic contributions from overseas (particularly from the United States) to appropriate pro-

grams in Israel. Such contributions were defined as nongovernmental, and hence eligible for tax-exempt aid. Thus the Jewish
Agency for Israel (JAI) became a philanthropic political instru-
mentality, a governmentlike body, funded from abroad primarily
for social and educational purposes (Elazar and Dortort 1984).
First and foremost it is concerned with the "ingathering of exiles"
through immigration and absorption activities. Second, it is concerned with the improvement of the quality of life for immigrants
from previous years, and the closing of social gaps which still exist
between many of them and the rest of the citizens of Israel (JAI
1985).

After the attainment of statehood, many of the volunteer
organizations transferred their functions to governmental sponsorship. Those remaining, whether political or nonpolitical, had a
supplementary character. By the early 1950s, it was apparent that
the new government could not by itself handle the massive demands of defense, housing, economic development, and the major
waves of immigration and their socioeconomic absorption. Many
new volunteer service organizations began to form to fill this
service gap. These agencies differed from those that had existed
prior to statehood in the Yishuv. They were more autonomous,
problem-oriented, nonpolitical in nature, highly specialized in
function, and more egalitarian. They often employed professionals, with at least a core of paid staff members, and were dependent
on the general public for funds.

One of the immediate tasks of the new government was
the resettlement of over a million immigrants from eighty countries, whose entry quadrupled the country's population. In addition to all of the problems inherent in such major immigrant
waves, there was no special ministry at that time for the absorption
of immigrants into Israeli society. Israel's major social ministries,
such as the Ministry of Housing, Health, Education and Welfare,
carried much of the responsibility for immigration integration in
their respective fields, financed with government monies.

In 1968, after the Six Day War (1967) and the realization
of the potential threat to the existence of Israel, increased Jewish
concerns from abroad brought about a rise in immigration to Israel
and growing expectations about additional increases in the future.

Thus the government decided on the creation of a new Ministry of Immigrant Absorption to play a more central role in the absorption process. The modus operandi provided for continued Jewish Agency responsibility for the staging of immigration abroad, while the new ministry was to deal with most areas of reception and integration within the country. It was anticipated that this ministry would eventually unite under one roof the absorption functions not only of the Jewish Agency but also of the other major social ministries—and do so more effectively. But this was not to be, for two reasons. First, the social ministries affected, having been unwilling to cede any of their functions to the Jewish Agency, were now equally reluctant to turn them over to the MIA. Second, the Jewish Agency was able to marshal a potent argument in support of its continued independent existence: the fact that contributions of American Jewry (and of some other communities as well) must be distributed by a nongovernmental, voluntary organization in order to enjoy exemption from income taxes. Jewish leadership in the United States asserted that to transfer responsibilities from the agency to the government would jeopardize their fund-raising structures in the United States. Their position held, and the key role of the Jewish Agency was maintained, but differences between the Agency and the MIA exist to this day.

Paradoxically, the Israeli government has transferred some of its own activities to the Jewish Agency, rather than the other way around. Some programs that had previously been financed by the government have become in part the financial responsibility of the Jewish Agency, including programs in the fields of health, welfare, housing for immigrants, and education. Operational responsibility, however, has remained with the government ministries.

Immigration Statistics

The process of immigration in Israel is strictly recorded since its scale is regarded as a major indicator for both the strength of the nation and the fulfillment of the ultimate Zionist ideal of "ingathering of exiles." Illegal immigration is nonexistent, because Jews are always welcomed and few non-Jews have good reasons to settle permanently. Furthermore, several budgets are determined by the actual size of the overall immigrant community and by the size of its various subgroups. Thus immigration statistics in Israel are regarded as relatively reliable, contaminated only by the less precise statistics of emigration.

From the establishment of the independent state in 1949, through the end of 1983, 1,737,653 persons immigrated to Israel. Fifty percent of them came from Europe and North America, 44 percent from Asia and Africa, and 6 percent from South America and Oceania (see table 4.1). The general trend of recent immigration to Israel, however, is that of a steep decrease. Only somewhat over one-quarter (28 percent) of all immigrants arrived between 1967 and 1983, while almost three-quarters (72 percent) arrived between 1948 and the end of 1966.

The Six Day War is regarded as a turning point in immigration to Israel. Until 1967, almost 90 percent of the million and one-quarter immigrants arrived from Asia, Africa, and Eastern Europe. After 1967 immigration from Russia increased to 34 percent, from North America it increased to 13 percent, and from South America to 9 percent, while the proportion of immigrants from Asia and Africa decreased to 19 percent. The peak years of immigration after the Six Day War were 1972–73, with an average of 55,000 immigrants per year (about half of them from Russia), whereas in the 1980s the numbers declined. The low was 13,000 immigrants per year in 1981–82, and the high was 20,000 in 1984 (including about 8,000 Ethiopians).

Characteristics of Recent Immigrants

The major immigrant groups after 1967, and in particular in the last ten years, were of very varied backgrounds and differed in many ways from earlier arrivals (MIA 1984).

Eastern European immigrants include the Russians and the Romanians. The Russians are divided into two major groups. Sixty-four percent of the 165,000 Russians came from Russia's European parts and 36 percent arrived from its southern republics in Asia: 18 percent (31,000) from Georgia, 9 percent (16,000)

from Buchara, and 7 percent (11,000) from the Caucasian moun-
tains. Since 1977, the majority of the Russian Jewish emigrés
dropped out in Vienna, most of them heading to North America.
The last six years have also been characterized by a significant
drop in the scope of emigration from Russia. Whereas the majority
of the European Russians are characterized by their higher education and by a nuclear-type family, immigrants from the southern
republics are mainly industrial workers having strong communal
ties.

Immigration from Romania since 1967 was small, approximately 1,000–5,000 persons per year. The majority of this group
consists of small nuclear families with higher education and the
highest numbers of elderly (23 percent) of all other immigrant
groups. Immigration from Iran grew significantly in 1979 after the
Khomeni revolution. Many of this group are professionals or are
involved in sales.

Recent Sephardic immigrants (also knows as Orientals)
include those from North Africa, Iran, India, and Ethiopia. Immigration from North Africa (86 percent from Morocco) decreased
after 1967 to fewer than one-tenth (28,000) of its earlier levels.
Most of those are large families employed primarily in industries
or in clerical work. The immigrants from India are divided into
three different subethnic origins: Bnai-Israel, the largest group
(14,000), who regard themselves as the descendants of the ancient
tribes of Israel; the Baghdadians, who arrived in India as mer-
chants from Iraq and have higher levels of education; and the
community of Kutchin, the smallest group (1,500) who were
primarily farmers.

The Ethiopians are the most recent group of immigrants to
arrive in Israel on a large scale. Their numbers in Israel were 287
until 1979, but from 1980 immigration grew significantly and by
the end of 1983 there were over 4,000. The 1984 rescue airlift
from Sudan brought an estimated additional 8,000 Ethiopian Jews
to Israel. Since the rescue mission maintained a high level of
secrecy, despite recent public exposure, attention focuses more on
the absorption complications of the Ethiopian than on their numbers. However, officials estimate that about 12,000 Ethiopian Jews
still remain in that country.

Table 4.1. Immigrants in Israel by Country of Origin, 1948–1983

Continent and Country of Origin	1948–1966		1967–1983		1948–1983 Totals	
	Number	Percent[a]	Number	Percent[a]	Number	Percent[a]
Asia	300,634	24	50,520	10	351,154	20
Iran	60,662	(20)	19,620	(39)	70,282	(20)
India	11,899	(4)	11,713	(23)	23,612	(7)
Other	228,073	(76)	19,187	(38)	257,260	(73)
Africa	367,189	29	45,315	9	412,504	24
Morocco	251,695	(69)	23,799	(53)	275,494	(67)
South Africa	5,106	(1)	10,161	(22)	15,267	(4)
(Ethiopia)	N.A.[b]	—	N.A.[b]	—	N.A.[b]	—
Other	—	—	—	—	—	—
Europe	528,758	42	270,596	56	799,354	46
USSR	15,234	(3)	164,868	(61)	180,102	(23)
Romania	228,309	(43)	37,523	(14)	265,832	(33)
France	9,423	(2)	35,090	(13)	44,513	(6)
U.K.	6,512	(1)	16,482	(6)	22,994	(4)
Other	269,280	(51)	16,633	(6)	285,913	(34)
North America	12,080	1	64,923	13	77,003	4
United States	9,387	(78)	58,694	(90)	68,081	(88)
Other	2,693	(22)	6,229	(10)	8,922	(12)
South America	22,422	2	45,364	9	67,786	4
Argentina	14,328	(64)	25,576	(56)	39,904	(59)
Other	8,094	(36)	19,788	(44)	27,882	(41)
Oceania	24,902	2	4,950	1	29,852	2
Total	1,255,985	100	481,668	100	1,737,653	100

SOURCE: Adapted from Ministry of Immigration and Absorption, Research and Planning Division, "Know Israel." (1984). (Hebrew).
[a] All percentages rounded to the nearest whole number.
[b] N.A. = nor applicable.

Most Ethiopian Jews arrived from villages where they had lived a traditional Jewish life, based on primitive agriculture and on small-scale trade. The large majority of arrivals are illiterate and young, with only 5 percent over sixty years of age. This group of immigrants raises, for the first time, the question of whether color differences will have any special effect on absorption procedures in Israel.

The recent flow of Western immigrants to Israel is composed primarily of North Americans, British, South Africans, French, and South Americans. Immigrants from these countries are relatively young (mainly between eighteen to twenty-nine years old), and a high proportion are singles who are highly educated and hold professional jobs. These characteristics, however, do not apply to the French immigrants, the majority of whom originate from North Africa and for whom immigration to Israel means a second major migratory move, after a stay in France.

Field Survey of Associations

The exact number of immigrant associations in Israel is not known, but those that have official status register with the Ministry of Interior as nonprofit groups. A list of twenty-nine national associations who have registered was provided by the Ministry of Immigrant Absorption (see list) and since these would be most of those involved in the provision of social services, this list was used to draw a sample for the field study. Ten associations were chosen, based on several criteria. Size was considered, and both large and small groups were selected; ethnic dispersion was important, to assure a broad range of cultural representation; class dispersion was also a criterion, to reflect different help-seeking patterns and needs; motivation to immigrate was considered, to include both groups who were attracted to Israel and those who were forced to migrate ("push-pull" motivation); and finally, key informants involved in absorption activities were consulted for recommendations of which associations to include.

The ten groups interviewed, representing over one-third of the registered associations, are listed in table 4.2 by ethnic origin, motivation to immigrate, numbers, and percent of recent arrivals. The names of the associations in both the list of 29 submitted by the MIA and table 4.2, which indicates associations interviewed, have been translated by the author from Hebrew. In some cases names have changed because of mergers, and in some cases the common usage may be different from the official listed designation. Those groups which have been interviewed have been starred on the list so that they can be identified.

History and Goals of the Associations

Since the history of Israel is strongly associated with major waves of immigrants who arrived soon after independence, it can be expected that the great majority of the immigrant associations came into existence in the early 1950s. Changes in the volume of immigration, countries of origin, and sociopolitical context, however, meant that some associations chose to merge along linguistic or broader ethnic lines, whereas others preferred to split up, primarily for political reasons.

The French, North Africa, and French-Speaking Immigrant Association is an example of a group that merged. It was established in 1950, and merged in 1968 with its ex-French, North African colonies and with other immigrants from French-speaking

Table 4.2. Immigrant Associations Interviewed, by Ethnic Origin, Motivation to Immigrate, Numbers Represented, and Percent of Recent Arrivals

Association	Predominant Ethnic Origin	Motivation to Immigrate	Number of People Represented	Percent of Recent Arrivals
Immigrant Association of America and Canada (Association of Americans and Canadians in Israel)	Ashkenazi	pull	60,000	40
Immigrant Association of the United Kingdom (British Settlers Association)	Ashkenazi	pull	45,000	50
Immigrant Association of Brazil	Ashkenazi	pull	7,000	15
Immigrant Association of Latin America (Latin American Immigrant Union)	Ashkenazi	pull/push	75,000	15
Immigrant Association of USSR (Russian Immigrant Association)	Ashkenazi	push	500,000	5
Immigrant Association of France, North Africa, and the French-speaking	Ashkenazi/ Sephardi	pull/push	150,000	20
Immigrant Association of Georgia	Sephardi	pull/push	38,000	8
Immigrant Association of Iran (Iranian Immigrant Umbrella Organization)	Sephardi	push	70,000	20
Immigrant Association of India	Sephardi	pull	25,000	4
Immigrant Association of Ethiopia (The Organization of Ethopian Jews)	Sephardi	push	12,000	95

origins such as the French Canadians, the French-Swiss, and the Belgians. On the other hand, the Immigrant Association of the USSR interviewed and the Immigrant Association of Georgia illustrate the splitting up of organizations. Russians originate from different geographic locales and from different political heritages. Their major reason to split up, however, was their different political affiliations in Israel. Of the associations sampled, the Georgians and the Immigrant Association of Ethiopia comprise recent waves of immigrants, in 1969 and 1984 respectively.

Six of the associations are based on membership, primarily for the purposes of internal elections and the distribution of general information. Most of the associations represent one ethnic group from a single country, whereas others are based on a common language, including three associations of English-, French-, and Spanish-speaking people. Nine of the ten associations reported that the proportion of recent arrivals (after 1980) among their constituents was 50 percent or less. Only the Ethiopians differed, with recent arrivals at 95 percent.

All the respondents reported that more recent arrivals were different from earlier arrivals however, this is not applicable for Ethiopians. The greatest differences were reported to be in religiosity and motivation to immigrate. The Immigrant Association of America and Canada, the French, and the Russians reported a significantly more religious wave of recent immigrants, whereas the Immigrant Associations of The United Kingdom, of Brazil, and of Latin American reported a decrease in the centrality of traditional Zionist pioneering ideals. These ideals are reportedly replaced by more realistic motives such as escape from totalitarian regimes (Brazil), and economic reasons (Latin America). Recent arrivals among the Iranians are reported to be better off financially than were previous waves. They came to Israel by free choice after comparing options in the United States and in Israel. However, the Zionist spirit was reportedly being revived with the arrival of the Ethiopians.

Not all immigrant associations spell out their goals, aims, and purposes in a detailed manner. The Association of Americans and Canadians in Israel (AACI), however, did so in Article 2 of their constitution, which states that the aims and purposes of the AACI are:

1. To assist members and prospective members to become integrated and to participate in the life of the country as rapidly and fully as possible.
2. To extend to members and prospective members such advice, guidance, assistance and services as will facilitate such integration. The services of the Association shall include but shall not be limited to: reception, housing, job placement, loans, counseling, social and cultural and educational activities.
3. To represent the interests of members and prospective members in their dealing with the Government and National Agencies on matters affecting such integration.
4. To encourage Americans and Canadians to come to Aliyah, and to work for conditions in Israel fostering this end.
5. To help Americans and Canadians better understand Israel, and to help Israelis better understand American and Canadian Jewish life. (AACI 1986)

Five of the ten associations interviewed reported that their goals had not changed since their inception. The goals of the other five reportedly did change. The Latin Americans, for example, have recently extended their goals and included the initiation of *aliyah* (immigration) in country of origin by creating "friends of the association" groups. Among the Georgians in the past the major goal was family reunification and helping their own poor. Today, since immigration is very slow, emphasis is placed on social absorption, especially through the sharing of information on Israel with the Georgians and by providing information on their own group to the Israeli society. The respondent from the Iranian Immigrant Umbrella Organization stressed that in the first years, the association's goal was to preserve group culture, while at the present it is rather the initiation and absorption of the latest waves of immigrants.

The first immigrants from India had traumatic experiences which shaped the goals of their association. They faced the humiliating effects of racial discrimination, with the attempts to segregate the Bnai-Israel sect from the general Jewish community in Israel. Early after their arrival, they had to learn new ways of organization and struggle. It took almost a decade until, in the early 1960s, the Israeli Rabbinate pronounced that these colored immigrants were truthful Jews, and thus should be allowed to intermingle with "greater Israel." After this political goal was accomplished, the aims and purposes of the Immigrant Association of India changed in the direction of the total integration of the Indian community within the Israeli society.

A decade after the Bnai-Israel incident, Jews from Ethiopia were involved in a similar political-religious debate. In 1973, the chief Sephardi rabbi ruled that the Ethiopian tribes claiming to be Jewish were indeed Jewish—thus they had to be saved. A small group of Israelis of Ethiopian origin started a public movement to open up Aliya from Ethiopia. As a consequence, in 1974 the Israeli government decided to apply the "law of return" to Jews from Ethiopia. The first two groups arrived in Israel in 1977 just before military aid by Israel to Ethiopia was publicized and emigration halted. It took two years of secret political exchanges to reopen the borders with the Sudan, and by 1984 a secret rescue mission was in full swing until publicity brought about a total halt to the mission.

During the last two years, about ten groups of Ethiopians created their own immigrant associations, each one claiming to represent their community. In 1985, for example, the Association of Ethiopian Immigrants registered as a nonprofit association with the general goal "to promote mutual support and cooperation within the Ethiopian Jewish community in Israel and abroad." This group is part of the sample survey. They seek to implement their goals as follows:

1. To always be at the side of those who have not yet reunified with their families in Israel, and to help find a solution to their predicament.
2. To promote the rights of Ethiopian Jewish immigrants in Israel in the areas of housing, education, religion, welfare, and employment.
3. To serve as a support system for members of the community by addressing emotional and practical needs, and to encourage members to come to each other's aid.
4. To provide orientation and information for newly arrived Ethiopian Jewish immigrants to prepare them for the transition into a new country.
5. To develop better understanding and communication between the Ethiopian Jewish community and interested outside groups or individuals.

6. To perpetuate the unique aspects of Ethiopian Jewish culture.
7. To coordinate collective economic endeavors for those interested
    members of the community. (AEII 1985)

The first priority of the association is to rescue Ethiopian Jews for immigration to Israel. This entails dialogue and cooperation with the Israeli government. The second priority is to promote the rights of Ethiopian Jewish *olim* (immigrants) by negotiations with various ministries and publicity in the media, and through legal services. Simultaneously, the association is planning to develop a support system through the establishment of local offices where Ethiopian Jewish olim may come for information, advice, and referrals. Thirdly, orientation will be provided for new olim by arranging seminars in coordination with the Jewish Agency, beginning at the airport immediately upon arrival. Next, the association will seek to improve understanding of their needs through public-speaking engagements and use of the media. Lastly, collective economic endeavors are planned, including founding a *moshav* (small landholders' cooperative settlement) and an artisan's cooperative, as well as a music and dance troupe composed of Ethiopian Jewish olim.

Association Structures and Major Activities

The ten associations sampled differ significantly in the ways they are set up, how they function, and in their major activities. They could vary from the well-organized associations offering a broad spectrum of professional social services, to the less-organized associations, offering hardly any services. The major factors that appear to differentiate the associations on such a continuum are the number of people represented; the proportion of recent arrivals; the level of public interest in the group as expressed through level of public funding; whether there was time to preplan or whether the people were pushed out from their country of origin; the level of ethnic cohesion or rivalries; the level of independent wealth; and the closeness of the sociocultural backgrounds of the immigrants.

The Association of Americans and Canadians in Israel is an example of a full-fledged, professionally staffed association. It represents a community of 60,000 North Americans (with a membership of over 16,000) through one national and five regional offices. Its officers, who represent the regions, are elected in a national convention held every two years. A detailed constitution describes their aims and purposes, membership base and procedures, list of officers, board of directors, committees and their powers, structure, and finances. The association employs about forty paid personnel and has a nationwide list of about 2,000 volunteers. Both are organized within twenty-two committees, at least half of which offer general and personal social services. For example, there are special committees for seniors and young adults, housing—with special subcommittees for singles and seniors, and education and absorption. The rest of the committees deal with more general issues such as relations with hometown groups, public relations, membership and organization, and the budget and finance.

The British Settlers Association is also a full-fledged association, incorporated in the British Olim Society. It represents a community of 45,000 through the Zionist Federation of Great Britain, Australia, New Zealand, and the Scandinavian countries. The association has twelve branches, each run by a chairman elected by the national executive committee. These branches arrange to have an "old-timer" volunteer greet newcomers either at the airport or, within a few days, in the newcomer's place of residence. Advice and referral is also offered on these occasions, primarily by their ethnic social service agency, the British Olim Society, which provides information, counseling, and advice on employment, housing, and social absorption.

The smallest immigrant association sampled, that of the Brazilians, represents a community of about 7,000, only 15 percent of whom are recent arrivals. Since the public funding of most associations is based on the number of immigrants represented, the Brazilian association is staffed only by fifteen active volunteers in the greater Tel Aviv area. They receive lists of expected arrivals from Jewish Agency officials, broken down by age, profession, family status, and expected area of settlement. Efforts are then made to match old-timer volunteers to the characteristics and needs of the newcomers.

The Immigrant Association of Latin America in Israel represents approximately 75,000 South Americans, through a national directorate and twenty-two branches. Each branch is run by a chairman and a local board. Except for the administrative aides, this association operates with about three hundred volunteers. In addition, a paid employment counselor was hired recently to help the association with finding jobs for their immigrants.

The Immigrant Association of France, North Africa, and the French-speaking claim to represent the largest conglomerate based on common language (500,000, of which over 200,000 originate from Morocco). In recent years they have had a membership list of 5,000. An average of 2,500 immigrants, many of whom were originally from North Africa, arrive each year, primarily from France. This association pays for two full-time positions (director general and national secretary) and five part-time positions, and is helped by 150 active volunteers. It has recently computerized its activities to connect immigrants to jobs and newcomers to absorbing old-timers.

The Central Organization of USSR Immigrants demonstrates a recent effort to unite a community of 150,000 Russians (6,000 members) from the European republics (also known as "White Russians"). Previous associations were initiated by ex-political prisoners who were divided among themselves by their political affiliations while still in Russia. In Israel, the Central Organization, as well as its fragmented predecessors, devotes most of its time to a variety of political activities aimed at maintaining contact with Russian Jews and promoting their emigration. In addition to such political involvements the association helps its members in translating their official documents and in seeking employment options.

The Immigrant Association of Georgia represents 38,000 people and is run by a twelve-member board of directors and a national council of forty members—both selected every four years. Eighteen local branches are run from the members' private homes. With the financial assistance of the Ministry of Absorption, the association runs a cultural club for children and youth in Jerusalem, in which Georgian Jewish heritage is taught and practiced through arts and crafts, exhibits, dance groups, and choirs.

The Immigrant Association of Iran is an Umbrella Organization of a recent merger of several small, independent, but not very active Iranian associations. The merger was initiated after the 1979 rise of the Khomeni government which caused a significant increase in Jewish emigration. The Iranian organization, which represents a population of 70,000 people, appoints its board of directors according to political party affiliation. The board is then subdivided into committees, the more active ones being concerned with employment, education, immigration, and absorption.

The Federation of Indian Immigrants reports hardly any recent arrivals (fewer than 5 percent). Most of the 25,000 people it represents arrived during the early and mid 1950s. This organization was hardly active in 1985, although it did have an elected national secretary and a council comprising the regional representatives. Most of the present activities of the federation are organized around local synagogues and a few women's chambers, where lecture series are held on general educational topics as well as on more specific issues related to the heritage of Bnai-Israel.

In 1985, the 12,000 Ethiopian Jews in Israel were not yet organized in a clear structure of an all-Ethiopian association. Depending on definition and source of information, there were from four to fourteen immigrant associations. Some were operated by a single person from his own home, while others claimed up to 1,000 members or 5,000 supporters. Some groups were formed from within the Ethiopian Jewish community, whereas others were formed and operated by veteran Israeli politicians and professionals on behalf of the Ethiopian Jews. International Jewish philanthropy (primarily from North America) is also involved in the efforts to promote the interests of this new community in Israel. Efforts are being made to set up an umbrella association, however, with local branches to primarily handle questions about personal status in relation to religious issues of the Orthodox rabbinate. In addition, the umbrella association will handle basic programs such as continued rescue and immigration; family reunification; promoting human rights; developing formal support systems; general orientation, information, referral, and advice services; and public relations, through the media. More specialized programs will have to deal with the severe matrimonial issues caused by the separation of tight family networks.

Joint Activities

Immigrant associations reported that they cannot accomplish their various aims and goals unless they cooperate with several organizations and coordinate their activities in areas of mutual interest. Two major types of coordination, at both the local and national levels, were identified. The first dealt with areas of mutual interest among the immigrant associations themselves, and the second was concerned with other organizations in both the voluntary and public sectors.

Among the immigrant associations, joint activities were initiated on social as well as political issues. A common base of language was the major unifying reason for the Council of English Speakers, serving immigrants from North America, Australia, the United Kingdom, and South Africa. This council provides general information on rights, benefits, and available services, and specializes in occupational and social-recreational opportunities. The council is especially active in geographic regions with high numbers of English-speaking immigrants. In the region north of Tel Aviv, an English-Speaking Residents Association (ESRA—the Hebrew acronym for "help"), is actively developing a countrywide group called the English-Speaking Sixty-Plus Council, by relying on scores of elderly volunteers who plan for and participate in their own services. Immigrants of Anglo-Saxon origin also run a Council of Concerned Citizens which initiates national projects related to issues of quality of life in Israel. A more "establishment"-initiated type of cooperation is the umbrella body of all immigrant associations under the auspices of the Jewish Agency. This group meets to discuss topics related to the absorption of immigrants, such as subsidized housing for singles who cannot afford the market price, and employment problems.

The second type of cooperation identified was in relation to other voluntary or public organizations. Joint activities with the Ministry of Immigrant Absorption and the Jewish Agency are the most common examples. Most associations have formal joint forums with these organizations on housing and the obtaining of mortgages. However, several interviewees reported that too often the absorption workers at the MIA feel helpless in the face of the problems raised by the immigrants, and in such cases it is the workers' common practice to refer the immigrants to their own corresponding associations. As one association chairperson said: "Basically the ministry is left with a romantic Zionist ideal, but with no professional or political power." Another respondent said: "The official absorption agencies are too complex, politicized, specialized and bureaucratized; thus they have to rely on our less-formalized, faster, primary-type ethnic networks."

When the issues become more complex, however, or when larger financial investments are needed, the MIA and the Jewish Agency become the significant organizations, with the Jewish Agency helping in the coordination of *aliyah* activities in the countries of origin, and the MIA financing and supporting acculturation.

On a smaller scale, there are additional organizations co-operating with immigrant associations, such as the Women's International Zionist Organization (WIZO). Several local authorities, major political parties, and the Israeli Federation of Labor Unions (Histadrut) have set up absorption committees or have appointed an absorption coordinator. Furthermore, the Israeli Labor Party has set up a joint project with the Histadrut for local, ethnic-community workers to encourage participation from the more recent immigrant communities in future party activities.

The Budget and Its Sources

Immigrant associations have three major financial sources: 1) the public sector, through the Ministry of Immigrant Absorption and through those local governments that have a high proportion of immigrants; 2) the voluntary and the quasi-public sector, through the Jewish Agency and the major political parties; and 3) the private sector through personal donations in Israel, from abroad or by the means of membership fees.

It was difficult to obtain a reliable picture on the associations' total annual budgets from these three sources, however, because most respondents were either not sure if all promised monies were in fact received, or they were unfamiliar with the various and complex aspects of their budgetary procedures. The best available budget estimates reveal a broad range of annual budgets from a low of $1,500 for the Georgians to a high of $627,000 for the North American association. Except in two cases, the Ministry of Absorption and the Jewish Agency account for most of the budget. Membership fees hardly count at all, with only two associations (the British and Latin American) reaching a maximum of 10 percent on this item. Private donations from country of origin or from abroad were reported by half of the respondents, and in the case of the Immigrant Association of Iran a single donation of $22,000 raised the proportion of this item to 75 percent of its total budget. In the United States and in some other democracies, there is a growing phenomenon of support organizations of parents, Zionists, or donors in the country or city of immigrant's origin, for example: the Cleveland Volunteers for Israel (CVI), the Parents of Americans in Israel (PAI), and others. Private donations in Israel are rare, with the AACI receiving a high of 7 percent. The Georgian and Indian associations received 20 and 50 percent respectively from Israeli formal organizations such as the local authorities, the Histadrut, the umbrella Sephardic Federations organization, and/or major Israeli parties.

Both the Ministry of Immigrant Absorption and the Jewish Agency face the problem of multiple minor groups trying to represent all immigrants from a certain country of origin. While there is a general effort to unify the factions, there may be exceptions for either political or cultural reasons. When a single country of origin is represented (i.e., an officially registered group with the Ministry of Interior) by more than one association, the budget appropriated for that country is divided among the groups. The criteria used by the Jewish Agency in supporting various associations includes:

1. The overall population represented in Israel by the country of origin.
2. The number of immigrants who arrived during the last three years.
3. The receipt of an annual report on last year's activities and next year's plans.
4. The number of Jews still in the country of origin and the measures taken by the association to promote their immigration.

5. The proportion of the budget of the association allocated for administration versus that allocated for programs.

The budget of the MIA to immigrant associations for 1985/1986 was divided into three main items: administration, $22,000; program activities, $200,000; and publications, $20,000. Administrative monies are allocated to the associations according to criteria similar to those of the Jewish Agency. However, monies for program activities are allocated by contracts, based on specific written plans submitted three months prior to the designed program activity. This item is the largest in the ministry's budget and it is more discretionary, since it is based on the special interests and initiatives of the associations. The ministry supervises and inspects the proper expenditures of those funds.

Immigrant associations from "distressed countries" tend to be poorer and weaker than those of the "free world." The associations from Russia, Buchara, Kaucas, Romania, India, Syria, Chile, Uruguay, and Ethiopia thus receive special treatment from the ministry both in cash (better terms for loans) and in kind (furnishing their offices). One innovative idea in the ministry is to advocate the adoption of weaker associations by stronger ones, thus enhancing voluntarism on an interethnic organizational level.

Identity and Acculturation Issues

As part of the replication of the New York study, issues of identity and acculturation of immigrants to Israel were examined.

In analyzing the responses of leaders of immigrant associations to questions about what distinguishes their own group from Israelis, three differentiating dimensions emerged. First, at the macro-social or national level, there were those respondents who emphasized the democratic and Zionist aspects of Israelis, since in their country of origin such motives were either supressed or lacked an acceptable means of expression. The British respondent, for example, felt that the Israelis can be themselves in their own right, that they developed a "survivor's mentality" both spiritually and mentally. One dimension of this is the right to military self-defense and to hit back if attacked. The Russian respondent emphasized freedom of speech and the freedom to organize in Israel, whereas in Russia, emphasis was placed on cultural factors through musical enrichment, literature, theater, and sports. The Zionist ideal of "feeling in Israel like being one big family" was reported by the Ethiopian respondent, meaning the sense of Jewish mutual aid. In Ethiopia, close tribal allegiance had been the dominating motive of their lives.

The second distinguishing factor between the Israelis and the respondents' own groups emerged in the interpersonal area. In this category the Israeli image was not flattering. Rudeness, toughness, pushiness, and shamelessness ("chutzpa") were noted as characterizing Israelis, whereas tenderness, good manners, and courtesy were claimed to be the predominant characteristics of the respondents' own groups. These stereotypes did not hold for the North American respondent, however, who saw the Israelis as more hospitable and more flexible in terms of combining family, work, and reserve service in the army; Americans were reported by this respondent to be more closed, money minded, and "square," or conservative.

The third and final differentiating dimension was at the family level. This dimension was predominant among the representatives from traditional Sephardic origins (Georgia, Iran, and Ethiopia). They stressed the cultural clash upon arrival, which has created a decline of authority of the man as traditional leader, and the breaking up of the partriarchic role of the family-unifying father. This painful process was reported to hurt families, primarily during daily joint meals, at times of family gatherings, and when an elderly member had to be removed from the extended family.

An empirical approach involved asking the association leaders to respond to a twenty-item identity-acculturation scale, adopted for Israeli use. Scores could go from 1 (lowest) to 5 (highest). The results indicated that, on the whole, the leaders saw new members as more committed to the encouragement of acculturation (M = 3.7) than to the preservation of group identity (M = 3.1).

Items highest on the acculturation scale were the importance of getting to know Israel by touring it (M = 4.7), and making new Israeli friends and getting involved in Israeli organizations (M = 4.1 for both). The lowest item on the acculturation scale was the importance of liking Israeli food (M = 1.9). On the identity scale, the highest items were keeping contacts with others from one's own ethnic group (M = 4.3), belonging to an ethnic club or association (M = 3.7), and retaining the native language (M = 3.4). The lowest score on the identity scale was on the importance of marrying someone from one's own group (M = 2.3).

Comparing the mean scores of the immigrant associations by country of origin, only two were substantially more committed to maintain identity than to promote acculturation, as noted by the scale items. These were the Ethiopians and the Iranians, and they represent recent large-scale immigrations.

Immigrant Needs and Services

The needs of immigrants for social services should be viewed within the general context of the social-welfare system of the absorbing society. In this study information on needs was obtained through the "key informant" method. All ten respondents were asked a general introductory question about the major problems their ethnic groups were facing. Eight of the ten respondents mentioned employment as the most problematic issue for new immigrants. Employment was reported both in terms of the need to find jobs, and as a problem of job security for employed new immigrants. North Americans, many of whom hold a bachelor's degree, stress the need to find jobs, and the Georgians, who have less formal education, are reported to be restless and in fear of layoffs.

General social problems, housing, and the need to learn the Hebrew language were each mentioned by four respondents. The mastering of the Hebrew language, for example, is a prerequisite for most jobs, primarily for those immigrants in special need of occupational retraining—i.e., those from Iran, India, and Ethiopia. Social problems included the need to adjust the dreams of Israel as a country of "milk and honey" to reality, the hardships involved in "breaking" into Israeli society, and the difficulties involved in adjusting to changes in the power structure in the family. While housing was mentioned as a general problem for immigrants, it was also stressed as a particular hardship for singles, for single parents, and for the elderly. A more detailed description of the major areas of needs explored during the interviews is noted below.

HOUSING

Major responsibility for housing in Israel lies with the central government through its Ministry of Housing. Its task is to plan the construction of new housing projects throughout the country and to provide assistance—primarily by loans and by long-term mortgages—in obtaining proper housing for selected groups of the population such as new immigrants, newly married couples, slum dwellers, and families living in overcrowded apartments (Doron 1976). Since standards adopted for public housing were rooted in Western culture, nuclear housing units were encouraged at the expense of the extended family. Housing policy thus became one major factor in weakening the bonds of kinship among Asian/African immigrants (Honig and Shamai 1978).

All but two respondents (from India and Iran) agreed that their ethnic group suffered from housing problems. A shortage of affordable apartments in Israel affects immigrants as much as the general public. The availability of public housing is decreasing as is the availability of affordable private housing, and the prices of apartments in the marketplace or for rent are much higher than in most countries of origin. Thus the expected amount of self-financing is much higher than the available mortgages offered by the banks. The terms of mortgages are specifically hard for singles. This situation means that less-wealthy immigrants experience continuous moves through temporary occupancy of privately rented apartments. In addition, about 20 percent of the tenants of absorption centers, which were set up initially as the first transitory stop for most immigrants, remain there as permanent residents due to the shortage of affordable permanent housing arrangements.

In the area of housing most immigrant associations are

limited to providing information, referral, advice, and guidance on options of rental and purchase in the private market. The AACI is the single exception, providing a loan to immigrants of up to $4,000, in addition to the government's mortgage.

A different type of housing problem exists in the settling of Ethiopians. The major issue here is whether to spread them out in Israel's major cities, thus breaking up some of their tribal ties, or to settle them together in one concentrated area. A second issue is the type of housing that best satisfies their needs within the options that exist in Israel. Constraints of time and of the availability of physical facilities have meant that this ethnic group has been spread out in several development towns, primarily in absorption centers and in publicly rented, high-quality hotels. There have been recent efforts to house some Ethiopians in Jerusalem, but only in immigrant centers.

EMPLOYMENT

Vocational guidance, vocational training, placement at work, and the provision of work are all the responsibility of the central government through the Ministry of Labor and Social Affairs. Employment bureaus have the exclusive authority by law to make placements through local labor exchanges.

Employment was mentioned as a problem by eight of the respondents (India and Brazil excluded). Although none of the associations ran a separate training program, they undertook different roles in locating and preserving jobs. The immigrant association of Latin Americans, for example, hired their own employment counselors in the big cities. In AACI self-help groups were created for lawyers and doctors to learn about Israeli practices. The French, Russians, and Georgians rely on voluntary help from their own groups to find jobs. Several Georgians and Iranians prefer self-employment in small businesses, but it is hard for them to invest both in mercantiles and in housing during their first period as immigrants.

Since unskilled laborers are usually the first to be fired, this was the major fear of the Ethiopian respondent. During their first three years in Israel, the Ethiopians enjoy some protection due to their immigrant status. However, anxieties are already high in expectation of the expiration of that period. In the meantime, among the first waves of the younger and better educated, several Ethiopians were selected, trained, and hired by the Jewish Agency as translators, mediators, and absorption guides, to aid doctors, nurses, teachers, and social workers in their interactions with this new group of immigrants.

HEALTH

Health services in Israel enjoy a high reputation in general, and specifically at the local delivery level. The Israeli National Sick Fund (Kupat Holim) is an extensive neighborhood network of quasi-governmental, subsidized health services in all communities, covering nearly the entire population. In addition there are universal-type health centers providing preventive family care for women during pregnancy and following childbirth, care for small children, guidance to their parents, and, more recently, communal health care for the elderly.

For these reasons, health problems were not reported by most respondents to be an area of special concern for the associations. The Ethiopians were the only exception. This group of recent immigrants suffered severe malnutrition and had experienced a series of epidemic diseases on their way to Israel. Particularly affected were those who arrived through the refugee camps of Sudan. Health services in Israel studied the special problems and assigned a newly specialized staff to those resident areas that had a high concentration of Ethiopians. Translators served as an important liaison in these encounters, alongside the newly trained nurses of Ethiopian origin. In addition to the efforts of modern medical services, traditional healers were reportedly turned to in times of personal or health-related crises. Elderly leaders and high priests (*Keissim*) provide advice, blessing, and prayer in crisis situations. The role of these traditional leaders is weakening, however, leaving a huge vacuum and a potential for the associations to develop new cadres of younger leaders.

PERSONAL SERVICES

Personal social services in Israel are offered by a large number of formal organizations, differing in their fields of activity, goals, auspices, and clients. They include both large bureaucracies serving large sectors of the population, and smaller ones which include volunteers at the local level. There is a need to interrelate this basically two-tier system, sorting out guaranteed baseline services from special ones in support of pluralism and exceptionalism. For Ethiopians different coping mechanisms were identified by their length of stay and by their cultural distance from Western traditions. According to the Ethiopian respondent, when disputes cannot be handled any more within the family, it is customary to turn to the tribe's elderly or to its rabbis (*Keiss*). Such problems are frequent among the Ethiopians because several families were separated during political persecutions, the migration to Sudan, and rescue missions. Thus large numbers of men and women lost contact with their spouses, which resulted in the stressful uncertainty of whether and when to start new relationships or to keep hoping for family reunification. Such uncertainties resulted in the hospitalization of several members of this community in Israeli mental institutions, where translators and social workers tried to relate routinized treatment procedures to the specific cultural and communication needs of the patients.

Among the Iranians, the handling of severe family disputes has already moved from family mediators to professional counselors in two major areas: marital disputes, affected by the changing roles of women in the family; and business disputes within the extended family, which are often handled by lawyers. Similar changes were reported by the Georgian respondent. In the early 1970s, the first waves of this immigrant group became known to Israeli society primarily by their young age of marriage and by their traditional abduction of brides, a central part of the young men's courting ceremony. The intervention of the Israeli-born chairman of the Georgian Immigrant Association was needed to help in acculturating this group to Israeli norms and legal regulations (i.e., age of marriage). His central role as unofficial judge and mediator of personal and family matters for the group continues and he functions alongside a similar role undertaken by the community's rabbis.

A different type of family problem was reported by respondents from the "free world" around the option of reemigration.

Among those (North America, Britain, Brazil, France), there is a large degree of intrafamily ambivalence about the permanency of their stay in Israel, leading to serious psychological conflicts, primarily between spouses or between them and their teenage children. "Free world" immigrants were also characterized by more intrapersonal types of problems. According to the North American and French respondents, recent immigrants have had more experience with mental health services in their country of origin than had previous waves of immigrants. They report cases of immigrants who came to act out the unfulfilled Zionist dreams of their parents, and broke down when they faced the harsh realities of life in Israel. Others in need of help in their country of origin made aliyah to solve their personal problems and to give themselves a "second chance" for life, while still others were sent to Israel by their parents to be "saved" from a variety of personal deviances.

Such problems of mental health become known to immigrant associations by two different routes. The first is directly from individuals in distress who prefer to share their problems with someone of their own ethnic group. The second is through social service workers in the general system who request consultation on the ethnic dimensions of their clients, the need for translators, and/or the wish to refer their ethnic client to a professional of the same origin via the ethnic association.

THE ELDERLY

In addition to all of the usual problems the aged face such as increased physical impairment, diminished capacities, inadequate incomes, poor housing, and social isolation, the Israeli aged are also characterized by limited mastery of the nation's Hebrew language and by lower levels of education than that attained by the younger generation. The respondents were unaware of the exact proportions of the elderly among their various immigrant groups, but they emphasized that this age category presents a broad range of problems with special needs for ethnically sensitive social services.

The AACI for example, estimates that about twenty percent of its members are elderly, many of whom came to Israel upon retirement. They present a need for English-speaking socialization, information, and advice. Although they came to retire within their own ethnic group—i.e., Jews—they cope with loneliness and with having been uprooted. Several social clubs have been set up with a strong spirit of self-help. According to the chairman of the British Immigrant Association (BIA), the elderly comprise the majority of the participants in the various social events organized by the association. He states, "Basically we are here to serve the lonely and those who have difficulties assimilating." The BIA had established its own social clubs in certain geographic areas, whereas in other areas they join the activities of the English-Speaking Residents Association (ESRA).

The Immigrant Association of Brazil emphasized advocacy functions as central in helping to deal with the special needs of its elderly. They write letters and accompany their members to various bureaucracies, specifically health and housing authorities, to ensure discretionary entitlements or services. For example: elderly immigrants are not entitled to be hospitalized through the National Sick Fund (Kupath Holim) since they have not contributed insurance fees during their younger years. However, immigrants who were involved in Zionist activities in their countries of origin may become eligible for such coverage. Thus the Immigrant Association of Brazil assumes the role of collecting, verifying, and certifying evidence on their members' Zionist activities in their country of origin.

Assuming the role of advocate is reported to be most necessary and helpful in dealing with Israeli bureaucracy. The Latin American Association is intensively involved in advocating for the housing needs of their single and lonely elderly. The French are involved in helping their elderly to transfer their retirement benefits to Israel through general counseling and through referral to lawyers of French origin in more complex cases.

Elderly immigrants from Russia are mostly the survivors of the Holocaust and several are also the survivors of either Nazi or Russian concentration camps. The aftermath of these traumatic experiences left many of the survivors with a strong need for support systems in their own language—which is primarily Yiddish. Social clubs for the elderly serve this purpose and the common Yiddish language often draws Latin American immigrants to these events since many of them originate from Eastern Europe.

Among the Georgians, Iranians, and Indians, a significant decrease in family responsibilities is reported toward elderly parents. Even more problematic, however, are the cases of childless elderly, or those whose children have moved far away. In such cases, efforts are made to prevent placement in homes for the elderly by organizing local volunteers of the association to assume visiting and follow-up responsibilities. Referral to the general social services system is thus delayed as long as possible. Placement in homes for the elderly is feared by Ethiopians, although to date, no such cases have been reported.

YOUTH

Only half of the respondents felt that their ethnic adolescents were experiencing special problems. Those problems were strongly related, however, to the social context in their country of origin.

Following the Khomeni revolution, hundreds of children and youth of Iran came to Israel by themselves. They were absorbed by the institutions of Youth Aliyah, a department of the Jewish Agency, one traditional purpose of which is to provide general care, education, and social and cultural integration to overseas youth brought to Israel without their parents. Youth Aliyah appointed a specially trained Iranian absorption worker to improve communication and enhance sensitivity to culture.

The Georgian immigrant association is closely involved with the problem of its youth. These youngsters face ethnic ridicule and stereotyping in Israeli public schools. To handle this problem, the association developed special programs in which the unique Georgian history was taught, with the aim of strengthening the ethnic pride of the young Georgian-Israeli generation.

The French respondent reported special problems with their younger adults, most of them visiting students, of whom 80 percent had initially planned to stay in Israel. It was reported that about half of those students returned to France with grave disappointments about Israel. This situation was basically viewed as the failure of the country to fulfill the expectations of this group.

The association was planning to hire a professional to organize "absorbing foster-care" parents, to facilitate the acculturation of immigrant French students.

Both the British and North American respondents reported cases of youth depression due to the hardships of social adjustment—primarily among those who opposed aliyah on the part of their parents. While there are known cases of adolescents who return to their country of origin on their own, several others are referred by their associations to private therapists or counselors.

WOMEN

The role of Jewish women in the family underwent major reformulations in the Jewish state. For centuries, Jewish tradition had emphasized the family as the central unit in the social structure. Zionist egalitarian ideals, however, had direct implications for family reorganization, equality between sexes, female roles outside the family, and increased independence of children (Honig and Shamai 1978).

In this study only four of the ten respondents were able to identify problem areas specifically related to immigrant women. The problems they reported fell into two major categories. The first was changing family roles among immigrants from traditional patriarchic backgrounds. An example was the opposition of newcomer Georgian husbands to the idea that their wives join the labor force. To help with coping and adjusting, the Georgian immigrant association had mobilized its old-timer volunteers to explain, inform, and consult with new immigrants on the norms and cultures of Israeli society.

The second category of problems that immigrant women were reported to face in Israel related to their marital status. According to the British and Brazilian respondents, there are more single, divorced, and widowed women among the newcomers than in previous waves of immigration. Some are motivated to come to Israel primarily to solve personal problems, rather than for the traditional Zionist reasons. To assist these women, their immigrant associations engage in efforts to organize or to sponsor social events for singles within their ethnic group. Participation, however, has been at a low level.

GENERAL AND FINANCIAL AID

Income maintenance systems in Israel include a variety of national insurance programs (such as old-age, survivors, work injury, unemployment, and maternity insurance) and noncontributory benefits. With respect to this, all the respondents emphasized that, in principle, they expect the assistance of the government to provide for the basic financial needs of immigrants. During the immigrants' first three years, most of these expectations are carried out by the Ministry of Immigrant Absorption. With the expiration of the "new-immigrant" status (Oleh Chadash), expectations are transferred to the general social service system of the major ministries.

In spite of these general provisions, four of the ten associations were making efforts to become more responsive to the life cycle and financial needs of their immigrants. The North Americans and the Georgians provide guidance in cases of death to kin, with help in all relevant procedures, i.e., funeral, legal, and financial matters. The North Americans, British, and Latin Americans also manage special funds for emergency loans such as second mortgages for housing on easier terms than those available in the market; loans to help start a new business; and emergency help, primarily during the first phases of absorption. Among the North Americans, these loans are strongly based on home town group relations, namely funds are available by community for immigrants from that particular area—a well-known philanthropic method of the pre-State era.

LEGAL AID

Legal aid and consultation through public bureaus are provided in Israel primarily to lower-income families; for others, legal advice is strongly based in the private sector. Six of the ten associations provide legal aid and consultation to their members on a voluntary basis: the Iranian, Russian, French, Latin American, British, and North American associations. They have organized lists of lawyers of their own ethnic group by area of residence, and people in need are free to select any one of them for advice. Such advice is available outside of the court only, since voluntary legal aid services within the courts is forbidden by Israeli law. Thus in cases dealt with in the courts, a fee for service is requested. In certain specialized areas—such as labor disputes or discrimination against women—referrals are made to the legal services of the Histadrut (General Federation of Labor), its women's organization (Na'amat), or to WIZO (Women's International Zionist Organization).

A special case of obtaining voluntary legal advice is that of the Ethiopians who are helped by non-Ethiopian veteran Israeli advocates. Case and class advocacy among the Ethiopians relates primarily to issues raised by the Israeli rabbinate against their Judaizing Ethiopians, who in turn have strongly protested the fact that their Jewishness was not recognized by the official Jewish authorities. The majority of Israelis have become increasingly sensitive to growing political attempts by the Orthodox establishment to exercise religious coercion on the newcomers.

CHILDREN AND SCHOOLS

All too often the problems caused by the migration of school-age children—whether the move is halfway across the city or halfway across the world—are not given sufficient attention. In Israel, all parties involved in immigrant absorption have long recognized the educational problems faced by newcomers, and the educational system has developed several programs to ease the diversified ethnic, religious, and cultural stresses of the transition period. Israel has adopted a three-category schooling system involving: 1) the Secular State (Mamlachti) and 2) the Religious State (Mamlachi Dati) schools, both of which are public; and 3) the strictly Orthodox private schools which are substantially subsidized by the Ministry of Education and the local authorities in which they function. Three major kinds of problems were reported: the normal problems of adolescence; special problems of adjustment and integration for immigrant youth; and gaps between immigrant parent expectations and the general level of the Israeli educational system.

According to the North American respondent, immigrant parents from the United States face a hard time adjusting to what they consider to be a mediocre educational system which prefers group solidarity over individual achievement. To overcome this, several families seek the development of after-school enrichment programs, which are often not available in an era of decline in public resources. In spite of this, immigrants are reported to reject the idea of private schools and support the public system.

The transition to the Israeli educational system requires that immigrants from traditional origins (Georgia, Iran, India, Ethiopia), adjust to a system that emphasizes national responsibilities and allegiances over ethnic loyalty. The ideal, however, has not always been consistent with experience. The first waves of immigrants from India in the 1960s, for example, were segregated in separate classes until the immigrant association of India demanded their integration in the general educational system. Presently, in the 1980s, a similar process is taking place with the Ethiopian community during their acculturation period.

In summarizing, many of the respondents focused primarily on the general process and structure of the absorption system in Israel, rather than on their own group's needs. The major criticism was aimed at the marginal role of the Ministry of Immigrant Absorption, which lacks, according to most respondents, both an adequate structure and human sensitivity to the special needs of immigrants. According to the respondent from India: "Israelis just do not have a mature appreciation of the civil service, and that includes serving its immigrants." On the other hand, according to the Iranian respondent, there are inadequate mechanisms linking the formal absorbing organizations and the immigrant communities both in their country of origin and in Israel.

The Iranian respondent also commented on reasons that may prevent adequate preparation in the country of origin during the preimmigration phase. First, totalitarian regimes do not permit "alien propaganda," which they consider to include the dissemination of information on the destinations of emigrants. In the Western societies, such a task is traditionally performed by Israeli emissaries (*schlichim*) of the Jewish Agency. The second reason for not being prepared prior to immigration could be the result of crisis events in the country of origin, such as in the cases of Iran and Ethiopia. The respondent from Latin America suggested abolishing the MIA, and replacing its functions by strengthened immigrant associations. This would create separate "mini-ministries" of absorption for each group of immigrants, with direct subsidy from the government.

Social Service Delivery for Immigrants in Israel

Social services for immigrants in Israel have been shown to be complex, often uncoordinated, and highly fragmented. In developing a rational model for such services, four factors should be considered: the ideological base; levels of delivery; the auspices of delivery; and the organizational continuum.

From an ideological perspective, different countries may express different levels of commitment to the absorption of various groups of newcomers. Unlike the United States, which does not officially aid in the adjustment or assimilation of immigrants (except in the cases of political refugees), Israel is ideologically committed to aid all Jewish immigrants in the absorption process. Western European countries often commit themselves to services for some immigrants for a limited period only (for guest workers, for example). Thus, they temporarily care for the basic needs of those immigrants while encouraging them to maintain their ethno-national identity in the expectation of their return to their countries of origin.

These differences in absorption policies can be conceptualized on a continuum. On one end there is the "melting pot" ideology, stressing a highly valued public commitment for a fast absorption and assimilation of all immigrants. This was basically the dominant ideology behind immigration and absorption policies in Israel during its first twenty years, but it is limited to Jews. At the other end of the continuum is a separatist "ethnic identity" position which may either be a national policy, as in the case of guest workers in Western Europe, or a voluntary personal or ethnic group choice. The latter is the case for several Israeli families in the United States, who see themselves as "sojourners," voluntarily maintaining an option to return to Israel by trying to segregate themselves and their children from mainstream American life (Korazim 1983, 1985).

In between the "melting pot" and "ethnic identity" positions is the policy of "cultural pluralism" in which the public sector recognizes and accepts ethnic diversity. This may be accomplished by legitimizing the incorporation, in certain areas of social services, of cultural content, by the matching of staff according to client ethnic characteristics, and by the representation of ethnic groups on the higher organizational levels of public bureaucracies (Jenkins 1981). The pluralist model is traditionally represented by the United States, and Israel has shifted in that direction since the late 1960s. By establishing the Ministry of Immigrant Absorption, Israel moved away from its official "melting pot" ideology into a more "pluralist" one which legitimized the incorporation of linguistic, ethnic, and cultural factors into the delivery of public services. However, a three-year time limit was introduced to the status of "new immigrant." During those three years, new immigrants are exempted from equal obligations by delaying their army service and exempting them from paying taxes on salaries and major commodities. At the end of that period, immigrants are expected to assimilate into the society at large and into its general social services.

The second factor to consider in this analysis is that there are three levels of social service delivery for immigrants: the national level, the regional-local level, and the neighborhood or community level. At the national level, there are the major ministries, the Ministry of Immigrant Absorption, the Jewish Agency, the national offices of each immigrant association, the larger political parties, and the Histadrut (the Israeli Federation of Labor Unions). These organizations set national policies, each in its own domain, allocate financial and personal resources, and supervise their programs. The delivery of the services themselves, however, is performed more on the regional, local, and neighborhood levels. Regional services include absorption committees with local governments, and the local chapters or branches of the national immigrant associations and those of the political parties and the

Histadrut. Community services include special programs for immigrants within local community centers, absorption centers, and local synagogues catering to special ethnic groups.

Social services for immigrants may also be described from a third aspect: their auspicies of delivery, i.e., public, voluntary nonprofit, private for-profit, or any mix of the above. Public services for immigrants are provided through the major ministries of government and through the specially established MIA. These services are "statutory" or "legislative" since they are enacted in laws and regulations, and they reflect the public responsibility for the newcomers. At the national level, the public sector is also responsible for functions such as planning, standard setting, licensing and inspection. Nonprofit and voluntary services for immigrants are of two major types. The first is the philanthropic, quasi-governmental Jewish Agency, which finances and operates programs for, for example, immigration and absorption, rural settlement, youth aliyah, housing, education, and special social programs. Under the second category are the immigrant associations. Although they do not represent a clear-cut voluntary service because of some mix with the public sector in funding, they do encourage the development of pluralism and provide opportunities for ethnic, cultural, religious, and other special interests to flourish without direct government interventions. Thus they function as "supplementers" and "improvers" of the public services. Private, for-profit (also known as proprietary) organizations offer services that immigrants buy in the "free market." This sector tends to develop in those areas that the public and the voluntary sector decline to take up, or when there may be a profit-making edge for private competition. Private therapists, physicians, lawyers, or private housing companies are available to all who are able and willing to pay. In the case of immigrants, as in the case of the general public, the affluent tend to benefit more from this sector.

For many years, the public, voluntary, and private sectors served as traditional categories of service auspice in the welfare state. However, these categories are not so clear cut as before, and it is increasingly difficult to distinguish what is public from what is voluntary or private. Some writers describe the emergence of a new mixed economy of welfare—a hybrid of the three sectors—intertwining all of the providers of social services (Utting 1980; Judge 1981; Kamerman 1981). Third-party payments, the purchase of service contracts, and voucher systems have become governments' preferred ways of mixing delivery of services, and Israel has followed this Western trend in its absorption policies. Immigrant associations, funded by the public, nonprofit, and private sectors serve as good examples of this hybrid intertwining.

Finally, the social service systems for immigrants in Israel may be examined through a continuum of organizational perspectives, i.e., how formal or informal are the service delivery structures. Formal organizations that originate in the bureaucratic model are characterized by workers hired by merit criteria, based on specialization and on the idea that egalitarian services have to be delivered according to universal organizational rules and regulations (Weber 1947; Kast and Rosenzweig 1979). Such organizations are also designed to maximize technical knowledge and large-scale resources. This model characterizes the major national ministries such as those for health, housing, education, labor, and welfare. Such formal and "rigid" bureaucracies are not the best forms to relate with empathy and comprehension to the idiosyncratic cultural and ethnic needs of immigrants, and they may even create barriers to access in cases of special needs. Thus the government's decision to create the Ministry of Immigrant Absorption can be seen as an attempt to retreat on certain criteria of "pure bureaucracy" and to make a public department more sensitive to the particular needs of newcomers.

At the other end of the organizational continuum are the immigrants' primary groups: the nuclear and extended family, friends, and neighbors. Here members enjoy frequent face-to-face contact, a positive and deep affect through permanent and instrumental relationships with unlimited commitment and with no detailed specializations (Cooley 1955). Primary groups are more effective where technical knowledge and large-scale resources are not required. In those cases, primary groups can take advantage of shorter lines of communication, of the immediate availability of their members, and of their low costs of maintenance. Thus they are able to make faster and more flexible decisions (Litwak and Figuera 1960). Such natural support systems which do not necessarily rely on professional skills help immigrants to cope and adapt in stressful situations.

Around the middle position between formal organizations and primary groups, there are the immigrant associations, trying to achieve a balance and integration between service and ethnic goals in a single delivery system. Since immigrant associations have a strong voluntary base they may share and mediate between the functions of primary groups and formal bureaucracies, thus creating—at least theoretically—a more efficient social-service delivery system.

Two additional structures may be identified on the organizational continuum. Between the formal bureaucratic delivery structure and the immigrant associations we could place the Jewish Agency, as a major philanthropic bureaucracy specifically catering to the needs of the Jewish population in Israel. Between the immigrant associations and the primary groups there are various types of mutual-aid networks at the local level, particularly those that are based in ethnic synagogues. For them, ethnic and religious ties are the basis of the commitment to service.

The organizational continuum of the services for immigrants can be summarized in figure 4.1.

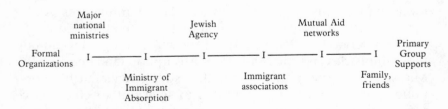

Figure 4.1. Organizational Continuum of Services for Immigrants

Summary and Implications

This paper has examined ethnic/immigrant associations in Israel within their broader societal context. Israel's history, ideology, economy, and social fabric have all shaped the policy and practice of immigrant absorption. The major roots of Israel's absorbing traditions lie in conceptions of Jewish charity and philanthropy, and the ideologies of the secular Zionist movement. Their interactions brought about a meshing of values which affected the absorption of immigrants in two contradictory directions—voluntarism and statehood.

Israel started its political history as an independent state, with a strong belief in the ideology of public statehood, and it advocated the idea of a cultural Jewish "melting pot" during the major waves of the "ingathering of exiles." Within two decades, this idealist goal turned to the idea of cultural pluralism, with the recognition that a gradually increasing separatist approach is needed to enhance integration and facilitate acculturation. The turning to cultural pluralism was forced, not premeditated; abrupt, not pre-planned; and originated from below, not from higher policy.

The interviews conducted with the key informants of immigrant associations revealed large differences among the associations in terms of their size, budgets, structure, and the variety of services they provided. The ethnic groups' length of stay, their proportion among recent arrivals, and their budgets are the best indicators of the extensiveness of their services.

This study of immigrant associations revealed gaps at three levels in programs to meet the ethnic needs of immigrants. At the macro level, there is little coordination between absorption policies and services delivered among the major ministries, among those ministries and the Ministry of Absorption, and between the Ministry of Absorption and the Jewish Agency. Furthermore, none of the above have attempted to spell out specific service expectations from immigrant associations. At the mezzo level, immigrant associations create a service dilemma about equity. Stronger associations (i.e., those that are wealthier, better organized, larger) can provide more for their ethnic group than can a weaker association. This inequity exacerbates the existing gaps among immigrants, further increases ethnic divisions, and impedes social integration. At the micro level, immigrants are often shunted from office to office according to their special needs (i.e., housing, employment, personal counseling), with no one agency taking the responsibility to integrate services and manage the cases. In spite of these constraints, immigrant associations in Israel do serve an important in-between function. Their ethnic bases serve as a meaningful intervening variable between the family, other types of primary groups, and the larger bureaucracies in Israel.

There are two complementary factors that will probably shape the future of absorption strategies and structures in Israel. The first is the severe decrease in the total number of immigrants to Israel (about 50,000 in 1982–84 compared to about 70,000 in 1979–81). For fiscal year 1985–86 the projected amount is 15,000. Thus (with the halt of Ethiopian immigration), some Israelis question whether it is still legitimate to regard their country as one that absorbs immigrants. The second threatening trend is related to requested retrenchments and cutbacks in the public sector as a major strategy of fighting the mid-1980s economic crises. These cutbacks necessarily affect public services for immigrants.

These factors raise at least three options that can be considered in relation to the future of immigrant associations in Israel:

One is to maintain the status quo, on the grounds that either there is no need to change absorption policies and procedures, or that such changes are not feasible due to political constraints among Israeli and Jewish Diaspora politicians. Those who believe that total accommodation and stagnation to political "realities" may be wasteful, unfair, and inefficient, however, do not find this acceptable.

A second option is to strengthen the public sector, which could be accomplished by transferring numerous programs from the Jewish Agency to the government. Some of the present Jewish Agency programs, such as the Student Authority program, the Hebrew Schools (Ulpanim), the hostels and absorption centers, the Hostels and Homes for the Elderly and the Welfare Services, duplicate those of the Ministry of Immigrant Absorption.

A large-scale reorganization in the direction of strengthening the government could also include the dismantling of the MIA itself and the transferral of its functions (and those of the Jewish Agency mentioned above) back to the major ministries as they were prior to its establishment in 1968, thus reducing fragmentation. This option could strengthen the in-between functions of immigrant associations by appointing them to handle a variety of issues in which ethnic dimensions play a central role.

A third and final option would be to strengthen the voluntary sector. This option would take an opposite direction from the former one in two alternative steps. It would support the idea of dismantling the MIA and transferring many of its functions to the major ministries and either to the Jewish Agency or to each association separately. Under such a plan, immigrant associations would emerge as a major in-between structure. In an era of voluntarism, however, their functions need not necessarily be as limited as they are at present. If immigration projections remain low, this option may be selected as the most viable alternative. One problem, however, would be the difficulties of developing a unified policy on the part of the associations, since they have not been able to establish strong coalitions in the past.

Regardless of which option will be followed, immigrant associations will continue to exist, incorporating important service roles which have to be further clarified and specified. They represent a unique organizational in-between structure which can function both as a formal service agency and as a primary age group–type ethnic service.

Immigrant Organizations and Associations in Israel

> The Immigrant Organization of USSR*
> The Immigrant Organization of USSR Prisoners
> Central Organization of USSR Immigrants
> The Immigrant Association of USSR and Eastern Europe
> The Immigrant Association of USSR
> The Immigrant Association of Georgia*

The Immigrant Association of Caucasia
The Immigrant Association of Bukhara
The Immigrant Association of Syria
The Immigrant Association of Iran*
The Immigrant Association of India*
The Federation of Sephardic Communities*
The Immigrant Association of France, North Africa and the
     French Speaking*
The Immigrant Association of North Africa
The Immigrant Association of Morocco
The Immigrant Association of Tunisia
The Immigrant Association of Egypt
The Immigrant Association of Ethiopia*
The Federation of South Africa
The Immigrant Association of America and Canada*
The Immigrant Association of Latin America*
The Immigrant Association of Brazil*
The Joint Organization of Romania
The Immigrant Association of Romania
The Immigrant Organization of Italy
The Immigrant Organization of Holland
The Immigrant Association of the United Kingdom*
The Immigrant Association of Hungary
The Coordination Committee of Immigration Activities

SOURCE: Ministry of Immigrant Absorption, Department of Social Absorption (1984). mimeo. 1.1. (Hebrew)
     *Association or key informant interviewed.

References

Association of Americans and Canadians in Israel, March 1986. "Constitution." Kfar
     Maccabiah (Mimeo).
Association of Ethiopian Immigrants in Israel, September 1985. "A Proposal for
     Strengthening an Indigenous Self-Help, Non-Profit National Association
     of Ethiopian Immigrants in Israel." Jerusalem: (Mimeo).

Cooley, C. H. 1955. "Primary groups." In Paul Hare et al., eds., *Small Groups*. New York: Knopf.

Doron, A. April 1976. "The Societal Context for Social Welfare." In Doron, ed., *Cross-National Studies of Social Service Systems—Israel*, pp. 1–27. Jerusalem: Ministry of Labor and Social Affairs.

Eisenstadt, S. N. 1956. "The Social Conditions of the Development of Voluntary Association: A Case Study of Israel." In R. Bachi, ed., *Scripta Hierosolumitana*, 3:104–25. Jerusalem: The Hebrew University.

Elazar, D. and A. Dortort, eds. May 1984. *Understanding the Jewish Agency: A Handbook*. Jerusalem: Jerusalem Center for Public Affairs.

Honig, M. and N. Shamai. 1978. "Israel." In S. Kamerman and A. Kahn, eds., *Family Policy: Government and Families in Fourteen Countries*, pp. 400–27. New York: Columbia University Press.

Jenkins, S. 1981. *The Ethnic Dilemma in Social Services*. New York: Free Press.

JAI (The Jewish Agency for Israel). Budget Division. 1985. "Proposed Budget for the Year 1985/86."

Judge, K. March 1981. "The Mixed Economy of Social Care: Purchase of Service Contracting in the U.S." Unpublished discussion paper.

Kamerman, S. B. 1981. "The Public and the Private Intertwined: The New Mixed Economy of Welfare." Paper presented at the Seventh NASW Professional Symposium, Philadelphia, Pa.

Kast, F. E. and J. E. Rosenzweig. 1979. *Organization and Management*. 3d ed. New York: McGraw-Hill.

Korazim, J. 1983. "Israeli Families in New York: Utilization of Social Services, Unmet Needs and Policy Implications." Unpublished doctoral dissertation, Columbia University School of Social Work. For a summary of the dissertation see: *Journal of Jewish Communal Service* (Summer 1985), 61(4): 330–41.

Korazim, Josef. 1985. "Raising Children in Ambivalent Immigrant Families: Israelis in New York." *Children and Youth Services Review*, 7: 353–62.

Kramer, R. M. 1976. *The Voluntary Service Agency in Israel*. Research Series, no. 26. Berkeley, Calif.: University of California at Berkeley, Institute of International Studies, pp. 10–14.

Litwak, E. and J. Figuera. 1960. "Technological Innovation and Theoretical Functions of Primary Groups and Bureaucratic Structures." *American Journal of Sociology* 73:468–81.

Macarov, D. 1978. "Service Delivery at the Neighborhood Level in Israel." In D. Thursz and J. Vigilante, eds., *Reaching People*, pp. 115–23. London: Sage.

MIA (Ministry of Immigrant Absorption). 1984. "Immigration and Absorption: Developments and Trends." Jerusalem: "Know Israel" Series.

Neipris, J. 1981. *Social Welfare and Social Services in Israel: Policies, Programs and Current Issues*, pp. 3–16. Jerusalem: School of Social Work, Hebrew University.

Utting, B. December 1980. "Purchase of Personal Social Services by Government Agencies in the United States." Report to the German Marshall Fund of the United States.

Weber, M. 1947. *The Theory of Social and Economic Organizations.* A. M. Henderson and T. Parsons trs. New York: Oxford University Press.

5.

Minorities Policies, Social Services, And Ethnic Organizations in the Netherlands

Hein de Graaf, Rinus Penninx, and Errol F. Stoové

Historical Background

In the period of reconstruction following World War II, public opinion in the Netherlands felt that the country was overpopulated. The emigration of Dutch inhabitants was therefore strongly encouraged: between 1946 and 1972 no fewer than 481,000 Dutch citizens went abroad for permanent settlement through the intermediary of the Directorate for Emigration. Immigration, on the other hand, was to be avoided and even prevented, a view that, frequently repeated in government documents, almost de-

Hein de Graaf is senior researcher at the Netherlands Institute for Social Work Research in the Hague and is responsible for this paper's section on "Recent Data on Ethnic Associations." Rinus Penninx is senior researcher at the Staff Department for Research and Development of the Ministry of Welfare, Public Health and Culture. He is responsible for the "Historical Background" and "Social Services and Ethnic Organizations" sections of this paper. Errol F. Stoové is director for the Welfare of Ethnic Minorities of the Ministry of Welfare, Public Health and Culture; he contributed to the latter section. Acknowledgment is made to the editor of *International Migration* for his permission to reprint part of the article by Mr. Penninx published in *International Migration* (Winter 1984), Vol. 22.

veloped into an ideology; the nonexistence of immigration was not unmasked as fiction until after the mid-1970s. Extensive immigration flows did in fact take place, even though newcomers were consistently labeled with terms other than "immigrant." They were called "repatriates" (although the greater part of them had never been in this *patria*); they included Amboinese (Moluccan) ex-soldiers of the Royal Dutch East Indies Army (KNIL), "guest workers," and former inhabitants of Surinam and the Dutch Antilles.

In order to describe the development from the above-mentioned situation to recent minorities policy, postwar immigration will first be discussed, followed by an analysis of factors that have contributed to the fundamental change in government policy.

Immigration to the Netherlands Since 1945

The first extensive immigration flow was that of the repatriates who went to the Netherlands prior to and after Indonesian independence. An estimated 250,000 to 300,000 people arrived between 1946 and 1962 (Kraak et al. 1957). The majority of this flow comprised people of mixed Indonesian-Dutch descent, who were entitled to settle in the Netherlands on the grounds of their citizenship. In colonial society they had belonged to the middle and upper levels of government and business, and their educational levels generally ranged from reasonable to high.

They were strongly Netherlands oriented (that is to say, oriented to the Netherlands such as it was known in the colonies). After a somewhat hesitant beginning, public authorities and private organizations provided an orientation program which aimed at the quick adjustment and assimilation of the newcomers into Dutch society. Favorable conditions prevailed, there was an expansive growth of the economy and the labor market and active support on the part of private organizations, and the migrants were well motivated (Ex 1966).

This process developed quite differently in the case of Moluccan ex-KNIL soldiers. Under pressure from political developments in Indonesia a number of soldiers in Java who had not yet been demobilized forced their own and their families' departure for the Netherlands in 1951 by means of a court sentence. They themselves, as well as the Dutch government, considered their stay as temporary and they intended to settle in a (never realized) free republic of the Moluccans at a later date. They were temporarily housed in camps and fully looked after. Ten years after their arrival this temporary housing had become untenable and, in a number of municipalities, residential areas were then built especially for Moluccans. In certain respects the conditions for adjustment or assimilation of this group to Dutch society were unfavorable: neither government policy nor the group itself was so oriented. The mode of housing—first the camps and later the usually closed residential areas—did not promote the mutual adjustment of newcomers and the surrounding society. This group's ability to participate in Dutch society was very limited: hardly any spoke Dutch and their level of education was low. Over the course of the years, the group of families that originally arrived—about 12,500 people in all—increased to an estimated 42,000 people of Moluccan descent in 1986.

The ambivalent government policy with regard to this group was not changed until 1978, after a series of dramatic occupations and train sieges by Moluccan youths had demonstrated its total failure. In a policy bill, published at the time, past mistakes were acknowledged and new lines were set—which may be regarded as a preamble to the general minorities policy which followed two years later ("Ambonezen in Nederland" 1959; Bartels 1986).

The arrival of massive groups of migrant workers from the Mediterranean countries was precipitated by a rapid economic expansion in the Netherlands after 1950. The government regarded "guest labor" as a means of removing temporary bottlenecks in labor supply. At first the initiative was taken by industry, but from 1968 onwards this labor migration became government controlled, and stricter rules came into effect for recruitment, admission and employment. The Netherlands has almost exclusively recruited unskilled and semiskilled workers, mainly from the countryside, whose education is poor. Their orientation is ambivalent; annual return migration decreased to low levels but percentages reporting desire to return remain relatively high.

After the 1973 oil crisis, the recruitment of labor became insignificant in the Netherlands. This was not the case for immigration, however, for in precisely that period family reunification began to increase, culminating in the peak years of 1979–1980. Since 1981 family migration has been strongly decreasing. By January 1, 1985, 335,000 people were living in the Netherlands who were nationals of one of the Mediterranean countries (as against 196,000 on January 1, 1976). The largest group is made up of Turks (156,000), followed by Moroccans (111,000) and Spaniards (21,000).

Until the end of the 1970s, the government policy for this group was passive and ad hoc, for it was assumed that they were only working temporarily, and therefore limited facilities were required for relief and assistance. The Ministry of Social Affairs was the first responsible department for policy, as "guest labor" was primarily a labor market policy. For a long time the Ministry of Welfare was the only department concerned with the effects of the (ever longer) stay of these migrants. Greatly increased family reunification, with the consequences arising from it, made a new comprehensive policy necessary (Penninx 1979, 1984; Shadid 1979).

Until 1965 migration from Surinam was small and mainly consisted of students. In the mid-1960s, however, more migrants arrived—mostly of Creole descent—in search of work. This flow reached its peak in 1973–75—the period prior to Surinamese independence, and included ethnic groups of Hindustanis, Javanese, and Chinese. A second immigration peak occurred in 1979–1980 before "the agreement with regard to settlement and residence of mutual subjects" was due to expire, after which date settlement in the Netherlands would become much more difficult. In all, about 140,000 people born in Surinam resided in the Netherlands on January 1, 1983, almost 90 percent of them Dutch citizens, and the number of people of Surinamese descent, including children born in the Netherlands, was estimated at about 185,000.

Since migration from Surinam is very recent, and the group is heterogeneous both ethnically and in levels of education, it is difficult to assess the adjustment process. It is clear that economic conditions at the time of their arrival and after can hardly be called favorable, and the Surinamese are more easily victims of stigmatization and discrimination because of their physical recognizability. At first there was almost no government policy with respect to this group; such policy did not really take effect until 1975. The mode of dealing with this group, as well as the facilities provided, are exact copies of those used for repatriates from Indonesia. However, the social basis for an adequate absorption policy and the mobilization of private organizations seems much smaller than at the time when the repatriates arrived (van Amersfoort 1982; Penninx 1979).

Migration from the Dutch Antilles, which form part of the kingdom so that migration is unrestricted, also started in the mid-1960s, stimulated by recruitment on the part of Dutch industry. In the 1970s, the group of Antilleans increased steadily—a migration surplus of some 2,500 per year. On January 1, 1983 the number of people of Antillean descent was estimated at approximately 42,000. The group is heterogeneous and there is not much well-founded information on the situation of Antilleans in the Netherlands.

In addition to the above groups, three categories are worth mentioning as minorities: the Chinese, the refugees, and the gypsies. The first settlement of Chinese in the Netherlands consisted of Chinese sailors who, after the shipping crisis in the 1930s, stayed behind in Amsterdam and Rotterdam. After the war they developed into a group of Chinese-Indonesian restaurant owners. The number of Chinese immigrants in the Netherlands is estimated at approximately 20,000.

The category of admitted and invited refugees in the Netherlands is very heterogeneous. Among the older refugees are the Hungarians (1956) and Czechs (1968). In recent years Ugandans, Chileans, Argentinians, Uruguayans, and Vietnamese have been invited to find refuge in the Netherlands. For these refugees the Netherlands as always had an intensive policy for reception and assistance; this is not true, however, for individual asylum seekers. The number of acknowledged refugees who have gone to the Netherlands after 1975 is over 10,000.

Finally, in the Netherlands there are 2,000-2,500 gypsies

who have been residing here for many generations and are Dutch nationals. A much smaller group of some 200 was admitted shortly after World War II, and most of them are now Dutch nationals. A group of some 700 foreign gypsies were legalized in 1977 and a policy aimed at integration was developed for this group.

Policy Before 1979 and the Development of New Concepts

The arrival of the different categories of migrants took place at various times, for various reasons, against the background of a generally accepted view that the Netherlands neither was, nor was to become, an immigration country. Attempts were made to restrict these migration flows as much as possible, but stopping them was politically unfeasible and unjustifiable. The immigrants were almost always defined as "temporary residents." This was particularly true for the "guest workers," but also for the Moluccans, the Surinamese, and originally even for the repatriates.

This idea of temporality led to a two-track policy: a certain amount of adjustment to, and participation in, Dutch society was considered necessary for the period during which these migrants were to stay in the Netherlands. This adjustment "while retaining cultural identity" was not aimed, however, at residence of long or possibly permanent duration, but rather at an expected return.

Responsibility for policy and coordination was placed with the department most involved with each group of migrants. In the case of the guest workers this was the Ministry of Social Affairs; in the case of the Surinamese, Antilleans, and Moluccans, the Ministry of Welfare; in the case of refugees, the Ministry of Foreign Affairs, and for other groups there was no policy at all.

In the 1970s it became increasingly apparent that government policy and its underlying views were inadequate. More and more the matter of temporality was brought up for discussion: the family reunification of foreign workers, the increasing period of residence, and a sharp fall in return migration of almost all immigrant groups were noted. Meanwhile the sharply increasing number of immigrants, combined with the turning economic tide, made it clear that a limited policy—mainly implemented in the welfare sector—was totally insufficient to guarantee the newcomers a reasonable position in the Dutch society: the more so because most of the recent immigrants came from the lower economic classes, had relatively little education and were, in many cases, badly equipped for quick absorption into the Dutch society. In addition, the majority of the immigrants settled in the four big cities and a number of industrialized centers and this exacerbated existing problems of unemployment, housing, and education.

Another matter of confusion was that policy and programs were different for each of these groups. Although each group did present different needs, it became clear that there was a common denominator for all of the newcomers. An important common source of integration problems appeared to be the Dutch society itself, selection mechanisms within it, and the inaccessibility to it on the part of the immigrants.

Research and public opinion polls have shown that the social climate, as well as the attitude of individual Dutchmen toward immigrants, have become more unfavorable during the past decade and that discrimination is demonstrable in a number of fields. In spite of this, however, quite a few Dutchmen show no signs of prejudice in their dealings with these immigrants and local groups, and by themselves or together with groups of migrants have often constituted themselves as defenders of the rights and interests of immigrants. Of even greater importance might be the fact that over the course of the years the Ministry of Welfare has granted considerable subsidies to private institutions on behalf of their reception of and assistance to immigrants.

Of quite a different order, but no less influential, have been the violent actions of a number of young Moluccans: the occupations and train sieges. These actions have clearly had a negative effect, but at the same time for many people they provided an eye opener to a long-suppressed problem and an impetus to a completely different policy.

The most important scholarly impetus in favor of a change of policy was provided in the report "Ethnic Minorities" (1979) by the Scientific Council for Governmental Policy. The reason why this report exercised such great influence was not so much that the ideas that it contained were new, but rather because the report gives a policy-directed synthesis of the state of knowledge, and a systematic confrontation of this knowledge with policy. The fact that controversies because of party politics did not occur with regard to the "minorities problem" seems to be of importance with regard to the development of minorities policy (Entzinger 1985; Ethnic Minorities 1979).

General Minorities Policy Since 1980

The main lines of minorities policy in the Netherlands and its development during the past few years can easily be followed with the help of three government documents: 1) the "Government's Reaction to the report 'Ethnic Minorities' of the Scientific Council for Government Policy" (March 1980); 2) the "Draft Minorities Bill" (April 1981); and 3) the final "Minorities Bill" (September 1983). The structure of these documents is generally similar.

The view of the position and the future of minority groups in the Dutch society—the analysis underlying government policy—is mainly derived from the report (see *Ethnic Minorities* 1979:1–40)of the Scientific Council for Government Policy. The government assumes that a great number of the members of minority groups who are at the moment residing in the Netherlands will stay there permanently, and also assumes that their number will increase considerably as a result of family reunification and births. (In the final bill this last supposition of growth has become less important due to the decrease of both immigration and births to immigrants since 1981.) The government states that enormous consequences for society and policy follow from this datum. The situation involves groups of different cultural backgrounds, different styles of living, and different standards and values, which might lead to cultural confrontations—at which point immigrants would form the weakest party.

There is a danger of cultural and social isolation of immigrant groups, unless a mutual adjustment of immigrants and the receiving society is pursued and realized. Furthermore, it is thought that this danger of social isolation and deprivation is relatively greater for immigrant groups than for the autochthonous population, because the immigrants have to secure a place in society from a very unfavorable starting position. At times of economic stagnation, or even economic decline, selection mechanisms usually work to the disadvantage of the socially deprived. Immigrants have to cope with an added number of handicaps; they are insufficiently familiar with Dutch society and the Dutch language; the foreigners among them often have a weak legal position; organizations and institutions in charge of granting work, housing, and educational facilities often appear to be less accessible to these newcomers and, lastly, prejudice and discrimination may form serious impediments. Essentially, the possibility of minority formation is clearly acknowledged. The term "minority" is defined here as a group, a vast majority of whom have had—measured by objective standards—a low position for generations and for whom effective participation in regular political decision making is impossible, a group that has its own culture, or at least particular cultural characteristics, and that the rest of society considers to be a separate group. Minority formation is the process leading to such a situation (van Amersfoort 1982). Consequently a policy is needed to counter such minority formation.

The following quotation shows the objectives of the minorities policy: "Minorities policy aims at establishing a society in which the members of minority groups who reside in the Netherlands, both individually and as a group, take an equal position and have full-fledged opportunities for developing. This main objective has been divided into three points. . . . a) creating such conditions as are necessary to enable minority groups to emancipate and participate in society. The possibility of mutual adjustment and acceptance of all groups within the total population must be promoted . . . ; b) decreasing the social and economic deprivation of members of minority groups; and c) preventing discrimination and fighting it wherever it occurs, and also improving legal positions where necessary" ("Draft Minorities Bill" 1981:35–36; "Minorities Bill" 1983:10).

Some aspects of these formulations are obvious: they are fundamental and also very ambitious. It is not surprising, therefore, that these objectives are not brought up for discussion among either the minority groups themselves or among the Dutch, by whom they are widely endorsed. The discussion is rather about the matter of priorities within the ambitious objectives and about the interpretation of these; in the practical execution of policy the government emphasizes the fight against deprivation, whereas representatives of organizations of minority groups strongly support policy measures that aim at the "strengthening of identity" and "emancipation within the group."

Of importance is the use of the term "minorities." In the Minorities Bill the term "minority formation," as developed by van Amersfoort (1982), is referred to implicitly. According to van Amersfoort's terminology, one can only speak of minorities once it has been demonstrated that for a number of generations immigrants have chosen, or have been allocated, a fixed, socially low, and politically and culturally isolated position. In the government documents, however, the term is used differently: all groups who, in van Amersfoort's definition, would be in danger of minority formation, are called minority groups. Thus the Dutch minorities policy is not an immigrant policy as such, but a policy aimed at particular deprived groups with a separate culture who are supposed to be different and who, on the basis of these two characteristics, are in danger of stigmatization, or have already been stigmatized.

The policy enunciated also included the goal of a pluralistic society. In practice this is not easy to achieve, and raises the question of whether cultural pluralism is not at odds with fighting and abolishing social deprivation. More funds need to be made available for the execution of this minorities policy. It has ambitious goals; the government states that the policy should be aimed at reducing the amount of deprivation of minority groups within the framework of a general antideprivation policy for all groups; special group-specific facilities would only be created where nothing else is possible.

A further aspect of the situation is that the government considers a restrictive admissions policy to the country to be an important condition for the success of the minorities policy. New settlement would be prevented, but family reunification of legal residents would be granted on humanitarian grounds. In practice, this is a difficult policy to execute.

A further condition for the policy's implementation is co-ordination at various governmental levels, in particular with the municipalities taking a major role in its execution. Finally, the new governmental policy is explicit on the issue of the participation of minority groups in policy. There has been heated discussion on the shape of this participation; a diverse group of national organizations have been consulted, ranging from special advisory councils for each ethnic group, to representatives of the various welfare organizations, to leaders of organizations of minorities that have developed on their own. In the final Minorities Bill a general advisory council of minorities, with subcouncils for the various groups, was proposed, and in 1985 such a structure, with eight subcouncils, was realized.

Research continues to play an important part in the formulation, preparation, and adjustment of policy. The Advisory Committee for Research Concerning Minorities, which was set up by the Minister of Welfare in 1978, has the status of an external advisory body with respect to programming all minorities research. The fact of government funding is both an advantage and a disadvantage in this enterprise.

Social Services and Ethnic Organizations

Students of the process of the absorption of immigrants into a new society have noted that the absorption process is largely determined by the receiving society and its institutions. One relevant question is therefore whether existing institutions will cooperate in attaining the desired final situation. Another is what part organizations of immigrants will play in this process. In the Dutch context it is important to understand the rather special relations between minority policies, social services, and the part played by organizations of the target groups.

In the Netherlands two phenomena dominate the way in which social services are organized. The first is the religious polarization or compartmentalization of Dutch society, and consequently of social service delivery. This means that in every city or town social service institutions of the major religious groups are functioning: one for Protestants, one for Catholics, one for "humanists," one for Jews, and so forth. The second peculiar characteristic is that all of these institutions began and are managed by private initiators who have joined forces in a foundation or an association. These foundations and associations are paid by national, provincial, and/or local authorities to perform certain tasks, such as offering professional social work services. In such a specific context—of a limited and ambivalent policy toward immigrants as it existed before 1980 on the one hand and a very specific structure of the welfare sector on the other hand—the resulting network of institutions is indeed complex. This can be seen from a few illustrations of the earlier period.

Social Services for Immigrants in the 1950s and Early 1960s

In the case of the repatriates from Indonesia a central reception plan, initiated and implemented by the national government, culminated in the assignment of housing for all repatriates. Social services to these newcomers after they had been permanently housed, however, were supplied by the existing social service institutions of the various religious denominations. The repatriates themselves were religiously rather heterogeneous, and each of the social work institutions was supposed to take up social work tasks for its own members. Indonesian repatriates never claimed special treatment or separate institutions with regard to social and welfare work; on the contrary, in general, they aimed at quick absorption and equal treatment by existing institutions (van Amersfoort 1982).

The situation of the Moluccan ex-KNIL soldiers was defined quite differently by themselves and by the government: they were here temporarily, placed in camps and fully cared for by a special division of the central government. There developed a strong political and religious organization of Moluccans within the camps and settlement areas, but policy implementation, including social services, was done by a national government institution.

In the case of social services for the temporary guest workers, the first initiatives were private efforts, usually in the form of Catholic community work or conducted by company representatives. In 1964 the Ministry of Welfare began to subsidize these organizations, which took on the form of foundations. The ministry itself did nothing to set up administrative bodies for the purpose of implementing social services, but relied completely on private initiatives. The percentage of subsidized social service activities of such foundations increased from 40 percent in 1964 to 100 percent in 1975. Later, when non-Catholic, mainly Muslim migrant workers also started to come to the Netherlands, the foundations for Assistance to Foreign Workers lost their initial Catholic image: they became group specific, working only for migrant workers. Organizations of migrants were virtually non-existent at that time and, as far as they existed, they were ignored in the network of social service institutions.

The first group-specific Foundation for the Welfare of Surinamese immigrants in the Netherlands was founded somewhat later. The procedures were the same, with private initiators starting social activities, which were subsidized by the authorities. The difference was that many of the initiators were themselves of Surinamese origin, from earlier migrations.

In none of the cases cited was it the philosophy of the governmental authorities or of the private initiators that organizations of immigrants could or should play an important part in the network of social services offered. Ethnic participants were present only in the case of the Surinamese Foundations, mainly because of the presence of a sizable established elite of that group already in the Netherlands.

Community Development as a Frame of Reference

In the second half of the 1960s the philosophy of community development became popular in the Netherlands: the general idea that all those living within a certain territory should form a community and that everybody should be stimulated to participate actively in the development of that community. This concept became the reference for a large part of the welfare policy developed at that time, and the special Community Development Division was created apart from the existing Social Work Division (which included all facilities aimed at repairing or easing the social problems of individuals) and also apart from the Cultural Work Division (which included all facilities contributing to the social, artistic, or scientific development of individuals).

The existing group-specific foundations were brought under the direction of the Community Development Division in the second half of the 1960s. Government attitudes became less passive than before, and a series of tasks were subsidized. These included: informing and educating the Dutch population about immigrants and minorities and their backgrounds and, conversely, informing and educating immigrants and minorities about Dutch society and their particular position in it; cooperating with groups of immigrants in the promotion of activities on their behalf; cooperating with organizations and services that offered effective assistance; managing and running meeting centers and other facilities to help achieve these goals; and in general cooperating with the authorities and organizations working for community development. Thus the essential work at hand was influencing group relations in a positive sense, and keeping this activity within the community development framework.

As it turned out, however, theory and practice clashed. The boundaries of social work, cultural work, and community development work were already debatable in cases where no immigrants were involved, and where immigrants were in the picture these boundaries became even more vague or did not exist at all. The foundations, which were group specific, took on all kinds of problems and did social and cultural work as well as community development. In fact the greater part of their work for the foreign workers and Surinamese was in helping individual immigrants not only with material problems but also with personal social services.

For the Moluccans the situation was different, since there were no historically evolved foundations at the end of the 1960s. When nationally controlled social service delivery was abolished in 1970, fifty-two new foundations for the Welfare of Moluccans were established and subsidized in nearly all settlement areas. These foundations differ from the ones for foreign workers and

Surinamese immigrants in that they do not engage in social-work activities, but concentrate almost completely on cultural and, to a lesser extent, community development tasks.

Welfare Policy as Part of the General Minorities Policy: 1980–1986

The introduction of a comprehensive general minorities policy as described earlier in this paper had very important consequences. The new definition of the situation (i.e., that the majority of the immigrants had come to stay) and of the goals of government policy (i.e., that the formation of a new underclass in society should be prevented) has led to two major discussions and developments in the welfare sector. The first one involves the part played by the immigrants themselves and their organizations in the formation and implementation of policies. The second is the renewed discussion of the division of tasks between group-specific foundations for immigrants and the public social service institutions.

Government policy since 1980 has been very explicit on the issue of participation in the formation of policy. Comprehensive advisory procedures, and a national advisory body of representatives of ethnic minorities, with eight subcommittees, have been established. The participation of minorities in municipal elections has been made possible and encouraged. Another important factor is that the Ministry of Welfare has demanded of the municipalities that they ask for the participation and advice of ethnic organizations in the formation and implementation of municipal welfare policies. Ethnic organizations should be stimulated, in the vision of the new policy, to act as a "link" between Dutch society and its institutions, on the one hand, and members of the immigrant communities, on the other. They can be subsidized by the municipal authorities and, in principle, a number of tasks formerly the prerogative of the foundations can now be carried out by local ethnic organizations.

This new situation is closely connected to the second important development: the reshifting and redistribution of tasks to be carried out by various organizations and institutions. The debate on reshuffling of tasks has two dimensions: the first is on the decentralization of the largest part of the welfare programs; whereas formerly funds were given directly from the ministry to institutions, in the new plan the municipal authorities receive funds to organize welfare programs. Secondly, the debate on the division of tasks among the different institutions on the local level was revived, and a new division was sought. New policies required that all public service institutions in the Netherlands should be accessible to immigrants, and should acquire the special expert knowledge to help them; the old group-specific foundations should give up their former social and cultural work activities, but continue community development activities and render service both to public service institutions and to organizations of immigrants; the municipal authorities should ask for participation and advice from ethnic organizations with respect to ethnic minority policies; and finally, ethnic organizations should be eligible for subsidization to implement these tasks and to carry out certain parts of the policy, e.g., cultural activities.

If this new formulation is looked at from a distance, it may be concluded that immigrants as a group and ethnic organizations have won quite an influence in the new situation in comparison with earlier periods. At the same time it is clear, however, that the term "emancipation," as applied to immigrant groups and ethnic organizations in Dutch policies, has a very special connotation. The greater part of the measures and facilities of the general minorities policy work on an individual level, aiming at the improvement of the position of the individual immigrant in Dutch society. The number of measures that could be said to have a bearing on a kind of collective emancipation of the group through their own institutions is limited. For example, ethnic organizations are asked to voice their opinions on minorities policies on the national and local level, but they are not asked to implement important parts of it. The idea of special schools for immigrants is vehemently discouraged, and the idea that ethnic organizations themselves could possibly run social services and welfare facilities in general for their own group did not occur to anyone in the pre-1980 period, and was still nonexistent afterwards. On the contrary the group-specific foundations, which actually performed part of these tasks before and which gradually became staffed with more and more people from the groups themselves, have been restyled and given limited and second-line tasks, while the primary functions have to be fulfilled by existing public institutions.

It is clear that the recent developments do not show an institutional pluralism; policy development is not directed toward separate institutions for different groups. This does not necessarily mean, however, that cultural pluralism does not or cannot exist; that depends on the openness and accessibility of the society as a whole. What is clear from the total picture of Dutch minorities policies is that equal opportunities and a reasonable social position have received more attention and support in policy than have collective emancipation measures.

Recent Data on Ethnic Organizations

This book is concerned with the way in which ethnic organizations function in welfare states, in particular with regard to the needs of new immigrants. For the Netherlands, the extended exposition of the particular nature of their immigration, and the resultant minorities policies generated by the population changes, was necessary background information to understand the actual operations of the many ethnic associations. This section will include material on the associations derived from three different sources. The first is a national survey conducted by the Ministry of Welfare of 2,158 associations. Second, the questionnaire used in the New York study, reported on in paper 2, was used in a special interview sample of eight associations, and the results are reported. Finally, data from an investigation of Turkish and Moroccan associations in Holland is drawn on for a case example of the issues and problems of an ethnic association for one group of guest workers.

National Survey of Ethnic Associations

Early in 1985 the Ministry of Welfare requested its civil servants in the provinces to complete a questionnaire on ethnic associations in the Netherlands. The reason for the request was to obtain more knowledge on how they functioned. Presumably the development of the new minorities policies had generated interest in an expanded role for these groups.

In filling in these questionnaires, different sources were used. These included the associations themselves, the local authorities, and data of the provincial offices of the ministry. This mix of sources may have affected the results, and this needs to be taken into account. The data were analyzed by one of the authors of this paper (de Graaf), and the outcome of this survey was published by the ministry in February 1986, in a limited number of copies.

Of the 2,158 associations included in the survey, 19 percent were Turkish, 17 percent were Surinamese, 15 percent were Moluccan, and 10 percent were Moroccan. In addition, 19 percent had members of different nationalities. Nearly all of the associations functioned on local levels; only 2 percent, or 49 associations, functioned on a national level.

As can be expected from the numbers, most associations have but a few active members. Seventy percent report having about twenty active members. In addition to their own group, 17 percent, or 457 associations, reported having voluntary workers of Dutch background among their members.

Most of the associations claim to be of service to their whole ethnic group, or to the whole group with the exception of the elderly. There are not many youth clubs among them (12 percent or 250 associations), and only 4.5 percent, or 96 associations, reported special groups for women. Eighty percent said that their association had a place where they could meet, but only half of these had the place to themselves; the other associations shared their meeting centers with other groups. Seventy percent of the total number of over two thousand groups reported receiving some government support.

The associations were requested to state their three major activities, in order of importance. The results are shown in figure 5.1. The majority of associations stated that the socio-cultural aspects of their activities, mainly recreational programs, were the most important. Second in importance was representing the interests of the group. Giving advice and information was noted to

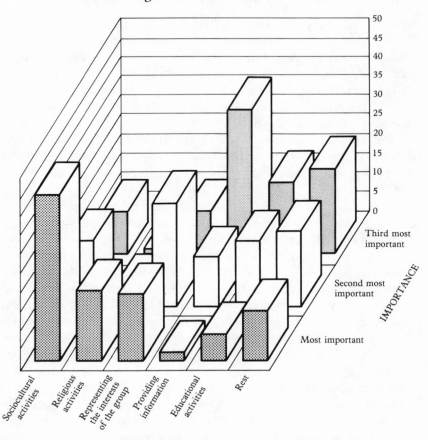

Figure 5.1. Activities of Ethnic Associations by Activity and Importance

SOURCE: This diagram was constructed by Hein de Graaf using the data of the questionnaire of the Ministry of Welfare, with its permission, for the purpose of this paper.

be the third most important activity. Only about 10 percent of the associations in the survey mentioned the delivery of social services as an important part of their functions.

Of those associations that felt that providing social services was an important part of their activities only 10 percent rated this as their most important function, and 45 percent each rated it as second and third in significance. Of the associations that did provide social services, 30 percent are Moluccan, although they make up only 15 percent of the total number of ethnic organizations. People of Moluccan origin are known for providing social services for their own group, and the earlier discussion of their circumstances upon arrival in the Netherlands and thereafter may explain this phenomenon.

In general the national survey confirms the existence of many different organizations of persons of the same ethnic background, but these organizations tend to be small, local, and primarily concerned with recreational activities, advocacy, and information and advice, rather than the delivery of personal social services.

Interviews with Eight Associations

In order to compare the Dutch associations with the American group, a sample of eight organizations was selected to be viewed, using the same instrument that was used in the New York study. The associations will be described briefly, and information given on their goals, activities, membership, and responses to the items on identity and acculturation. The group of eight included three Turkish organizations, two with members who were Moluccan, and one each with members who were Moroccan, Surinamese, and Antillean.

The first Turkish association was a federation, an umbrella organization established in 1979. Its members are local Turkish Islamic associations. There is a board of three leaders, each with a special assignment. One keeps contact with the Dutch authorities, one keeps informed on developments in Turkey, and one concerns himself with the Turkish people in the Netherlands. This organization is supported by contributions from its members, and the group does not receive any government grants.

The second Turkish association is a left-wing organization of Turkish laborers, which has local associations in several Dutch towns, and an umbrella organization in Amsterdam. It is a relatively small organization, putting its emphasis on representing the interests of Turkish laborers in the Netherlands. This group, which started in 1974, does receive government grants.

The third Turkish association started in 1981, and is essentially a local group. It has no formal members, but the leadership committee consists of seven men. It organizes many activities for the benefit of local Turkish people, keeps in contact with the local authorities, and has recently started a translating center. It has its own meeting place.

A Moluccan church organization was also interviewed. This group was founded in 1973 by the Evangelical Protestant Moluccan church. They had five trained social workers on their staff. They used to be supported by their church, but since 1978 they receive government grants. Their main goal is reported to be providing social services for their members. Also interviewed was a Moluccan women's organization. This is a loosely organized group consisting of seven active members. They report their main goal to be "representing the interests" of all Moluccan women in the Netherlands. They got started in 1979, and receive government grants for their working expenses.

A Moroccan youth association, begun in 1985, was based on the unification of three former Moroccan youth clubs in Rotterdam. They receive government grants and their main objective is "representing the interests" of the local Moroccan youth. Their most important activity, however, is organizing social evenings in their meeting center.

A Surinamese women's association, with the ambitious goal of the emancipation of Hindustani women, was also interviewed. This group, which began in 1983, has a total of forty-five members and a leadership committee of three members. They receive a small government grant. Until the present, they have not had a meeting place of their own.

Finally, an Antillean organization was interviewed. This is one of the older associations, having started in 1963. Its main purpose is to organize social gatherings. It also fulfills the function of representing the interests of the local Antillean people. In principle every man or woman in the city and the surrounding area is a "member." There are forty voluntary workers who organize social activities, but the final responsibility lies with their committee, consisting of five people.

GOALS AND ACTIVITIES

It should be stressed that the ethnic associations in Holland are relatively young. Although the Antillean association was founded in 1963 and the Moluccan church organization in 1973, the other associations have just started. All of them, except for one, claimed that representing the interests of their group was their main goal. The Moluccan church organization was the only association that claimed that providing social services was their main objective. All associations see every member of their ethnic group as a possible member of their own organization.

Most of the associations do not have formal members. Some do not have any members at all. Others consider that everyone belonging to their ethnic group in that area is a member of their association. In general, these are small groups. Most of the associations actually have from ten to fifty active members, and five to ten who do the actual work. The majority of them may be considered to be instrumental leaders; in other words they were elected leaders because they are good organizers and not because of their family backgrounds.

The Turkish Islamic federation mainly concerns itself with negotiations with the authorities and supporting its local member associations. The Moluccan church organization has trained social workers on its staff who are primarily engaged in providing services for members. All other associations claim to be fulfilling all kinds of functions, from organizing courses and social evenings, to giving information, to maintaining contact with the local and national authorities. All of those interviewed, except for one, received government grants for their social activities and working expenses. The Islamic federation received its necessary funds from members. Contacts among groups are rarely made. They only come together at demonstrations against unwelcome government measures.

IDENTITY AND ACCULTURATION RESPONSES

Although the sample is small, there was interest in seeing how the association leaders would respond to the same questions on identity and acculturation asked in the New York study. For each of the items noted they were asked how important they were in their orientation to Dutch society, or how important they were in maintaining identity with the country of origin. Possible responses were "important," "unimportant," or "neither" (see table 5.1).

As can be seen from these responses, both acculturation and maintaining identity are considered to be important. The single item of most importance in both categories related to language—both retaining one's own and learning that of the host country.

It was interesting to find from questions pertaining to appreciation of the Dutch that, despite great differences in background and culture among the various immigrant groups, they were all more or less agreed on their perceptions of the Dutch people. They saw the Dutch people as less hospitable, less emotional, and less spontaneous than their own groups. They considered themselves to be more family minded than the Dutch, and saw the Dutch as having less respect for persons in authority. All

Table 5.1. Acculturation and Identity Items

Acculturation Items	Important	Neither	Unimportant
Speaking Dutch at home	3	2	3
Learning to speak Dutch	7	—	1
Celebrating Dutch holidays	2	4	2
Making Dutch friends	6	1	1
Learning to like Dutch food	—	5	3
Allowing teenagers to date Dutch friends	4	3	1
Belonging to Dutch associations	5	3	—
Moving to a neighborhood where only Dutch live	1	3	4
Identity Items			
Retaining the native language	7	—	1
Celebrating native holidays	6	1	1
Keeping in touch with the country of origin	6	1	1
Teaching children native customs	7	—	1
Preparing traditional food	3	3	2
Keeping contacts with people from the native village	3	3	2
Living in a neighborhood with people from the same ethnic group	2	2	4
Belonging to ethnic associations	6	—	2
Marrying in the same ethnic group	2	3	3

informants emphasized wanting to preserve their own values. They did not have definite ideas on the promotion of mutual tolerance.

According to the respondents, the major problems of the immigrants were unemployment and housing. Some expressed the opinion that, since younger people have no future prospects, they will cause trouble in the future. They did not feel that problems concerning education, divorce, or health could be solved by the ethnic associations.

Case Studies: Turkish and Moroccan Associations

With its changing stance on minorities and immigrants, two or three years ago policymaking related to immigrants came to be the chief responsibility of the local authorities. They also became the chief suppliers of government grants. National, and later, local policymakers expressed the hope that the ethnic associations themselves would primarily concentrate on representing the interests of their groups and, furthermore, would participate in decision making, give information and advice to their group, and organize courses.

This section of the paper will report on a field study conducted by one of the authors (de Graaf) in one large and six small towns in the Netherlands. The purpose was to see the new policy in action, to describe the proceedings of the associations, and to analyze the expectations of various parties, notably policymakers, of the association activities. Material presented draws on the report published on the local Turkish and Moroccan associations by de Graaf (1986).

Before discussing the study outcomes it is important to note how the word "association" has been used. In the de Graaf report that word is used even for those cases where it is only a matter of groups of people wanting to get together socially, groups who are tied by friendship or family bonds, place of origin, or language. To the outside world these groups call themselves associations because they are expected or requested to do so. Nevertheless these groups cannot be equated with the formal Dutch associations. They may more appropriately be compared to the informal

Dutch social clubs which would not necessarily consider themselves to be associations. Most of the time these Dutch social clubs do not feel the need to register as official associations, because that would imply having to go through all kinds of formal procedures—proving that they have a place to meet, the necessary supports, and money for the rent. On the other hand the ethnic groups, in more or less the same situation as these Dutch social clubs, actually do have important reasons to show themselves to be formal associations. They need government grants and, particularly in the case of the Islamic societies, they have to handle the contributions brought in by their members.

Given this conflict, it is understandable why the informants' replies to questions concerning their internal hierarchical structure, their procedures, and regulations with regard to elections tend to give a distorted view of the reality. The leaders feel obliged to translate the informal and haphazard activities of their associations into formal terms, because they are in fact seeking the association designation. The problem becomes most apparent when they are questioned about the number of members on their books. Most associations seem reluctant to answer this question, because they do not usually have formal subscribing members: they are faced with having to decide to declare as members only those on committees, those participating in club activities, or even all fellow countrymen in their area. Depending on how much importance seems to be attached to the response, and depending on the choices made, the number of association members may be reported as going all the way from about five to one hundred or more.

ASSOCIATION FUNCTIONS AND TARGET GROUPS

The ethnic associations fulfill a number of functions, which relate to four target groups. They can be classified as follows:

Club members. There are three main activities for this target group. These are giving shelter, giving support, and organizing sociocultural activities restricted to those members who participate. In giving shelter, the association fulfills the emotional needs of members by offering a meeting place where they can feel at home and be in familiar surroundings with like-minded people.

This creates an atmosphere of solidarity and togetherness. In supporting club members the association may supply goods and money, and also give advice and help with personal or family problems. This activity is most closely related to the issue of providing social services, as discussed earlier in this paper. This is a function fulfilled in only a limited sense by the Turkish and Moroccan associations. In the main, they give shelter and organize sociocultural activities.

Other ethnic group members. The association provides general, informal, noncollective activities which may indirectly affect others of their own ethnic group in their area. The objective is to influence the values, moral codes, and customs of the ethnic group, without the members of the group directly taking part in the club activities.

Local authorities. With the local authorities, the main focus is on representing the interests of the group. There are in fact two groups to represent. One is the ethnic association itself, and the other comprises also some, or all, of the fellow ethnics in the area.

Dutch population. This involves activities intended to influence the values, moral codes, and conduct of the Dutch population by means of social action or through the media.

CONFLICTING EXPECTATIONS

In accordance with the new policy mandates, the local authorities expect the ethnic associations to fulfill the following three functions: representing the interests of their group, organizing courses, and giving information. From the field study, however, it appears that there are in fact two main kinds of associations: recreational clubs and Islamic societies. These groups are, respectively, primarily engaged in either organizing recreational activities or furthering programs associated with their religious interests. Herein lies the conflict in expectations between what the authorities see as ethnic association functions, and the basic interests of the groups themselves. This is demonstrated in various ways, for each of the expected activities.

Representing group interests. The leadership of the associations have an important role to play in their activities, and they reflect their basic interests. The Islamic societies, for example, are concerned with promoting their religious beliefs. On the local level they have traditional leaders, mostly middle-aged men of prominent families, who hardly speak the Dutch language. They become leaders because they already have some authority in their local Islamic community. In contrast, the recreational clubs have leaders who are good organizers of social activities. They are an example of "instrumental" leaders. It is questionable, however, whether either of these leadership types are capable of representing their groups to the Dutch authorities. The religious leaders usually do not speak Dutch and religious matters are their only concern. As a rule they are not sought out by the Dutch authorities. The leaders of the social clubs, although good organizers, are not experienced negotiators. Nevertheless the local authorities and other Dutch institutions as well tend to consider them the spokesmen for the Turkish or Moroccan community in their area. This misconception is further promoted by the fact that the social clubs include the objective of representing the interests of the group as part of their association purpose. In most cases this may have been inserted at the suggestion of the Dutch advisers who may have indicated that this would be a better route to the receipt of government grants.

There are unfortunate consequences to this procedure. Social-club leaders seldom turn down offers to sit on decision-making bodies and advisory committees, positions that carry prestige and status. The advantage is not only personal, but appears to offer opportunities to advance group interests. Once involved in this way, however, leaders must give proof of their qualifications, and this often means reporting on the numbers of persons involved in their associations. Since the social clubs are by nature small and informal, the need to build up membership figures could lead to the padding of roles, and to subsequent accusations and investigations. All of this would be detrimental to the chosen leaders, who risk losing face with their own group as well as with the Dutch authorities.

There are other potential problems. Members of social clubs may have different opinions on policy issues, and could divide into separate groups in a struggle for representation. Furthermore, local authorities may be confronted with several different ethnic associations, all claiming to represent the interests of the ethnic group in their area. Thus instead of one well-organized and functioning social club, there could arise several badly functioning pseudo–interest societies.

The ill effects of wrongly regarding social clubs as societies of interest could induce concerned civil servants to look upon these ethnic associations as standing for nothing at all. Thus social clubs and religious societies would be well advised to avoid the designation of societies of interest, since it could negatively affect their functioning in their appropriate roles.

Course offerings. All social and religious associations reviewed had course offerings on their programs. These included language courses as well as those that teach a trade, such as typing or mechanics. The elaborate course offerings did not seem to be appropriate in view of the main purposes of these organizations. Furthermore, there are many educational courses presently given by the Foundation for Assistance to Immigrants, the local authorities, and Dutch voluntary workers. A possible explanation for this activity is that the leaders of these clubs anticipated that the subsidizing institutions preferred for them to organize educational courses, among their other activities, and that this would lead to larger subsidies than if they limited themselves to recreational or religious activities. There are problems involved, however, in this approach. For one thing, social and religious societies are not organized as educational institutions; furthermore, they lack qualified instructors, and this is not what the membership is interested in. They compete with other qualified educational institutions. If they are forced to recruit from outside their membership, club members will feel that the purposes of the association are being distorted. When an association or a club has a specific goal, but feels obliged to perform other functions that it cannot fulfill, the consequences will be negative both for the subsidizing institution and the ethnic association.

Information and advice. This is yet another area that associations are led to believe they should mention when reporting on their activities, since it is likely to lead to government subsidies. However, few are qualified to fulfill this role. It can be expected that there will be an exchange of information during social or religious gatherings. With regard to the religious groups, however it appears that Turkey is the main topic of discussion in the Turkish centers and mosques. The Islamic societies do reach many of their own people, but they have no contact with local Dutch institutions and therefore are not equipped to give information on Dutch society. Although some associations do give information they reach only small groups of people, and usually in a single session on a specific subject. The investigation led to the same conclusion as the previous ones: the social clubs and the Islamic societies are not suited, because of their nature, to give information on Dutch society.

EXTERNAL RELATIONS OF ASSOCIATIONS

There are several ways in which the ethnic associations interact with institutions in the Dutch society. These will be discussed, together with some of the attendant problems.

The Foundations for Assistance to Foreign Workers. As we have seen in section 2 of this paper, the Netherlands has organizations called Foundations for Assistance to Foreign Workers (FAFW), which are Dutch-run institutions whose purpose is to help foreign workers and their families in various ways. In the past few years there have been policy changes affecting their operations. In January 1986 the FAFW transferred to the local authorities their function of supplying government grants to ethnic associations. They also transferred their "direct support" to foreign workers to the regular social-welfare institutions. The FAFW was left with the task of engaging in the "structural support to ethnic associations."

This shift in function has led to some problems. For one thing, FAFW specialists who had been used to working with individuals and giving direct help were now supposed to work in the community with the ethnic group as a whole. This requires different skills and contacts, and a grasp of group problems. The relationships between the FAFW and the Turkish and Moroccan associations are often quite poor. The reasons are complex, but one could be that the people who have been giving direct services are now forced to play another and unfamiliar role, and one where they have limited capabilities.

Dutch voluntary workers. Only one club of all the ethnic associations studied in the six small towns had Dutch people directly involved. Matters are different in larger towns, however. From the beginning of the 1970s Dutch voluntary workers have been very concerned about the immigrants, and have started organizations intended to represent their interests, and have organized courses and recreational activities and supplied information. Without intent these Dutch "support organizations" and the ethnic associations who offer the same services became rivals. This has led to dissension, and to the gradual loss in importance, in conflict situations, of the ethnic associations made up of immigrants.

Two main categories of voluntary workers who are Dutch have appeared on the scene. The first are the Dutch who want to join existing organizations or start their own. These volunteers tend to be "leftish," progressive, and intellectual, and their motivation to help is political. They would be prepared to take second place in this effort to the leader of the ethnic association. The second kind of voluntary workers are Dutch people who want to do something for the immigrants out of compassion. They are eager to help, and want to support the immigrants, preferably in a material sense. This type is active mostly in the large towns, and will not cooperate with the ethnic associations, being more concerned with charity. The first kind of volunteer is likely to say about the immigrants that "they have less opportunities than we have; that is unjust, and we are going to help them make up for lost opportunities." On the other hand, the second type would say that "it is our duty to help the underprivileged because we have the opportunity and because they cannot help themselves."

In practice, the Turkish groups can manage their own mosques and run their own meeting centers, even if they speak little Dutch or don't speak Dutch at all. Those associations who do make contact with the Dutch authorities do so by means of interpreters or through the Dutch-speaking members of their clubs. In the small-town social clubs, the activities are strictly geared to the ethnic group itself and do not require the "helping hand" of Dutch voluntary workers.

Local authorities. The responsibility of policymaking with regard to ethnic minorities lies with the local authorities. They can decide to form formal committees on which representatives of ethnic groups can participate in decision making. The disadvantage of this procedure is that individual members of ethnic groups not so appointed may be restrained from having direct contact with the local authorities because their representatives are already heard on advisory committees. Although the local authorities are supposed to aim for representative committees of immigrants, the random choosing of such representatives can have certain dangers. If the authorities are not aware of the immigration situation, do not sympathize with the ethnic group, and are not prepared to spend enough time to make and keep up contacts, then the plan will not work. Not all civil servants are capable of fulfilling these functions.

The civil servants most directly concerned with the Turkish and Moroccan groups are the so-called "municipal minority-groups coordinators." It is interesting to distinguish between the different types of coordinators and their manner of going about their jobs. The first type is the office clerk, who is at his best behind his desk. He knows the movements of the municipal machinery and he knows all about policymaking with regard to ethnic minorities. The second type is the expert on ethnic minorities. He is not used to working in city hall; on the contrary he is often engaged in a battle with the municipal bureaucracy and various political bodies. He is well informed on the various ethnic groups and usually has valuable contacts with them. The third type of coordinator is a fairly progressive type of civil servant. He is focused on stimulating those groups in society who are being excluded from opportunities, such as women and younger people. Finally, type four is the kind of civil servant who, from either incapacity or unwillingness, does not become at all active with regard to ethnic associations.

All four types described above are operating in the system. The civil servants have just recently been confronted with the necessity of actually working with the ethnic associations. They do not as yet have a ready-to-consult set of rules at their disposal. Each has to find his own solutions to the problems, and these differ substantially depending on the knowledge, personality, and ideas of the responsible minority-groups coordinator and the circumstances in the various municipal departments.

Grants and subsidies. The subsidizing institutions give grants to ethnic associations who are capable of fulfilling certain conditions. In this manner they are able to influence their activities. The grants are supplied to help these associations run their own meeting centers. They cover working expenses such as gas, electricity, water, and rent, and educational and cultural activities including expenses for courses, information evenings, and other activities. Grants for social activities are much smaller than grants for running a meeting center. This discussion will deal mainly with the latter.

Having a meeting place of one's own turned out to be the first priority for all the associations in the survey. This was not surprising, since most associations are social clubs who need a place to meet. But the Islamic societies as well wanted meeting centers next to their mosques.

Ten of the twenty associations reviewed received grants for their expenses. There is only one Islamic organization among these ten. The remaining ten unsubsidized associations consisted of the other four Islamic societies, three committees who did not need a regular meeting place, two youth clubs who were under consideration for a center, and an ethnic committee for the unemployed. Assuming that the youth clubs will get their meeting place, it was found that only the Islamic societies have to raise money to pay for their operations. The mosques are supported by contributions from members.

The subsidization of a meeting center is a critical goal for the ethnic association. In order to be approved it needs to make a claim to represent a local ethnic group large enough to justify the request. The association must also prove that it is capable of running a meeting center, and show that its group is of long standing and solid. Finally, the group has to prove that the place it gets will not just be used as a gathering place, but that it will also organize social activities, information evenings, and courses. The existence of a variety of organizations often means that ethnic groups will compete against each other for support. If the local authorities, for example, will only subsidize one Turkish association in a town, the various groups may be polarized and compete. The struggle for meeting centers in the large towns is not restricted to ethnic associations only; Dutch voluntary workers as well need a place to organize activities for the immigrants. It appears to be evident that the Dutch organizations are more successful in getting subsidized meeting centers than the ethnic associations. This is not surprising, because Dutch voluntary workers have more experience in dealing with local authorities than have the immigrant groups.

The local authorities, in following government policy, made promoting the participation of women and younger people from minority groups their first priority. This will certainly affect the various existing associations, when they apply for subsidized meeting centers. The mosques are regularly visited by women. There are also special Koran classes for younger people. In principle the imam is the trusted representative for women as well as men, and any activity organized for women by whatever institution will need the consent of the imam if it is to succeed. However all Islamic societies and their imams in the six small towns studied (as opposed to the one large town) happen to be so conservative that they sometimes have gone so far as to advise against women taking courses organized by other associations. The local authorities are aware of this situation, and this stance will undoubtedly affect the role in decision making that will be allotted to the Islamic societies, as well as their chances for receiving grants for additional meeting centers. The Turkish meeting centers are almost exclusively more or less teahouses for older men, and women and younger men are not encouraged to attend.

Until the present the ethnic cultural beliefs of the Islamic societies have prevailed, and these have clashed with the policy intentions of the local authorities. If the latter will actually make it their priority to supply grants for activities for women and younger people, the Turkish associations will have to weigh their position against their desire to have a meeting place of their own.

CONCLUSIONS OF THE FIELD STUDY

For the sake of analysis, the functions that the associations studied fulfilled can be divided into four categories:

Function 1   a. Giving shelter
             b. Giving support
             c. Organizing sociocultural activities
Function 2   a. Influencing fellow countrymen (ethnic)
Function 3   a. Representing the interests of ethnic
                 associations
             b. Representing the interests of fellow coun-
                 trymen (ethnic)
Function 4   a. Influencing the Dutch

It was found that neither the Turkish nor the Moroccan associations, with one exception, is engaged in representing the interests of its group in the area in relation to the local authorities. The fact that both groups lack leaders who speak good Dutch, are capable of negotiating with the Dutch authorities, and at the same time enjoy the confidence of their own group, may account for this. In addition the Turkish and Moroccan people whom we met in their meeting centers have little interest in Dutch society, but on the other hand are very much concerned with their home country and their countrymen. Taking this into consideration, it is not surprising that the associations mainly fulfilled the function of giving shelter to their fellow ethnics. Of the twenty associations studied only one fulfilled almost all of the four functions mentioned above. The others gave shelter and organized social activities or exerted influence on the ethnic group for religious purposes.

These conclusions contradict the current view in the Netherlands on the role of ethnic associations, i.e., that of expecting them to represent the interests of their group, organize courses, and give information. It is important to explore why these associations are not capable of fulfilling the functions set for them by the Dutch authorities.

The fact that the ethnic associations mainly wish to give shelter to their members is revealing. It is significant that the Turkish and Moroccan people who belong to these groups are the first generation of immigrants; they were born abroad. Many do not speak the Dutch language and are not accustomed to Dutch ways. They are often not aware of what is being expected of them.

It is understandable that under these circumstances the immigrants will seek refuge within their own circles. This is the only place where they can speak their own language, do things according to their customs, and where they do not have to strain to relate to foreign surroundings. The family, of course, is the first resort, but that is not enough for many immigrants, and the meeting center and ethnic association becomes the place to get together with one's peers.

It is clear that what immigrants want to find within the association are opportunities to be with others of their ethnic group and perform religious duties or participate in social activities. It is essential to them that the frame of reference is their own language and culture and not the Dutch language or culture. Matters relating to Dutch society do not fit in, and are even in conflict, with their wishes. To get away from Dutch society is precisely the reason why immigrants get together.

It is now evident that attempts to have immigrants in their ethnic associations concern themselves with representing the interests of their group, organizing courses, and giving information, all of which concern Dutch society, are bound to be unsuccessful. The carrying out of these tasks could lead to the ruin of the associations, causing them to give up their primary function of giving shelter to the group.

These issues are not settled. Local authorities are now seeking to carry out policy mandated by the national government, as set forth a few years ago in the Draft and the Final Minorities Bills. But at the national level, there has been some recent reconsideration. In particular, it is proposed that the Turkish and Moroccan people should be allowed to go their own ways, and that authorities should be able to supply grants to associations even when they just fulfill the function of giving shelter. If this is the case, it may be that over time the associations could gradually be helped to fulfill other functions as well.

References

Ambonezen in Nederland. (Amboinese in the Netherlands) 1959. Ministerie van Maatschappelijk Werk, Staatsuitgeverij, 's-Gravenhage.

Amersfoort, J.M.M. van, 1982. *Immigration and the Formation of Minority Groups, the Dutch Experience 1945–75.* Cambridge: Cambridge University Press. Originally published in Dutch in 1974.

Bartels, D. 1986. "Can the Train Ever be Stopped Again? Developments in the Moluccan Community in the Netherlands Before and After the Hijackings." *Indonesia,* no. 2.

Entzinger, H.B. 1985. "The Netherlands." In T. Hammar, ed., *European Immigration Policy: A Comparative Study,* pp. 50–88. Cambridge: Cambridge University Press.

Ethnic Minorities. 1979. The Hague: State Publishers. Netherlands Scientific Council for Government Policy. Report no. 17.

Ex, J. 1966. *Adjustment After Migration; a Longitudinal Study of the Process of Adjustment by Refugees to a New Environment,* The Hague: Nijhoff.

Graaf, H. de. 1986 *Plaatselijke organisaties van Turken en Marokkanen* (Local Organizations of Turks and Moroccans). 2d ed. Den Haag: NIMAWO.

Kraak, J.H. et al. 1957. *De repatriëring uit Indonesië; een onderzoek naar de integratie van gerepatriëerden uit Indonesië in de Nederlandse samenleving.* (The Repatriation from Indonesia; A Study into the Integration of Repatriotes from Indonesia in the Dutch Society), 's-Gravenhage: Staatsdrukkerij.

Minderhedennota (Minorities Bill) 1983. Ministerie van Binnenlandse Zaken, Staatsuitgeverij, 's-Gravenhage. Stukken Tweede Kamer 1982–3, 16102, no. 21.

Ontwerp-Minderhedennota (Draft Minorities Bill) 1981. Ministerie van Binnenlandse Zaken, 's-Gravenhage.

Penninx, R. 1979 "Towards an Overall Ethnic Minorities Policy?" In *Ethnic Minorities,* pp. 1–170. The Hague: Netherlands Scientific Council for Government Policy. Report no. 17.

Penninx, R. 1983 *Migration, Minorities and Policy in the Netherlands: Recent Trends and Developments.* SOPEMI report for the O.E.C.D., Ministerie van WVC, Rijswijk.

Penninx, R. 1984. *Migration, Minorities and Policy in the Netherlands: Recent Trends and Developments.* SOPEMI report for the O.E.C.D., Ministerie van WVC, Rijswijk.

Regeringsreactie op het rapport 'Etnische Minderheden' van de Wetenschappelijke Raad voor het Regeringsbeleid (Government's Reaction to the Report "Ethnic Minorities" of the Scientific Council for Government Policy), 1980. Ministerie van Binnenlandse Zaken, 's-Gravenhage.

Shadid, W.A. 1979. "Moroccan Workers in the Netherlands." Ph.D. dissertation, State University of Leyde, Netherlands.

6.
Ethnic Associations and Service Delivery in Australia

John Casey

An extensive post–World War II immigration program has brought almost two million immigrants to Australia from non–English-speaking (NES) countries. The influx of these immigrants has signified far-reaching changes for a society that had largely been made up of the descendants of English and Irish settlers. At first it was thought that the immigrants from NES backgrounds— initially from Europe and later also from the Middle East, South America, and Southeast Asia—would assimilate virtually unnoticed into the dominant Anglo-Australian culture, but they continued to be marginalized both economically and politically from mainstream Australian society, and virtually excluded from positions of decision making and power (Martin 1981).

Slowly, the NES immigrant communities acquired a fragile political base and began to demand a more equal participation

John Casey worked as the coordinator of the Botany Multicultural Resource Centre and later as the Immigrant Services development worker at the Local Community Services Association in Sydney, Australia. Acknowledgment is made to Desmond Crowley, project officer of the Ethnic Affairs Commission of New South Wales, who provided up-to-date data on immigration and contributed to sections of the draft.

at all levels of Australian society.* Early assumptions of assimilation were reluctantly abandoned and a begrudging recognition was given to the distinct ethnic identities that existed in Australian society, and the right of immigrant communities to maintain their language and culture.

A crucial element in the settlement process of these communities is the formation of religious, social, cultural, sporting, political, and service organizations. A recent publication, the *Directory of Ethnic Community Organizations* (DIEA 1984), lists 2,600 organizations among the NES immigrant communities in Australia. These organizations are only the more formal associations in their communities. If the small, less-formal groupings that exist in each community are included, it can be estimated that there are some 5,000 NES ethnic organizations in Australia, ranging from small fraternal associations and large social clubs to substantial social-service agencies.

This paper will concentrate on the role of the not-for-profit, human service–oriented ethnic associations. The role of all of the ethnic organizations in the delivery of what is loosely defined as "service," and their contribution to the settlement processes of their community cannot, however be underestimated. A study of the development of these organizations would reveal the strong link between their social, cultural, political, and service functions, which in the context of an immigrant community facing an uncertain future in a new country cannot easily be separated.

The paper does not replicate the field studies made in the other countries. Instead, it locates the ethnic service associations in the immigration and social-service history of Australia, and examines the role they play in social and human service delivery to their communities. Unlike the ethnic associations described in the papers on Britain and United States—which represent a continuum between social, cultural, and political activities and social services—the ethnic associations in Australia are part of a more clearly demarcated subset of ethnic organizations. Similar volun-

---

*For brevity, the term "NES immigrant" is used throughout this paper. It refers to immigrants and refugees from countries where English is not the standard language. It primarily refers to the first generation of immigrants but it is also used in the sense of the "NES immigrant community," which includes Australian-born descendants.

tary mutual aid associations have existed since the beginning of
NES immigrant settlement in Australia, but these ethnic associations are a relatively new phenomena which have emerged in
their current form only in the last few years. The associations are
quickly integrating themselves in the community-based service
sector and carving out their slice of the social service "pie" in
Australian society.

The associations have had an indelible impact on social
service delivery to NES immigrants, yet it is difficult to predict
what direction that impact will take. It is still little more than a
matter for speculation whether ethnic associations will be able to
fulfill their goal of providing effective, culturally appropriate services and assisting their community in participating more fully in
Australian society. Ethnic associations and the services they provide are as much a product of the political and human service
systems in Australia as they are an expression of the needs of the
NES communities. The restrictions inherent in these host systems
may yet frustrate them.

Although this paper speaks about Australia in general, it
concentrates on NES immigrants and their associations in Sydney.
Sydney, a city of 3.2 million, and the capital of the state of New
South Wales, is the largest urban concentration in Australia. The
state population of 5.4 million represents 30 percent of the total
population of the country, and the situation in Sydney is representative of the settlement of NES immigrants in urban areas
throughout Australia.

Immigration to Australia

The demographic impact of the postwar immigration program to
Australia has been massive. In a little over two generations the
prewar population of just over 7 million has doubled; 65 percent
of the increase is the result of immigration and the children of
immigrants. Although Britain had been the traditional source of
new settlers, 55 percent of the postwar immigrants are from NES

countries. Australia has moved from a British-dominated colony to a multiethnic society. In large areas of the major cities persons born in NES countries make up more than 30 percent of the population. No one ethnic group dominates among the NES communities. In Sydney there are substantial numbers of Greeks, Italians, Yugoslavs, Arabic speakers, and Chinese, as well as smaller communities of Turks, Latin Americans, Eastern Europeans, and Indochinese. Australian cities are mosaics of ethnic enclaves (see table 6.1).

White immigration to Australia began in 1788 when Britain established a penal colony on the site of present-day Sydney. Convicts were transported to alleviate the crowded state of the jails which had resulted, in part, from the loss of the American colonies. Aboriginal ownership of the land was not recognized and within a few years most of the native population in contact with the settlers had been displaced, died of introduced diseases, or had been killed by the soldiers and convicts. For the first thirty years the new settlement remained largely a penal colony, but by the 1820s substantial numbers of free settlers were arriving. Apart from short periods of "gold rush," Australia has not—until recently—been a popular destination for immigrants. Australia could never compete with the glittering lure of the New World, and the danger and cost of traveling the long distances meant that Britain remained the primary source of immigrants (Loh and Lowenstein 1977; Wilton and Bosworth 1984).

In 1851 the population of Australia was 438,000. The discovery of gold in the 1850s brought a large influx of immigrants, including some Europeans and the first large group of nonwhite immigrants, the Chinese. By the early 1860s the population was near 1.25 million, and after the English and the Irish, the Chinese were the third-largest ethnic group. These population figures do not include the substantial numbers of aboriginals who were not counted in the official census until 1971.

The Chinese laborers were seen as eroding the working conditions of white workers, and their presence culminated in anti-Chinese riots on many of the gold fields. Partly in response to the Chinese, and to the use of Pacific Islanders in the sugar cane fields of the north, the ideal of a "white Australia" emerged in the late 1800s. Many of the Chinese and the Pacific Islanders were

Table 6.1. Birthplace of the Population: Sydney, Australia, 1981

Australia	*2,322,193*
U.K./Ireland	246,742
Austria	6,714
Czechoslovakia	6,024
Germany[a]	24,097
Greece	43,628
Hungary	10,822
Italy	62,682
Malta	21,265
Netherlands	16,780
Poland	14,134
Spain	4,956
USSR	9,319
Yugoslavia	44,351
Europe n.e.i.[b]	29,536
China	13,162
Cyprus	8,289
India	10,182
Lebanon	36,010
Malaysia	8,076
Sri Lanka	3,261
Turkey	9,480
Vietnam	15,385
Asia n.e.i.	51,871
Canada	4,935
U.S.A.	8,660
America n.e.i.[c]	25,257
Egypt	14,862
Africa n.e.i.	17,822
New Zealand	53,052
Oceania n.e.i.	12,885
Total	3,156,432

SOURCE: From Ethnic Affairs Commission, *Local Government Area Ethnic Population Profiles as at 1981 Census* (January 1984), p. 23.

[a] Includes West and East Germany.

[b] Not elsewhere included.

[c] Central and South America.

repatriated, nonwhite immigration was to be strictly controlled, and it was assumed that the remaining aboriginals would either die off or intermarry with the whites.

The "white Australia policy" was given official sanction in the form of the Immigration Restriction Act of 1901, one of the first acts passed by the Federal Parliament, a body formed when the separate British colonies on the continent merged into the Australian Federation in 1900. Although the act did not specifically exclude nonwhites, its mechanisms were used to ensure that only "desirable" immigrants were admitted. The most infamous of the act's provisions gave immigration officials the power to require a prospective immigrant to take a dictation test in any European language the official chose. If an immigrant could not pass a test in Gaelic, for example, at the discretion of an immigration official, he or she was excluded. The dictation test was regularly used until the late 1950s. Non-British immigration was not encouraged, but restricted numbers of Europeans—many of them refugees—who were deemed assimilable were admitted.

The end of World War II saw a major change in Australia's immigration policy based both on the need for labor to fuel the postwar economic expansion and on a fear of invasion from the north. The population at that time was around seven and a half million in a country the size of the continental United States, and the Asian nations were seen as coveting Australia's vast empty spaces. Fear of the "yellow hordes," and of the "domino theory" (Australia would be the last "domino" to fall as communism swept down through Asia) were constant themes in Australian politics of the 1950s and 1960s. Postwar governments embraced an immigration program aimed at attracting 200,000 immigrants per year, and exhorted Australia to "populate or perish" (Australian Population and Immigration Council 1977).

There were not enough British to fill the quotas and so, for the first time, white immigrants from non-English-speaking countries were encouraged to emigrate to Australia. In keeping with the earlier notions of desirable immigrants, only Northern and Eastern Europeans were accepted at first as they were seen as more easily assimilable into Australian society. By the early 1950s the economic situation in northern Europe had stabilized and the area ceased to be the major source of immigrants. Southern Europeans, primarily Greeks, Italians and Yugoslavs, were then accepted. Later, many Turkish, Middle Eastern, and South American immigrants also arrived. In the meantime, international pressure and Australia's regional obligations led to the unofficial dismantling of the "White Australia" Policy by the mid-1960s—it was not officially abandoned as government policy until 1972, under the Labor government—and substantial numbers of Asian immigrants and refugees began to arrive. The initial target of 200,000 immigrants each year was never met but, since 1948, Australia has admitted an average of 110,000 immigrants and refugees per year, about 45 percent of them from Britain and other English-speaking countries (see figure 6.1 and table 6.2).

It is important to note again that until the mid-1970s, Australia remained a relatively unpopular destination for immi-

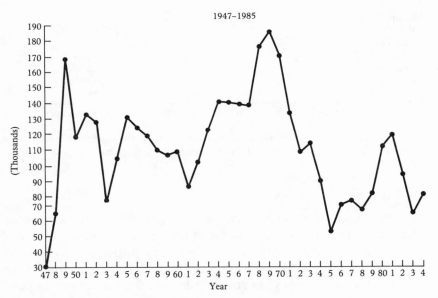

Figure 6.1. Immigrant Arrivals in Australia

SOURCES: For the years 1947–58: "Permanent Arrivals," from Australian News and Information Bureau, Department of the Interior, *Australia in Facts and Figures*, vols. 19, 24, 26, 29, 33, 37, 41, 45, 49, 53, 57, 61, 1948–59. For 1959–60 through 1982–83: "Permanent Settler Arrivals," from Department of Immigration and Ethnic Affairs, *Australian Immigration: Consolidated Statistics*, no. 13, p. 17 (Canberra: Australian Government Printing Service, 1984). For 1983–84: "Permanent Settler Arrivals (estimated)," from Department of Immigration and Ethnic Affairs, *News Release*, March 7, 1984. For 1984–85: "Permanent Settler Arrivals," from Department of Immigration and Ethnic Affairs, *Statistics Monthly* (April 1986), p. 6.

Table 6.2. Immigration by Major Source Countries to Australia, 1959–1982

United Kingdom/Ireland	854,244
Italy	176,708
Greece	154,389
Yugoslavia	154,119
New Zealand	84,279
Vietnam	62,561
Germany[a]	60,937
Lebanon	48,464
Netherlands	40,564
Malta	37,466
United States	36,592
India	34,247
South Africa	28,418
Turkey	27,605
Spain	25,842
Poland	24,348
Malaysia	20,995
Egypt	19,573
Cyprus	19,006
Philippines	17,062
Total (all countries)	2,285,935

SOURCE: Department of Immigration and Ethnic Affairs, *Australia Immigration: Consolidated Statistics (1982)*, no. 13, pp. 60–63.

NOTE: Prior to 1959, no distinction was made in the statistics between those intending to settle permanently and those arriving for a stay of one year or more (long-term arrivals).

[a] East and West Germany.

grants. Australia actively recruited immigrants and for many years had an assisted-passage scheme which paid the relocation expenses for eligible newcomers. Other immigrants, particularly in the 1950s, came under an indenture scheme whereby they were contracted to work on government-sponsored capital works programs for two years in exchange for their passage. Whereas the United States sees itself historically as a benign haven for the "huddled masses," and Britain sees itself as the reluctant mother country of its former colonial charges, Australia recognized the imperative it had to foster new settlement. It was not until around 1975 that applications to emigrate to Australia exceeded the annual immigration quota. For the first time since the 1930s strict immigrant quotas were reintroduced. The selection criteria for these quotas, however, were based on Australia's labor needs or its family reunion or humanitarian programs, and not on racial grounds.

Refugees have also been a major part of postwar settlement in Australia. In the late 1950s and 1960s Hungarians and other Eastern European refugees came in substantial numbers, and many of the South Americans that began to arrive in the early 1970s were fleeing military dictatorships. In 1975 the first boat-loads of Vietnamese refugees landed on the northern coast of Australia, precipitating a major overhaul of Australia's refugee policies. From 1975 to 1984, 114,100 refugees were resettled in Australia. With a refugee-to-population ratio of 1 to 138, Australia is the top receiving nation among the industrialized countries (U.S. Committee for Refugees 1986). The vast majority of the current refugees are Indochinese, with smaller numbers of Eastern Europeans and Latin Americans (see table 6.3).

Table 6.3. Refugee and Special Humanitarian Programs: Country of Birth of Arrivals to Australia, July 1984–June 1985

Refugee Program	
Kampuchea	1,208
Laos	188
Vietnam	5,819
Eastern Europe	1,183
Latin America	578
Middle East	558
Other	146
Special Humanitarian Program[a]	
Indo-China	52
Eastern Europe	270
Latin America	1,261
Middle East	1,352
East Timor	777
Sri Lanka	436
(White) Russian	837
Other	185
Total	14,850

SOURCE: Department of Immigration and Ethnic Affairs, *Statistics Monthly* (April 1986), Canberra, p. 18.

[a] Australia adheres to the UN definition of a refugee as someone who is, among other things, "out of his country of origin." The Special Humanitarian Program refers to people who are not refugees by the UN definition and some change-of-status cases in Australia.

Immigration levels over recent years fell from a peak in the late 1970s as both the Liberal and Labor governments attempted to respond to a high unemployment rate and an economic downturn. Recent research, however, has indicated that immigration can aid economic development and increase employment (Chapman and Miller 1986). The present Labor government—in a reversal of the party's traditional enmity to imported labor—is again strengthening the immigration program (see table 6.4). The projected number of immigrants for 1986 is back up to about 80,000, with proposals to increase the intake to 110,000 within five years (*The Sun Herald* 1986).

Finally, as an island, Australia has been able to control its borders fairly strictly. Illegal immigration has been restricted almost exclusively to persons overstaying visitors' visas. According to current estimates, there are 50,000 illegal aliens in Australia (Collins 1986).

Changing Attitudes to Immigration

The influx of NES immigrants created a crisis of identity for the British-colony mentality of pre–World War II Australia which had been based firmly on the belief of the superiority of white, English-speaking cultures. This crisis spurred significant changes in both public policies and "community opinion" towards NES immigration and settlement. These changes in attitudes have evolved through a number of identifiable stages.

Table 6.4. Immigration to Australia by Category, July 1984–June 1985

	Number	Percent of Total Immigration
Family migration	41,116	52.7
Skilled labor	7,019	9.0
Business migration	1,561	2.0
Independent migration	213	0.3
Refugee/special humanitarian	14,850	19.0
Special eligibility[a]	13,328	17.1
Total	78,087	100

SOURCE: Department of Immigration and Ethnic Affairs, *Statistics Monthly* (April 1986), Canberra, p. 6.

[a] Of this category, 10,587 are New Zealanders.

ASSIMILATION

The first postwar reaction to NES immigration was that the new immigrants should, and would, simply melt into Australian society and became just like Anglo-Australians. This firm belief in assimilationism was an important factor in convincing Australian society to accept the presence of a large number of non-British immigrants (Martin 1978). Only a few years earlier popular publications such as *The Bulletin* and *Smith's Weekly* had led vicious racist attacks against European immigrants (Dugan and Swarc 1984).

This attitude was reflected in an almost complete absence of support services for newly arrived immigrants. The federal government provided hostels to process and temporarily house immigrants when they first arrived, but once out of the hostels they were on their own. As it was assumed that the assimilation of NES immigrants would not be problematic, no need was seen for special provisions to ensure that they had access to existing social and health services. English classes and some orientation programs were provided in migrant hostels, but they were generally not available to people outside the hostels until the 1960s. Voluntary organizations receiving funds for working with immigrants concentrated their efforts on British immigrants and assimilating the "New Australians," as the NES immigrants were called.

INTEGRATION

By the mid-1960s it was becoming obvious that assimilation was unworkable in practice. Large concentrations of NES immigrants in the inner urban areas of Sydney and other major cities were becoming more visible; health and human services organizations were starting to be embarrassed by their inability to reach NES immigrants; the few isolated advocates for the rights of NES immigrants were starting to come together and advocate collectively; and the immigrants themselves had achieved a political base from which to lobby.

Assimilationism slowly started to give way to new ideologies. It became acceptable to assert that there was a legitimate role for the preservation of immigrant cultures and languages. The civil rights movements and the reemergence of ethnic identities in other parts of the world were having their echo among the aboriginal and NES immigrant communities in Australia. At first ethnic identity was only seen in an integrationist sense (Martin 1981). The preservation of culture was seen as a "cushion," softening the blow of culture shock and smoothing the path to eventual integration. The end product of this integration could be one of two things; it could either be a delayed assimilation into Anglo-Australian culture, or the creation of a new Australian culture which would be the synthesis of all the old cultures—the "melting pot." In the early 1970s, the confirmation of the rights of NES immigrants to preserve their language and culture began to take on a more permanent, pluralist sense (EAC 1978).

MULTICULTURALISM

The early 1970s also saw the emergence of the "ethnic vote"—NES immigrants for the first time were seen as a significant sector of the voting population. The first Labor government in over twenty years was elected partly by successfully wooing the NES immigrant communities, and by offering a hope for a wide-scale social reform. In 1973 the Whitlam Labor government launched its manifesto for immigrant affairs in *A Multicultural Society for the Future* (Grassby 1973), which entrenched the new pluralism as the basis for government policies. "Multiculturalism," a term borrowed from Canada, quickly became a bipartisan approach and was continued by the subsequent Fraser Liberal (conservative) government.

Multiculturalism acknowledges the more permanent role for self-expression by ethnic groups, and claims to grant equal status and access to all ethnic groups in Australia. It recognizes that Australian society is no longer defined only in terms of the Anglo-Celtic culture of the British colonizers, and that monolingual and monocultural services discriminate against NES immigrants. Multiculturalism has meant that existing services are being adapted to meet the needs expressed by the ethnic diversity of Australian society. The existence of interpreting services, migrant service units in government departments, the Migrant Resource Centres, more English classes, and grants to ethnic associations are all part of an overall strategy to give NES immigrants equal access to services. Federal funding has established the Special Broadcasting Service which has television and radio networks broadcasting in the languages of immigrants, and more funds are available for immigrant cultural groups.

Despite the bipartisan commitment to the general concepts of multiculturalism, its policies and practices continue to be controversial. The conservative approach stresses that immigrants can maintain their identity only as long as it doesn't interfere with a commitment to an "Australian ethic" and narrowly defined social cohesion (Australian Council on Population and Ethnic Affairs 1982), and to the extent to which it can contribute to the "problem-solving" tasks of social and human services. Too much ethnicity is seen as destabilizing. A liberal approach stresses the "rights" aspects of multiculturalism, claiming that a recognition of diversity must be accompanied by a recognition of the rights of all residents to full and equal participation in cultural, social, economic, and political life. Critics from the right claim that multiculturalism undermines the fabric of Australian society, while critics from the left assert that it only serves to gloss over the structural differences and true causes of discrimination (Jakubowicz, Morrisey, and Palser 1984).

These changes in attitude have not occurred without resistance from influential sectors of Australian society. Each successive wave of immigrants has been treated with a certain amount of suspicion (Loh and Lowenstein 1977). In the 1950s the labor movement closed ranks against the influx of "wogs" (a derogatory name for European immigrants), and "Asians out" graffitti is all too common in Sydney in the 1980s. Hostility toward immigrants has always increased during periods of economic recession, and the current climate of uncertainty has witnessed the reemergence of many of these sentiments. In early 1984, a speech by an eminent historian, Geoffrey Blainey, sparked off a bitter, and at times racist, debate about the "Asianisation" of Australia (EAC 1984b; FECCA 1984).

Current Demographics

Despite the "success" of the postwar immigration campaign and the rhetoric of "rags to riches" stories, many NES immigrants—

as measured by a range of social and economic indicators—are concentrated near the bottom of the Australian socioeconomic ladder.

1. *Occupational Distribution:* Australia has the second-largest overseas-born work force in the world (after Israel). Twenty-six percent of the labor force was born overseas; 17 percent in NES countries. NES immigrants are not, however, evenly distributed throughout the occupational categories. Forty-five percent of employed NES immigrants work in manufacturing or construction industries and 25 percent of all unskilled blue-collar workers in Australia are of NES migrant extraction. In comparison, 15 percent of the Australian born work in manufacturing. The Australian born and migrants from English-speaking countries are more likely to be employed in skilled, white-collar, or professional occupations (Storer and Papadopoulos 1982).

2. *Unemployment:* Manufacturing and construction industries are the first affected and hardest hit during economic downturns. As a result some NES immigrant groups are carrying a large part of the burden of current unemployment. NES immigrants who arrived in the 1950s and 1960s have an unemployment rate close to that of Australian-born workers—in March 1984 the unemployment rate for the Italian born was 8.4 percent, while for the Australian born it was 9 percent. However recently arrived communities and those with a large proportion of youth are particularly vulnerable. In 1984 the unemployment rate for the Vietnamese born was close to 34 percent, and it was 27 percent for the Lebanese born (EAC 1984a).

3. *Income:* The Henderson (1975) report on poverty showed that 30 percent of the Italian born and 23 percent of the Greek born, but only 9 percent of the Australian born, were under the poverty line. Every study of income distribution by ethnic origin has shown that workers born in NES countries have a significantly

lower average wage than the Australian born and workers born in English-speaking countries (Lever-Tracy
1981).

4. *Accommodation:* NES immigrants tend to live in areas that
reflect their work and income. In the cities they are
concentrated in poorer, "less-desirable" inner-city or
outer urban areas. In some Sydney local government
areas (Marrickville, Botany, and Fairfield) NES immigrants are more than 33 percent of the population (EAC
1984c).

These demographic facts outline the extent of the effects of
discrimination against NES immigrants, who were imported
largely as unskilled labor. As factory fodder for the postwar economic boom, their position has become that of a new working
class in Australia (Collins 1978). Although above the aboriginal
population on most social indicators, they remain very much a
disadvantaged minority in Australian society—a minority very
likely to be in need of the human services.

Social Services in Australia

Individual effort and independence from government intervention
are important values in Australian society. At the same time,
however, the rights of Australians to receive services and the
obligation of the government to provide them are recognized. The
Australian government—federal, state, and local—takes a major
role in human service delivery. Higher education, primary health
care, income maintenance, and employment services are either
directly run as government entities or receive the large majority
of their funding from government sources. Currently there are no
tuition fees at Australian universities, and Medicare, the government health insurance plan, provides free health care to all Australian residents, including immigrants.

The *New York Times* (1986), in an article on Australia, referred to the "cradle to the grave welfare system" which "has not enhanced competitiveness." This description may reflect the perception by many conservatives of an overly intrusive government involvement in service delivery, but it also distorts the extent of such government involvement. Jones, in his book *The Australian Welfare System* (1983), calls Australia a "welfare laggard" in relation to European countries. Labor struggles of the late nineteenth century and the early part of this century laid the groundwork for a welfare state more akin to the countries of northern Europe than to the United States, but conservative forces have restricted the extent of the benefits. Australian social services are more liberal than these in the United States, but fall short of the benefits available in northern Europe.

Because of the extensive government involvement in services, privatization has not occurred on the scale that it has in the United States and, unlike the United States, large private philanthropic foundations and corporate sponsorship are limited as alternate sources of funding for social services. At the same time, the voluntary tradition in Australia is strong and a large nongovernment sector plays an important role in service delivery in a number of key areas. With the exception of a small group of large, established—mostly church-based—charities, and organizations working on specific disabilities and illnesses, however these organizations deliver only a small minority of "hard services." Moreover, the expectation remains that, even though services are provided through the nongovernment sector, the vast bulk of the funding will come from government sources.

Only a small cartel of long-established nongovernment organizations have the resources to provide services such as income maintenance or other major direct services. The vast majority of organizations in the nongovernment sector deliver "soft services," self-help, and community development. The restriction on the services that nongovernment organizations deliver is a result not only of a government commitment to services, but also of barriers within legislation governing the nongovernment sector. Only a small minority of nongovernment agencies are eligible for charity status, or tax-deductible status for contributions. Agencies that do not qualify for these narrow categories are in effect denied access to private funding. Without status as a charity, organizations have only a limited right to seek and collect private funds; without the tax-deductible status on contributions, organizations cannot expect to attract them. Until last year, legislation on incorporation as a legal entity virtually excluded small nongovernment organizations. The organizations had no legal status beyond that of their individual members. Without corporate status, organizations are restricted in the property they control and in their business transactions, and members are personally liable for any debts incurred. Recent legislation has made incorporation more available.

The postwar immigration program began in the period in which Australia was shaping its welfare state. Keynesian economics had supposedly provided the tools to end poverty, and the economic boom would ensure that all Australians prospered. The agitation of the 1960s shattered that myth somewhat, and showed that not all were sharing equally in the supposed wealth, but it was not until 1975 that poverty was "officially rediscovered." The report *Poverty in Australia: Report of the Commission of Inquiry into Poverty* (Henderson 1975) confirmed what some advocates had been claiming for nearly a decade: that large numbers of Australians were living below the poverty line, and that NES immigrants, along with the aboriginals, were disproportionately represented among the poor.

The federal Labor government, elected after the Henderson inquiry had begun its work but before the report was published, brought with it a greater commitment to social issues. In an attempt to respond to the needs highlighted in the Henderson report and to demands for more control over services by the recipients of those services, the Labor government encouraged local service initiatives through the Australian Assistance Plan (AAP). The AAP created a large number of community-based services aimed primarily at community organizing and advocacy. In keeping with the expectation that the government take responsibility, the community-based services were almost entirely government funded.

A state Labor government elected in 1975 extended these initiatives to services funded through state government bodies. In 1979 the New South Wales Department of Youth and Community Services funded the network of Neighbourhood Centres, managed by locally elected management committees, to provide local information and referral, community development, and advocacy services to localities throughout the state.

The return of a federal Liberal (conservative) government in 1975 saw the abandonment of much of Keynesian theory and the introduction of austere Monetarist policies but, despite the dismantling of the AAP and general social-service cutbacks, many of the community-based initiatives started under the Labor government have survived. The first flush of progressive hope that accompanied the introduction of these initiatives had subsided and even the conservatives had seen the value in promoting self-help. A Labor government was elected again in 1983 and removed some of the fears of further wholesale cutbacks, although by 1986 it too was engaging in a number of "austerity measures."

Immigrants and Social Services

Australian immigration policy has always been based on the premise of new settlers and never that of guest workers (Australian Population and Immigration Council 1977). Immigrants were brought to Australia to build a new, permanent life there for themselves and for their children. An immigrant or refugee, having gone through a selection process in the home country or country of first refuge, generally arrives in Australia with a permanent-resident visa. Permanent residents have essentially the same rights and access to services as do citizens. They cannot vote or hold certain offices and they have a three-year restriction on their length of stay outside the country, but most immigrants have unrestricted access to government benefits and services. Permanent residents can apply for citizenship after two years of residence in Australia.

Social service law generally does not refer to immigration status, but to length of residence or intention to reside. To be eligible for sickness or unemployment benefits,* an applicant must have resided in Australia for one year immediately prior to application or be likely to remain permanently. Most recent legal immigrants are deemed to satisfy the second requirement and can receive the benefits if they satisfy other income or medical requirements. Other benefits or pensions for widows, supporting parents, and the elderly have more-restrictive residence requirements, but immigrants who don't meet the criteria may still be eligible for Special Benefit, which is decided on individual circumstances and is paid at the same rate as unemployment and sickness benefits (DSS 1986).

Even in cases where the Department of Immigration and Ethnic Affairs (DIEA) has sought to restrict the access to benefits to certain groups of immigrants, administrative decisions within the Department of Social Security (DSS) have tended to grant them income maintenance through Special Benefit. The DIEA, for example, introduced the Assurance of Support Scheme to allow the entry of relatives who were eligible for immigration under the family reunion policy but who were liable to become a public charge. The potential immigrant's sponsors in Australia signed an agreement with the DIEA to fully support the relatives for ten years during which they were ineligible for pensions or benefits. In 1985 the DSS stated that the Assurance of Support would lapse when the assured persons become Australian citizens or are "absorbed into the Australian community." No clear rules have been adopted for "absorption" but substantial residence (two years) is thought to satisfy the requirement (WRC 1986).

In the first decades of the immigration program, and in keeping with the assimilationist philosophy of the time, no special accommodation was made in social and health services for the needs of immigrants. It was assumed that NES immigrants would quickly assimilate and that universal services were fully accessible to all sectors of the population. By the late 1960s, the validity of this assumption was being questioned both by Anglo-Australian

*Pensions and benefits in Australia are noncontributory. All costs are met by the federal government from general revenue.

advocates of immigrant rights and by the NES immigrant communities themselves. The inability of government services to reach NES immigrants was becoming an embarrassment, and researchers were demonstrating that while services remained monolingual and monocultural they were, in effect, discriminating against NES immigrants. NES immigrants were missing out on benefits and services for which they were legally eligible (EAC 1978).

Although multiculturalism was adopted as a government policy by the Labor government in 1973, it was not until 1977 that a comprehensive federal review of the services available to immigrants was undertaken. The federal Liberal government's *Migrant Services and Programs* report (Galbally 1978) recommended a major overhaul of many services, and recommended the abandonment of universality to a large extent, and the incorporation of principles of a minimalist, problem-solving brand of multiculturalism into service delivery. The assumptions implicit in this approach were that needs or problems were temporary, and once they were met, programs could be stopped and funds diverted to other new need areas. Needs were closely linked to an initial settlement period. The principles of the Galbally report were later reconfirmed in the *Evaluation of Post-Arrival Services and Programs* (AIMA 1982). In New South Wales, the state Labor government's *Participation* report (EAC 1978) had provided a more expansive analysis of immigrant services, emphasizing the rights of NES immigrants to full participation in Australian society, and focusing more on the legislative and structural changes necessary to ensure those rights.

Current social and health services reflect both the expectation that the government will take major responsibility for services and the official commitment to multiculturalism. The federal Department of Immigration and Ethnic Affairs, as well as regulating the intake of immigrants, assumes the role of a major service provider. The DIEA includes the Settlement Branch, which deploys teams of bilingual case workers and administers the department's funding programs, and the Telephone Interpreter Service; a twenty-four-hour service in all major languages operating across the country. In addition, the DIEA funds the Adult Migrant Education Service which organizes English-language classes. Four of the six states have an Ethnic Affairs Commission to oversee immigrant issues, and most federal and state government departments with major service functions have a migrant services or ethnic affairs unit.

Most of the services for NES immigrants have only been in existence for, at the most, ten years. Despite their increasing presence, many generalist services have been slow to respond to the needs of immigrants. The New South Wales Department of Youth and Community Services was described in a report in 1982 as a "conservative and Anglo-Australian organization which was being forced slowly and at times reluctantly into accepting its contemporary responsibilities" (Jakubowicz and Mitchell 1982). This description is applicable to most government and nongovernment services in Australia. Lobbying by advocates for NES immigrants rights have forced many changes in service delivery, but the battles have often been long and bitter. At times the victories have been short lived. Groups that have fought to establish immigrant services units in government departments have witnessed how, instead of creating instruments to change the department, they have created bureaucratic backwaters where anything labeled "ethnic" is sent to be ignored (Casey 1985).

In December 1983 the premier of New South Wales sent memos to all state government ministers requiring their departments to submit ethnic affairs policy statements designed to "adapt existing programs and services to meet more effectively and equitably the needs of the multicultural community." This new policy, known as "mainstreaming," is a tacit acknowledgment that in the five years since the state government published the *Participation* report (EAC 1978), which chronicled the marginalization of NES immigrants and set out a blueprint for policies addressing NES issues, there has been only limited success in bringing NES immigrants into the mainstream of Australian society.

One of the major strategies in service delivery to NES immigrants has been the adoption of the community-based service models established under the Australian Assistance Plan (AAP). The *Participation* report (EAC 1978) and the federal *Migrant Services and Programs* report (Galbally 1978) advocated the creation of separate sources of funding for ethnic groups to establish their own service associations. The federal government withdrew funding from the fiercely assimilationist Good Neighbour Councils and funded a network of Migrant Resource Centres—community-based service centers which serve areas with major concentrations of immigrants. It also extended programs that provided funding to nongovernment organizations to employ social welfare workers to work with immigrant communities. The state Ethnic Affairs Commission established funding programs to provide "seed" funds for new ethnic associations. Traditional sources of funding also began to rethink their policies and sought to make their processes more accessible to ethnic groups. The availability of these funding sources has been the impetus for the growth of ethnic associations.

The support for nongovernment, community-based funding has always been promoted as being "nonpolitical," and service is somehow meant to be value free. Funds are allegedly granted to those who can best demonstrate their ability to provide service. Even the most casual analysis, however, reveals how funding sources bestow their favors on organizations sharing their ideologies. Among the NES immigrant communities, maintaining the semblance of being "nonpolitical" has at times proven to be especially difficult. Governments have been reluctant to admit that the NES immigrant communities are divided along political, religious, and ethnic lines. The emphasis on cohesion as the basis for multiculturalism has meant that governments have been particularly harsh on those organizations engaging in anything that could be remotely interpreted as "political," particularly with regard to the internal politics of the immigrant communities or their home countries. In the Italian community, an organization with roots in a wartime, pro-Mussolini group has grown, while an organization with union and Italian Communist party ties has had submission after submission rejected. In the Turkish community funders have had to choose between left- and right-wing organizations, in the Arabic-speaking community between Moslem and Christian, and in the Yugoslav community between Serbs and Croats. The return of the Labor government has seen a more "balanced" allocation of federal funds, but more overtly political organizations are still avoided.

The last ten years have seen a dramatic expansion of ethnic associations and their consolidation as a legitimate sector of non-government social welfare. They are funded despite an apparent duplication of services provided directly by government departments or through nongovernment organizations such as the Neighbourhood Centres, as they are seen as the link between their community and mainstream services. With restrictions on the possible extent of their work because of government involvement in social services, constraints on funding sources, and the legal barriers on nongovernment organizations, ethnic associations act primarily as information and referral agencies and advocates for their clients who have difficulty negotiating the system. Their role is seen to be complementary to the specialist immigrant services units in government agencies and the increasing numbers of multilingual staff.

The Work of Ethnic Associations

In New South Wales in 1985 there were sixty-five service-oriented ethnic associations representing thirty NES immigrant groups, according to a listing published by the Local Community Service Association (LCSA), a nongovernment, community service lobby organization. The LCSA list included only those associations that had a primary goal of providing social and human services, served one language or ethnic group, and had a relatively stable, sophisticated structure. Less formal organizations, organizations that had other aims but provided incidental social services, and broad-based organizations serving more than one group were not included.

These ethnic associations are a new addition to the network of the community-based services first established in the early 1970s under the Australian Assistance Plan. At first funding for establishing these community organizations was restricted to universal services, but the late 1970s saw the beginning of the systematic distribution of these funds to ethnic-specific associations.

The two government reports mentioned earlier also established separate sources of funding through the extension of the federal Department of Immigration and Ethnic Affairs' Grant-in-Aid and Migrant Project Subsidy programs, and the state Ethnic Affairs Commission's Community Funding Program. Although many of the organizations may have been in existence for a number of years—particularly among the longer-established communities—the large majority of them would not have had access to the funds to employ full-time workers until within the last five to seven years. Many of these associations were previously more socially or culturally oriented, and some were based in churches, but the availability of funds for social-service functions have drawn them into their current role.

Ethnic associations are also part of the large body of non-government organizations too small to deliver hard services. The associations tend to be small agencies, either entirely voluntary or employing at most a small professional and administrative staff. The largest association would employ around eight workers with a budget of $200,000, while the average budget of an ethnic association in New South Wales is $20,000 to $30,000 per annum. Eighty-five to 90 percent of the associations funding comes from either state or federal sources, and their survival as viable service deliverers depends on their ability to gain access to public funds. The associations, as a prerequisite to obtaining government funds, function on the typical "community management" model and a management committee is elected from the membership. They are usually low on resources, understaffed, and function from inadequate premises.

The political impact of multiculturalism has also meant that NES immigrant lobby organizations have formed which are able to provide support and advocacy for these ethnic associations. The three local Ethnic Communities' Councils, one in each of the major cities in New South Wales, in cooperation with Ethnic Communities' Councils in other states and the national Federation of Ethnic Communities' Councils of Australia bring together thousands of small NES immigrant organizations into an influential ethnic lobby.

The mainstay of a typical association's work is its drop-in/casework function. The office of the association is open during working hours—often only part-time—and clients present themselves at the association without appointments. The casework consists of informing clients of what services are available and how to obtain them; filling in forms; assisting clients in dealing with English-only government departments and businesses; and assisting them in finding work, accommodation, etc. Few associations provide ongoing casework or in-depth counseling, usually recognizing their lack of resources and trained personnel in this area. Some associations also take a more active role in advocacy work on social service and wider political issues that affect their community.

In both their organization and aspects of their service delivery the ethnic associations could be seen as the equivalent of the state's network of Neighbourhood Centres and Community Information Centres. Like the Neighbourhood Centres they are seen as providing a localized and responsive way of ensuring that a community has access to government services and the means to organize itself around the issues that affect it. Ethnic associations tend to emphasize their casework function more than do the Neighbourhood Centres, and instead of defining their "community" by a geographical boundary, ethnic associations define it as an ethnic or language group.

Without the hard data that a survey of the associations would furnish, it is difficult to accurately inventory the myriad of services that they provide. It is, however, possible to identify the major service needs the associations attempt to address.

INFORMATION AND REFERRAL

Many of the services in Australian society continue to be inaccessible to NES immigrants. This inaccessibility is expressed both in terms of the lack of information about available services and the inability of many of the services to cater to immigrant clients. The associations attempt to fill these gaps. They act as brokers, informing their community of what is available and referring clients to appropriate services. If the client cannot speak English the association often becomes the go-between for the clients and the appropriate government department or nongovernment agency.

Information about services is usually given on a one-to-one basis in response to individual inquiries, but associations also organize information sessions and talks on issues of interest to their community. Increasingly over the last four years, government and nongovernment services have become aware of the way in which a lack of information discriminates against non–English-speaking communities. Translated information material, advertising through the ethnic media, and outreach efforts are becoming more integral to community and public affairs units of services. The ethnic associations utilize these efforts to facilitate their own information functions.

At times, however, the quality of the information provided by the ethnic associations is questionable; the information providers themselves are often uninformed. Many of the staff in the ethnic associations have only limited experience in Australian social services, and have too little time to inform themselves of the current situation or to keep up with changes.

INCOME MAINTENANCE AND EMPLOYMENT

Figures quoted earlier in this paper identified the NES immigrant communities as more likely to be in poverty, and many NES communities are experiencing significantly higher rates of unemployment than the Anglo-Australian population. The hardest hit are the recently arrived immigrant groups (EAC 1984a). Government responsibility for income maintenance and the ethnic association's limited funds mean that the associations are not able to assume any income maintenance role beyond working with clients to ensure that they have access to pensions and benefits available through government departments and to emergency relief funds or goods in kind from the government and large charities.

Employment services are also organized directly through the federal and state governments. The Commonwealth Employment Service of the Department of Employment and Industrial Relations determines eligibility for unemployment benefits and provides local-level job-finding services through their neighborhood offices. As with income maintenance, ethnic associations faced with the high unemployment in their communities can do little except help members of their community to ensure that they have access to the services, benefits, and training that are available. Some ethnic associations assist members in finding employment through the informal networks that exist in the community, but few if any would provide a formalized job-finding service.

Since 1983 federal funds for job creation and training programs have been available through the Wage Pause Program, the Community Employment Program, and the Participation and Equity Program. A large proportion of the money has been given to government programs, but community organizations have also been given funds for local job creation initiatives. A number of ethnic associations have successfully petitioned for funds to employ workers in the associations and thereby expanded their services.

Occupational health is also a major employment concern for NES immigrants as many are employed in high-risk industries. The incidence of work-related injuries are higher among NES workers than among English-speaking workers, despite attempts to lower the injury rate. Although ethnic associations do not provide any direct services to injured workers, a significant proportion of their work involves clients receiving injury compensation payments and sickness benefits. A number of associations organize activities such as support groups for members with work-related injuries.

HOUSING

NES immigrants tend to live in the poorer inner-city neighborhoods or the new housing developments in the outer areas of Sydney. Moreover, their low income and proportionately higher rates of poverty have meant that many immigrants are eligible for public housing through the state Department of Housing.

Ethnic associations provide two main services in relation to housing. First, as with unemployment, some of the associations provide informal accommodation-finding services through networks in their community and through real estate agents they know to be reliable. Second, they assist eligible applicants in negotiating the bureaucracy of the Department of Housing, which—like public housing authorities throughout the world—is notorious for its long waiting lists and lack of responsiveness to tenants' requests. Tenant advocacy and the protection of tenants' rights have only recently made an impact on the work of ethnic associations. Nongovernment advocacy groups are making more of an effort to reach NES immigrants, and the Department of Housing has recently established a Multicultural Housing Policy Unit.

LANGUAGE AND CULTURE

The need to acquire English skills is the common denominator among the NES immigrant communities. English classes are available directly through the Adult Migrant Education Service funded by the federal Department of Immigration and Ethnic Affairs and the state Department of Technical and Further Education. Both departments and the state Board of Adult Education also provide teachers or funds to community organizations for classes. Most ethnic associations organize some classes, particularly for women and the elderly.

At the same time, ethnic associations provide a range of services and activities to preserve the language and culture of their country of origin, and to perpetuate them among the Australian-born children. Many associations sponsor music and dance groups, and most language grouups now have their own "ethnic schools." The ethnic schools function after school hours or on Saturday afternoons to teach language and culture to the children of immigrants. They are separate legal entities from the ethnic associations and receive their own funding from the federal Department of Education and the state Ethnic Affairs Commission, but many are organized under the auspices of an ethnic association.

LEGAL AND IMMIGRATION ADVICE

NES immigrants are often unaware of their legal rights and have limited access to legal services. Ethnic associations do not have the capacity to provide any comprehensive legal assistance. At best, some of the associations may have volunteer lawyers providing free legal advice for a few hours a week, but most associations rely on building links with community legal aid centers in their areas or upon government bodies providing legal advice.

Immigration inquiries—regarding citizenship, the sponsorship of relatives, and change of status—also account for much of the work of ethnic associations, particularly among those communities still coming to Australia in substantial numbers. An immigration law "industry" has not developed in Australia and, in the absence of lawyers seeking the work, ethnic associations find that they are expected to carry much of the burden of answering inquiries and assisting clients in filling out forms. Moreover, despite the government's commitment to permanent settlement, there has been a significant return rate of immigrants to their home countries, particularly those immigrants of retirement age who see retirement "back home" as more appealing. Requests for repatriation assistance, and inquiries on the portability of pensions and benefits, have also become part of the work of ethnic associations.

SERVICES FOR SPECIAL GROUPS

Women often bear the greater burden in immigration. Male immigrants have a greater degree of social and economic freedom and more job-related opportunities to learn English. Many immigrant women work outside the home as well as carrying the domestic duties, and differing cultural expectations between the old culture and Australian society create stresses in relationships.

Many of the associations reflect the male-dominated stereotypes of their communities and avoid services that could in any way be interpreted as undermining the role that that culture ascribes to women. A number of associations do, however, organize women's social and information sessions and refer women to other organizations for health and counseling services.

As demographic forecasts map the aging of the general population, the elderly are increasingly recognized as a needy sector of the population. NES communities are also having to come to terms with what is essentially the first generation of NES elderly. Poverty, lack of care for the infirm, isolation, and homesickness are the main concerns facing the NES elderly. Language regression—the tendency of the NES elderly to lose their command of English—also serves to accentuate those needs.

Apart from their usual referral and advocacy role to ensure that existing resources are responding to the needs of the elderly, ethnic associations attempt to address the isolation of the elderly in their communities. Nearly all ethnic associations organize gatherings, classes, group outings, and home visiting for isolated elderly. A number of associations are also examining the possibility of establishing nursing homes catering to their own ethnic group.

Issues in Service Delivery

As a relatively new phenomenon, both within the Australian social-service scene and to many of the NES immigrants involved in them, ethnic associations remain controversial. The question of integration into Australian society is a major issue facing ethnic associations. While, on one hand, the associations advocate that members of their ethnic group acquire those aspects of Australian society necessary to survive and prosper, their very existence is rooted in the preservation of a separate ethnic identity.

The White Australia Policy was based on the premise that other races and cultures would only serve to taint a purely British colony. Later the fiercely assimilationist policies and rhetoric of the 1950s and early 1960s made an attempt to reconcile the Anglo-Australian past with the reality of the diverse immigration of the postwar era, and were a defense against the perceived threat to the British way of life. With the new pluralism of multiculturalism, and the seemingly greater acceptance of diversity, the issue has only become less complicated by degrees and ethnic associations are still finding themselves walking the thin line between acceptance and rejection. At the same time as policymakers are increasingly recognizing the validity of making ethnic associations partners in service delivery, the associations and the government departments that fund them find themselves under attack for dividing Australia. The influential weekly magazine *The Bulletin* (1986) carried an article on "How the Bloated Ethnic Industry Is Dividing Australia" which, in a throwback to assimilationist thought, described how government monies to ethnic organizations were undermining the cohesiveness of Australian society.

Ethnic associations and their advocates constantly find themselves having to justify the existence of the associations. Do they provide better services than mainstream organizations? Can they contribute to a better access to mainstream services for their communities? The advocates of service delivery through ethnic associations claim that only through linguistically and culturally appropriate services can the needs of NES communities be met. While generalist providers of services can do much to ensure that their services are accessible, there will always be those sections of the community whose needs can only be met through associations organized through their own communities. It is not a question of either mainstream or ethnic services. Both types of organizations have complementary roles to play in service delivery (Casey 1985).

How exactly the ethnic associations can best fulfill their role is another area of controversy. Far from being consensual groups, NES immigrant communities are "dynamic, contested arenas of ideas and values" (Jakubowicz and Meekosha 1986). The debates between conservative and liberal forces in the wider social-services community are also evident among the ethnic associations. With limited resources, a constant tension is kept between what are seen as the competing priorities of "direct-service" work and organizing and advocacy work. Ethnic associations generally tend to lean toward direct service. This more conservative approach is imposed by a combination of a number of factors. First, the sheer pressures of their high client loads and lack of resources leave most associations struggling to handle their day-to-day work. Second, many of the staff and management in the associations lack experience in social service issues and alternative service delivery strategies. Third, there is a fear of "biting the hand that feeds them"—associations are reluctant to take on work that may be perceived as antagonizing funding bodies or bringing criticism of the association or the NES communities.

The ethnic associations have a high profile among their respective communities and there is little doubt that they are drawing on the best resources and energies of the NES immigrant communities to maintain their current level of service. Further, by accepting without question the constraints imposed by the Anglo-Australian funding structures and by the separation of services, ethnic associations are compartmentalizing service delivery in a way that may be denying the essential connections between

culture, politics, religion, and services in the immigrant experience. Given the restrictions on their resources, these services may
ultimately have only a limited impact on the current situation.
Like the wider social services in Australia which have had restricted success in reducing inequities (Jones 1983), ethnic associations will find that their goals of equal access and equal opportunity for their communities are difficult to achieve.

   In December 1985, the Committee of Review of Migrant
and Multicultural Programmes and Services was established by
the federal government (Jamarozik 1986). The committee com-
missioned a study on "the present and potential further role and
effectiveness of the voluntary sector in the provision of services to
immigrants" which focuses on the work of forty ethnic associations in Sydney. Preliminary findings of the study highlight areas
of concern in the service delivery of the associations. In particular,
Petruchenia (1986) reports that there is a big gap between the
policy and the practice of multiculturalism, and that many associations feel they continue to face a lack of understanding and
sensitivity. Funding was also a major concern. Most ethnic-specific
funding tends to be for a period of one year or less, and the
associations considered that it resulted in insecurity and inflexi-
bility which greatly restricted service development.

   Another major concern is that expressed earlier in regard
to the information services of the associations. Just as the associations are, at times, struggling to provide accurate information on
services to their clients, their lack of information hinders their
ability to advocate for themselves as agencies. Over the last few
years, for example, funds for job creation programs have injected
millions of dollars into nongovernment services. While ethnic
associations have gotten access to some of the funds they rarely
have known about them by the first round of funding.

Conclusion

Ethnic associations in Sydney, as defined in this paper, form a
distinct subset within the multitude of organizations that exist
among the NES immigrant communities. Although many of the

associations have their roots in social, cultural, political, or religious organizations, the availability of funding for community-based ethnic organizations to take on a service function has prompted these associations to redefine their roles to coincide with the expectations of the funding bodies. The paper has demonstrated how this small number of associations provide community-based social services to their own ethnic groups within an Australian framework. Conclusions about these ethnic associations must consider what effect these services have, and what advantages or disadvantages they offer to NES immigrant communities.

The associations are the result of the struggle of advocates, both NES immigrants and Anglo-Australians, to create services that will be more sensitive to the particular needs of the separate NES immigrant communities while also providing a means by which members of those communities can get access to mainstream services in the Australian society. NES immigrants in Australia are more likely to be unemployed, to work in low-paying jobs, and to suffer discrimination in access to goods and services. Can these ethnic associations meaningfully address these imbalances?

Ethnic associations are indeed providing a more responsive form of service delivery to their communities, and their advocacy work can help ensure that mainstream services also become more responsive to all their constituents. There are dangers, however, which may signify that in the final balance the ethnic associations may only serve to perpetuate the marginalization of NES immigrants.

The ethnic associations suffer from a lack of resources which severely curtails the effectiveness of their services. Moreover they are currently still at the edges of the nongovernment social-service sector and have found it difficult to lobby for their own interests, or even to gain access to the expert knowledge necessary to function efficiently. In their present format many of the ethnic associations are condemned to providing second-class service, and this inadequate service may maintain immigrant "ghettos," shielding mainstream services from future criticisms of unresponsiveness.

The report of the Committee of Review of Migrant and

Multicultural Programs and Services will undoubtedly determine the direction of public policy regarding ethnic associations for at least the next decade. Whatever the direction the committee's recommendations take, the associations themselves will have to develop their political acumen and the ability to promote their interests and that of their communities; capacities that many do not presently possess.

References

Australian Council on Population and Ethnic Affairs. 1982. *Multiculturalism for All Australians*. Canberra: Australian Government Printing Service.

Australian Institute of Multicultural Affairs AIMA (/). 1982. *Evaluation of Post-Arrival Services and Programs*. Canberra: Australian Government Printing Service.

Australian Population and Immigration Council. 1977. *Immigration Policies and Australian Population: A Green Paper*. Canberra: Australian Government Printing Service.

The Bulletin. February 18, 1986. "How The Bloated Ethnic Industry Is Dividing Australia."

Casey, J. 1985. *Non–English-Speaking Migrants and Community Centers—A Handbook*. Sydney: Local Community Services Association.

Chapman, B. and P. Miller. 1986. "Immigration and Unemployment." *Current Affairs Bulletin* (September), vol. 63, no. 4.

Collins, J. 1978. "Fragmentation of The Working Class." In E. Weelwright and K. Buckley, eds., *Essays in the Political Economy of Australian Capitalism*, 3:42–85. Sydney: Australian and New Zealand Book Co.

Collins, J. 1986. "Migrant Welfare and the Workplace." In Jamarozic, *Provision of Welfare Service to Immigrants*, pp. 23–26.

DIEA (Department of Immigration and Ethnic Affairs). 1984. *Directory of Ethnic Community Organizations in Australia*. Canberra: Australian Government Printing Service.

DSS (Department of Social Security). 1986. *A Guide to Department of Social Security Payments*. Publication CL001 (L.D.). Canberra: DDS.

Dugan, M. and J. Swarc. 1984. *There Goes the Neighbourhood*. Melbourne: McMillan.

EAC (Ethnic Affairs Commission of New South Wales). 1978. *Participation*. Sydney: EAC.

EAC. 1984a. *Immigrants and Unemployment*. Occasional paper no. 2. Sydney: EAC.

EAC. 1984b. *The 1984 Immigration Debate*. Occasional paper no. 4. Sydney: EAC.

EAC. 1984c. *Local Government Area Ethnic Profiles as at 1981 Census*. Sydney: EAC.

FECCA (Federation of Ethnic Communities Councils of Australia). 1984. *The Great Immigration Debate*. Sydney: FECCA.

Galbally, F. 1978. *Migrant Services and Programs: Report of the Review of Post-Arrival Programs and Services for Migrants*. Canberra: Australian Government Printing Service.

Grassby, A. 1973. *A Multicultural Society for the Future*. Immigration reference papers. Canberra: Australian Government Printing Service.

Henderson, R. 1975. *Poverty in Australia: Report of the Commission of Inquiry into Poverty*. Canberra: Australian Government Printing Service.

Jakubowicz, A. and H. Meekosha. 1986. "Migrants, Marginality, and Community Work." In Jamarozik, *Provision of Welfare Service to Immigrants*, pp. 3–4.

Jakubowicz, A. and G. Mitchell. 1982. *Community Welfare Services and the Ethnic Communities*. Sydney: NSW Department of Youth and Community Services, Planning and Research Unit.

Jakubowicz, A, M. Morrisey, and J. Palser. 1984. *Ethnicity, Class, and Social Policy in Australia*. Sydney: Social Welfare Research Centre.

Jamarozik, A., ed. 1986. *Provision of Welfare Service to Immigrants (Proceedings of SWRC Seminar, May 26, 1986)*. Report no. 60. Sydney: Social Welfare Research Centre.

Jones, M. 1983. *The Australian Welfare State*. Sydney: Allen and Unwin.

Lever-Tracy, C. 1981. "Labour Market Segmentation and Divergent Migrant Incomes." In *Australian and New Zealand Journal of Sociology* (July 1981), 17(2):21–30.

Loh, M. and W. Lowenstein. 1977. *The Immigrants*. Melbourne: Hyland House.

Martin, J. 1978. *The Migrant Presence*. Sydney: Allen and Unwin.

Martin, J. 1981. *The Ethnic Dimension*. S. Encel, ed. Sydney: Allen and Unwin.

New York Times Magazine, "Being Australia." September 29, 1985, pp. 20–32.

Petruchenia, J. 1986. "The Role of the Non-Government Welfare Sector." In Jamarozik, ed., *Provision of Welfare Service to Immigrants*, pp. 5–7.

Storer, D. and G. Papadopoulos. 1982. "Some Dimensions of the Occupational Health and Safety Situation of Migrants in Australia." In *Communicating with Migrant Clients*. Canberra: Migrant Services Unit, Department of Social Security.

The Sun Herald. "Labor Courts New Aussies," April 13, 1986, p. 52.

U.S. Committee for Refugees. 1986. *World Refugee Survey: 1985 in Review*. New York: American Council for Nationalities Service.

WRC (Welfare Rights Centre). 1986. *Newsletter*, vol. 4, no. 1. Sydney, Australia.

Wilton, J. and R. Bosworth. 1984. *Old Worlds and New Australia*. Melbourne: Penguin.

7.

Conclusion: The States and the Associations

Shirley Jenkins

During the field study in New York, one of the social-work interviewers said of the ethnic associations, "This is the best-kept secret in social work." Not in the mainstream, not taught about in the school curriculum, not integrated into the formal social service system, and not run by established professionals, nevertheless, uncounted numbers of ethnic associations are giving support, counsel, training, referrals, and refuge to other members of their own ethnic groups. Slowly their work is being recognized, and gradually both the public and voluntary service systems are beginning to respond to the potential that exists in ethnic associations for improving service delivery, in particular for new immigrants.

An inescapable conclusion of this study has been that new immigrants are not "born again" when they arrive at their destination. Instead they carry with them the heavy baggage of language, culture, values, and life-styles from their former circumstances. Retaining their ethnic identity and seeking acculturation to the new environment are not antithetical. If achieved in appropriate proportions, both efforts may complement each other in the struggle for satisfactory functioning. Ethnic leaders express a stronger bent for preserving identity than for promoting acculturation, which is to be expected since it is this that reflects their special role in their own communities. In addition, ethnic leaders in all countries studied almost universally characterize their own group as having positive traits, and the people of the host as having negative ones. But they recognize the need to adapt in order to survive. They also cling to their native culture and language, not only for historical reasons, but to provide the social supports that make the effort of adaptation possible.

The detailed exposition of the services offered by ethnic associations to new immigrants in New York City is impressive, in particular because these activities occur at a time when there is a dearth of family supports for low-income people. A familiar language, the sense of advocacy on behalf of members, and some evidence of "know-how" in dealing with the formal system, are all important ingredients in the attraction the ethnic associations have for new immigrants.

The thirty ethnic associations in the New York City study vary among themselves, and the typology shows a range from the highly professionalized service agency to the community focussed association, to the self-help primarily social or cultural group. But there are many needs that most new immigrants have in common, and these are recognized to varying degrees by the ethnic associations. Since the associations are broader than the family, but smaller than the bureaucracy, they can serve as linkages between those two systems. Litwak, Meyer, and Hollister (1977) have paid particular attention to the issues of linkages between primary groups and bureaucracies, and developed the "balance" theory of coordination between these two institutions. Ethnic associations qualify as providing such linkages on a number of grounds, one of them being the capacity to reduce the social distance between the family and the bureaucracy. For example, they have high "sender initiative," defined as "the amount of capacity to reach a target group and have it listen to the message" (Litwak, Meyer, and Hollister 1977: 125).

A broader view of the ethnic association as a social institution can be gleaned from the cross-national material. Looking at ethnic associations in five countries suggests ways in which they are dependent on their social and national contexts. One way to approach this analysis is to refer to the four variables suggested by Cox (1985) as affecting ethnic group development, discussed in paper 1. These are: 1) the nature of the immigration; 2) the nature of previous contact; 3) socioeconomic political contexts on arrival; and 4) the prevailing host society attitudes.

Among the five countries reviewed, there are three different patterns of immigration and, following Cox's paradigm, each appears to affect the way in which the ethnic associations function. In two countries, Australia and Israel, new immigrants were sought as part of a national policy to populate the countries and increase their labor supply. Those were the two countries in which ethnic associations for immigrants received formal approval, and were incorporated into the network of community supports. With regard to Israel, Korazim has raised the question of how independent the associations really are, and in Australia Casey has asked whether the official link with the bureaucracy may stultify ethnic development and marginalize services. Thus it appears that, in these cases at least, the fact that the ethnic associations are part of the official policy of relating to new immigrants can truncate or at least inhibit their advocacy function.

There are some parallels between Britain and the Netherlands with regard to the recent immigration. In Britain this has been primarily an aftermath to the break-up of former colonial empires and the desire of former subjects to avail themselves of the presumed advantages of "home country" residence, in particular economic opportunities. There was time-limited legal protection for the entry of the former colonials and their relatives, but the immigrants were not necessarily welcomed as new populations that would add to the national stock. The Dutch situation is more complicated. Most of the ex-colonial migration had political roots, but some of it was economically determined. In addition, there was a sizable entry of guest workers who were Europeans and who came for economic reasons. In both countries, however, the impact of differences in race and culture were underestimated, and there were and are many problems in acculturation. According to de Graaf, Penninx, and Stoové, most efforts of the new Dutch minorities policy to solve problems of immigrants are aimed at improvement of the position of individual migrants in Dutch

society and there is relatively little attention paid to the culture of
the new immigrant groups. Ethnic associations, as presently developed in these countries, appear to be less effective as linkages
in social service delivery. In the Dutch case, according to de Graaf,
this may be because associations are selected randomly and functions actually applicable and those wished for by the receiving
society may clash. In the British case, according to Cheetham, it
may be because of the pattern of strong universal services and
because the associations appear to represent a perpetuation of
diversity, a position antithetical to the presumed national ideology
of a homogeneous state.

The United States has not sought immigration in recent
years, but it did respond to political pressures to redress inequities
in its immigration policies by liberalizing immigrant legislation in
1965 and introducing new refugee legislation in 1980. The consequences were an ethnic shift in residential aliens, and a heavily
dependent refugee population, mainly from Indochina. There
were two sets of laws (1965 and 1980), two types of immigration,
and, not surprisingly, two different policies for ethnic associations.
The 1986 legislation, which will have a special impact on the
undocumented Hispanics, may also have unintended consequences for the closing of ethnic ranks.

Associations of new immigrants who were resident aliens
proliferated, affected in their organizing patterns by previous
waves of immigrants of similar backgrounds, by class, language,
national origin, and special interests. These groups receive no
special attention but function in the same way as do other voluntary associations. For the refugees, however, there was a commitment to encourage the development of self-help groups, and
there were specific provisions for the support of mutual assistance
associations. The rationale was that such groups could help refugees become self-supporting. The outcomes of these efforts varied,
depending on leadership, the needs of the group, and available
resources.

The development of ethnic associations with responsibility
for some service delivery is too recent a phenomenon for precise
evaluation, but the New York study did raise three questions about
their future functioning. One is whether the MAAs might become
so "grant-driven" that they will veer toward a bureaucratic stance

rather than retain their "linkage" position. A second question is how their functioning will affect the established voluntary sector for social service delivery. Finally, it is interesting to speculate whether the current dichotomy between refugee associations and associations of other immigrants can be breached in order to develop common goals and mutual supports for newcomers, regardless of national origin or legal immigration status.

The next factor suggested by Cox as affecting ethnic-association development is the nature of previous contact. This is difficult to evaluate since contact can be of different types, and the effect can be positive or negative. One example of previous contact is the relationship of former colonial subjects to the ruling power. This kind of contact involves obligations on the part of the host, and expectations on the part of the immigrants, both of which are often unfulfilled. Another kind of previous contact is the impact on new immigrants of earlier waves of immigration from the same sending countries. This also is complicated and can have varying effects. If the earlier wave was successful in acculturation, and has established strong ethnic organizations, these may be very helpful to the newcomers. In New York, for example, the Russian refugees received substantial support from established Jewish philanthropic agencies. In several cases, however, the new waves represented different political, religious, or class groupings than the earlier arrivals, and were looked down on by their own compatriots. An example were the "Marielistas" from Cuba. Where there were differences within the ethnic group there could be a multiplicity of associations that were competitive with each other. This occurred among the Ethiopian refugees. In these cases, the concept of the ethnic association as fulfilling a "linkage" function is weakened, because there is no reliable way for the bureaucracy to determine which association is the better representative of the ethnic group.

The context of welfare legislation and the pattern of service delivery in host countries affect the ways in which ethnic associations operate. In all of the countries reviewed, income maintenance is a public function, and although ethnic associations may give occasional help, they rarely assume fiscal responsibility for supporting new immigrants. Personal social services, however, are delivered in a variety of ways. In the United States, where there is federal, state, and local involvement in social-service delivery, public as well as voluntary services, and both secular and sectarian agencies, the ethnic associations have great maneuverability. They may receive public or voluntary funding, they may be free-standing or affiliate with the established voluntary sector. In New York City, their operations may challenge the long-time prominence of sectarian agencies in the delivery of social services, a challenge that has already been made by agencies representative of minority groups.

The last criterion suggested by Cox, host society attitudes, needs far greater specification for meaningful analysis. Immigrants may be welcomed in times of labor shortages, but attitudes can quickly change if there is unemployment. Political refugees may be hailed on arrival, and ignored shortly thereafter. Ethnic associations may be tolerated and even encouraged, but support may be withdrawn if they adapt strong advocacy or adversarial positions. Involved in any examination of host society attitudes should be an examination of issues of institutional racism, since a substantial portion of new immigrants in the countries studied involve persons of different racial as well as ethnic origins. This examination needs to be concerned not only with the structural absorption of new immigrants, in peopling areas and taking jobs, but in cultural absorption as well, and the openness of the social institutions in the new homeland. When only second-class status is offered, the development of ethnic associations will be affected.

In *Brown v. the United States* (1954), the Supreme Court decision that supported desegregation in the public schools, a cogent argument was that education could not be both separate and equal. The events of the 1960s brought forth a new ideology which challenged the integrationist position. Many ethnic associations today reflect the concept that equality can only be achieved from a base of being separate. The rationale is that a sense of identity and ethnic purpose can be the platform for political bargaining to achieve more favorable access to opportunity in the larger society. Thus the proliferation of the many ethnic associations in the current period has implications beyond the recreational, social, and humanitarian goals of earlier times.

This study has explored the specific role of the ethnic association in the delivery of social services. Some negative aspects have emerged: the varying structures of the welfare system obviate the possibility of a single model; there is the danger of cooption by the bureaucracy; there is the possibility of marginalization of services; and there are difficulties in identifying representative associations in an atmosphere of intraethnic competition. On the other hand, within the context of a broad definition of social services and social supports not prescribed by the formal welfare system, the ethnic associations have a very impressive performance record. In numerous cases examined, they represent the only access link for the delivery of entitlements to immigrant groups.

Cheetham offers two salient explanations for this. First, there is the centrality of language and culture, which is the basis of communication between new arrivals and host societies. Second, there appears to be a parallel acceptance of both preservation of identity and support for acculturation as dual aspects of successful functioning in the new society. The issue of whether or not there will be third-generation assimilation, or whether, as projected by Gans (1979) there will be a retreat to "symbolic ethnicity," is not very relevant for service programs for newcomers. Population movements are likely to persist and even intensify, and the new arrivals will be in need of help; ethnic associations may be the best way to communicate their needs to the formal bureaucracies. The functions of these ethnic associations will be worked out within the various national contexts. Their role as linkage institutions will depend on a delicate balance between the structure of the welfare state and the special needs and circumstances of their particular ethnic groups.

References

Cox, D., 1985. "Welfare Services for Migrants—Can They Be Better Planned?" *International Migration* (March), 23(1): 73–95.

Gans, H. J., 1979. "Symbolic Ethnicity: The Future of Ethnic Groups and Cultures in America." *Ethnic and Racial Studies* (January), vol. 2, no. 1.

Litwak E., H. Meyer, and C. D. Hollister, 1977. "The Role of Linkage Mechanisms Between Bureaucracies and Families." In R. Liebert and A. W. Immershein, eds., *Power, Paradigms, and Community Research*, London: Sage.

Index